Ballet
FOR
DUMMIES®

by Scott Speck and Evelyn Cisneros

WILEY

Wiley Publishing, Inc.

Ballet For Dummies®

Published by
Wiley Publishing, Inc.
111 River St.
Hoboken, NJ 07030-5774
www.wiley.com

For general information on our other products and services or to obtain technical support, please contact our Customer Care Department within the U.S. at 877-762-2974, outside the U.S. at 317-572-3993, or fax 317-572-4002.

Wiley also publishes its books in a variety of electronic formats. Some content that appears in print may not be available in electronic books.

Library of Congress Cataloging-in-Publication Data:

Library of Congress Control Number: 2003105854

1O/RS/QZ/QT/IN

ISBN: 0-7645-2568-9

Manufactured in the United States of America

10   9   8   7

WILEY   is a trademark of Wiley Publishing, Inc.

About the Authors

© Lisa Kohler

Scott Speck, award-winning conductor, has led the San Francisco Ballet in hundreds of performances at San Francisco Opera House, Washington's Kennedy Center, the Paris Opera, London's Royal Opera House at Covent Garden, and on tour throughout the United States. He is currently Music Director of the Mobile Symphony and the West Shore Symphony, and Principal Guest Conductor of the China Film Philharmonic in Beijing.

Scott Speck is in demand as a guest conductor of ballet, opera, and symphonic performances throughout the world. In recent seasons he has led the orchestras of Paris (Orchestre Colonne), Moscow (State Radio-Television Symphony Orchestra), Shanghai, Beijing, Baltimore, Buffalo, Florida, Honolulu, Houston, New Orleans, Oregon, Rochester, San Diego, Virginia, and Windsor, Ontario, among many others.

His commentaries have appeared regularly on National Public Radio, the Australian Broadcasting Corporation, the British Broadcasting Corporation, and Voice of Russia. A Fulbright scholar and *summa cum laude* graduate of Yale, he has written about the arts for several magazines and journals.

Scott Speck is the co-author (with David Pogue) of *Classical Music For Dummies* and *Opera For Dummies*, published by John Wiley and Sons.

© Marty Sohl

Evelyn Cisneros, legendary Prima Ballerina, danced with the San Francisco Ballet for 23 years, creating innumerable roles, performing nationally and internationally, and starring in several televised productions. She is the subject of the book *Evelyn Cisneros: Prima Ballerina;* the subject of the PBS special *Evelyn Cisneros: Moving On;* the former host of the PBS program *Bay Windows;* and the online ballet advice columnist "Ask Evelyn" for *Dance Magazine.* She has been featured on the covers of several major dance publications.

She has been honored for her activism as a role model for the Hispanic community as well as for her artistic achievement. She holds honorary doctorates from Mills College and from California State University at Monterey Bay.

When Evelyn Cisneros retired from the San Francisco Ballet with a gala performance in 1999, the Mayor proclaimed "Evelyn Cisneros Week" to commemorate the event. She is now Ballet Education Coordinator for the San Francisco Ballet Center for Dance Education, while continuing to teach ballet, stage ballets, and coach dancers.

About the Dancers

Stephen Legate (the male dancer featured in the studio demonstrations throughout this book) trained with the National Ballet School in Toronto and the School of American Ballet in New York City. While dancing with the National Ballet of Canada, he won the Erik Bruhn Prize as Best Male Dancer. He joined the San Francisco Ballet as a Soloist in 1991 and was promoted to Principal Dancer the following year.

His acclaimed roles include Prince Siegfried in *Swan Lake,* Prince Desiré in *Sleeping Beauty*, Romeo in *Romeo and Juliet*, Colas in *La fille mal gardée,* and Cassio in *Othello*. His immensely varied contemporary repertory includes leading roles in most of the Balanchine, Robbins, Kudelka, Morris, and Caniparoli ballets.

Stephen Legate has performed all over the world with the company and as a guest artist. In April 2000 he received the Isadora Duncan Award for best performance in an ensemble, with his wife and partner Evelyn Cisneros. Together they also performed in *A Supernatural Evening with Carlos Santana*, which aired nationally and was released on DVD. His most important role to date is that of husband and father.

Leslie Young (the female dancer featured in the studio demonstrations throughout this book) has danced with the San Francisco Ballet since 1985, and was promoted to Soloist in 1995. While studying at the San Francisco Ballet School, she won the Princess Grace Foundation Award.

Her memorable roles include the Lilac Fairy and the Fairy of Tenderness in *Sleeping Beauty*, a Princess and Big Swan in *Swan Lake*, Rosaline in *Romeo and Juliet,* the Sugar Plum Fairy, Butterfly, and Snow Queen in *The Nutcracker*. She has danced in numerous works of George Balanchine, Jerome Robbins, Mark Morris, and Helgi Tomasson, among many others. In addition to her work as Soloist, she now works closely with the emerging choreographer Julia Adam as Ballet Mistress.

Leslie Young participated in the development of Felissimo's Danseuse inner/outer wear. She was integral in developing San Francisco Ballet's *Nutcracker* outreach program for children in local hospitals.

Dedication

From Scott Speck:

To my parents, Gayle and Mort, and my brother Jeff.

To Giang Quach, for your eternal support.

To Emil de Cou, for inviting me into the ballet world in the first place.

And to the sweet and lovely Evelyn — my first and greatest ballet teacher.

From Evelyn Cisneros:

To my husband, friend and life-mate Stephen: Without your love, constant encouragement, and understanding, this adventure would have never been possible. Thank you for picking up the slack for our family while I was working, for your witty input, and for being my sounding board and strength. Thanks to my son Ethan, who is my joy; and to my parents Fred and Esther and my brother Robert, whose enduring support made my dance career a reality. Thanks to my artistic directors and choreographers for the opportunities; to my fellow dancers and partners for the support; and to my students and teachers for your faith in me.

To my co-author Scott: You have been a source of encouragement from before the first page to the final word. Your faith in me, patience, and sense of humor have made this project a pleasure. You have encouraged me to discover another form of silent expression. My deepest gratitude.

With deepest appreciation to my Lord Jesus Christ for my life, for all things are possible for those who love the Lord.

Authors' Acknowledgments

We gratefully acknowledge the help and encouragement of the staff of the San Francisco Ballet Association — especially Artistic Director Helgi Tomasson, Glenn McCoy, Carol Oune, and Jennifer French. We appreciate the work of Leslie Young and Stephen Legate, who appear in the studio photos throughout this book; and Gregory Cheng of Byron Hoyt Music, which made its Website available for our musical examples. We give special thanks to our loving and enthusiastic editors, Mary Goodwin and Natasha Graf of Wiley Publishing. We especially thank David Pogue for his original inspiration. And we truly appreciate the strenuous efforts of Kim Okamura, Tonya Cupp, Holly Gastineau-Grimes, and everyone at Wiley on our behalf.

Publisher's Acknowledgments

We're proud of this book; please send us your comments through our Dummies online registration form located at www.dummies.com/register/.

Some of the people who helped bring this book to market include the following:

Acquisitions, Editorial, and Media Development

Project Editor: Mary Goodwin

Acquisitions Editor: Natasha Graf

Editorial Program Assistant: Holly Gastineau-Grimes

Technical Editor: Kim Okamura

Editorial Manager: Michelle Hacker

Editorial Assistant: Elizabeth Rea

Cover Photos: © John Lamb/Getty Images/ The Image Bank

Cartoons: Rich Tennant, www.the5thwave.com

Composition Services

Project Coordinator: Kristie Reese

Layout and Graphics: Joyce Haughey, Stephanie D. Jumper, Heather Ryan, Erin Zeltner

Special Art: San Francisco Ballet

Proofreaders: John Tyler Connoley, Aptara

Indexer: Aptara

Publishing and Editorial for Consumer Dummies

Diane Graves Steele, Vice President and Publisher, Consumer Dummies

Joyce Pepple, Acquisitions Director, Consumer Dummies

Kristin Ferguson-Wagstaffe, Product Development Director, Consumer Dummies

Ensley Eikenburg, Associate and Publisher, Travel

Kelly Regan, Editorial Director, Travel

Publishing for Technology Dummies

Andy Cummings, Vice President and Publisher, Dummies Technology/General User

Composition Services

Debbie Stailey, Director of Composition Services

Contents at a Glance

Table of Contents

Chapter 17: Watching Ballet in Action 265

Part V: The Part of Tens 279

Chapter 18: The Ten Most Commonly Used Ballet Steps 281

Introduction

● ●

*O*oooooh. Well done!

With enormous strength, passion, and finesse, you've made a flying leap into the world of dance. Notice how deftly you hoisted this book; how stylishly you soared over the Table of Contents; how gracefully you flipped to this page.

Take that a step further, and you've got *ballet* — where women in tutus and men in tights leap across the stage, doing some very unusual things to their own bodies.

Ballet is a form of dance, and you've experienced it all your life: on TV, in the movies, at your junior high school prom. (Okay, maybe you skipped the prom.) If you've ever heard the names Fred Astaire, Paula Abdul, or Mikhail Baryshnikov, you know more than enough to get started.

Whether you want to *dance* ballet or just find out all about it, your ballet experience can remain as powerful and elegant as it began. All you have to do is take it one step at a time.

About This Book

To get one thing straight right off the bat: We take for granted that you're a highly intelligent person. After all, you've chosen this book from among a whole *shelf* of ballet books.

But in today's world, you're expected to be fully conversant with *millions* of different subjects. Clearly, even the greatest genius can't know *everything*. It happens that you, O Reader, are still in the first stages of ballet mastery.

That's why we've written *Ballet For Dummies*. Without presupposing any prior experience, this book gives you a thorough understanding of the basics of classical ballet. It broadens and deepens your appreciation for the art form. It helps you explore the steps yourself (if you want), within your own comfort level. It puts you at ease discussing ballet in any situation. And although this book is not a suitable alternative to a graduate degree in ballet, it's much more fun and costs about $90,000 less.

Conventions Used in This Book

As you leaf through this book, you may notice that we use French terms to refer to ballet steps. Ballet began in France, and you can't get very far in ballet without tackling a couple of these terms. But not to fear — we provide pronunciations for each term throughout each chapter. You can find a detailed list of the French terms, and others, in the glossary at the back of the book.

We also use letter-and-number combinations, such as D-1, D-2, or D-3, to refer to different directions in a room. These combinations help guide you as you do the steps, allowing you to face the right direction at the right time. Turn to Chapter 9 for more information about this room layout. You also find it printed on the Cheat Sheet at the front of this book, just in case you get lost along the way.

Foolish Assumptions

We don't make any assumptions about you, O Reader. For example, we don't assume that you have any previous experience with ballet — although if you do, you can still find plenty in this book to keep you busy. We explain everything from the beginning, so that you can go farther, faster, in your exploration of this great dance form.

However, some people do make some unfortunate assumptions about ballet before they know much about it. In the following list, we can help you ward off a few ballet misconceptions that are quite common — especially in America.

- ✔ **You need to be rich to enjoy ballet.** Not at all! As we show you throughout this book, you can discover the joys of ballet with nothing more than this book, a sturdy piece of furniture, and your own two feet.

- ✔ **You need to be skinny to dance.** Not true — unless you plan to audition for a huge ballet company like the Bolshoi tomorrow. Whether you're shaped like an hourglass or a clock, you can begin to explore the steps in this book.

- ✔ **You need to start young.** Again, if you want to be a world-famous professional dancer, it helps to start dancing as a kid. But if your goal is to master the steps and enjoy the art, you can start at almost any age. You should see what Grandpa did yesterday.

- ✔ **Ballet is just for girls.** Yes, it is for women and girls. But it's also very much for guys. Ballet as we know it was invented by a king, and at first, *only* men were allowed to dance it. Professional ballet dancers are just as fit as Olympic athletes — and in many countries, male dancers are revered as macho national heroes.

People of all ages, genders, colors, shapes, and sizes are discovering ballet — and having a blast doing it. Starting today, you can, too.

How This Book Is Organized

We divided this book into five different parts, for your reading pleasure.

Part I: Ballet Dancing from the Top

In this part, we ease you into the world of ballet. We show you what ballet is and how it started. We introduce you to the most popular kinds of ballet attire. We let you in on the warm-ups that the pros use. And we present the basics of ballet technique — things you can do right here, right now, without any prior training.

One of our favorite chapters tells you all about music. Besides being an incredibly rich art form in its own right, music is the inspiration for most ballet. We show you how to listen to music, count it out, and coordinate your steps with it.

Part II: Belly Up to the Barre

In Part II, we introduce you to the *barre* — that long, horizontal, wooden pole that ballet dancers use to start every single day of their lives.

In the three chapters of this part, we demonstrate just about everything a person can do at the barre — and even how to get along without one. Some of these steps are extremely simple to grasp — such as the *plié* ("plee-AY"), or knee bend. Others (in later chapters) are successively more advanced.

Part III: Center Floor, Anyone?

This part shows you the awesome steps that you can try out on the ballet floor — or in your living room. We start with the first tentative steps away from the barre and end with amazing *pirouettes* (spins) and thrilling jumps across the floor.

We even explain some very advanced steps that you often see the pros do — like the whip turn known as the *fouetté* ("foo-et-TAY") and the stunningly impressive *double tour,* or double turn in the air.

Part IV: Living the Ballet Life

In Part IV, we point out all the ways that ballet can change you. From performing a simple dance (alone or in pairs) to watching the great masterpieces onstage, this part is a complete guide to making ballet an important part of your life.

One chapter is all about *choreography* — the art of creating an original ballet. We introduce you to some of the world's greatest choreographers, and show you how to design your own dances.

Part V: The Part of Tens

Part V contains our picks for the Top Ten of ballet — everything from the most common steps to the best-loved ballets; from the most useful ballet terminology to the ten strangest (but truest) facts about those sleek and graceful animals known as professional ballet dancers.

Icons Used in This Book

Throughout *Ballet For Dummies*, we use several icons to point out important features worth noting.

This icon clues you in on a handy shortcut, technique, or suggestion that can help you get more out of your ballet experience.

This icon reminds you of an important point — something that appears elsewhere in the book, or something you should always remember as you practice ballet.

For especially complicated moves, or their descriptions, let this icon be your guide.

This icon marks an opportunity for you to get up and dance.

Sometimes you just gotta be *really* careful. We use this icon when we want to show you how to do a step without hurting yourself.

This icon lets you into the backstage world of ballet. It also signals great stories worth repeating.

Where to Go from Here

We designed this book so that you can start *reading* anywhere. Use the Table of Contents or the index as a starting point, if you want. Or, if you're in a romantic mood, put on a CD of *Swan Lake*, skip right to the chapter on partnering (Chapter 14) and discover what you'll be able to do in the not-too-distant future.

But if you want to actually *try* what you've read, we strongly recommend that you start at the beginning. In ballet, each exercise gives you the skills you need to try the next. As ballet dancers are always saying, "You gotta *plié* before you can *double tour*." (Oh yeah — there's a glossary at the back too.)

The reason that ballet becomes an obsession for so many people, including us, is that it has incredible power. If you're attuned to it and are within its sphere of influence, you simply cannot remain unchanged.

We hope that this book helps you to tune into the life-affirming force of ballet. We hope that you want to experience more. And we hope that this incredible art continues to move you and change you as long as you live.

Part I
Ballet Dancing from the Top

In this part . . .

You've seen ballet before. You've marveled at its beauty and grace. You've wondered what on earth was going on. Now you're about to watch it through different eyes — and maybe even prepare to do it yourself.

In this part, we ease you into this strange art form. We show you what ballet is, and even give you a little history. We tell you what you need to look good — both in the studio and onstage. And we tell you about music, ballet's great inspiration.

This is the part where you don't even have to sweat. (Well, except for the part about abs.) No nitty. No gritty. Just fun.

Chapter 1

Curtain Up! Welcome to the Ballet

*W*elcome to world of ballet — a universe of beauty and grace, aerial pyrotechnics, heroes, villains, and a fairy or two. Where the sound of tapping toes melds with the luscious strains of a full orchestra. Where true love always triumphs, evil is destroyed, and everybody has great legs.

This is the world of ballet. And by the way — don't be put off by the fact that all the guys are wearing tights. It's art, man, art!

Ballet for Life

Whether you want to participate in ballet or just watch it, the ballet experience can excite and inspire you. Ballet is one of the most beautiful forms of expression ever devised: an exquisite mix of sight and sound, stunning aesthetics, and awesome technique.

Though the professional ballet world may or may not be for you, the *practice* of ballet certainly can be. Ballet can give you more strength and flexibility, better alignment, and infinite grace — for life. It can counteract the aging effects of gravity, reduce stress, and prevent injury. And until you've tried moving your body to some of the most beautiful music ever written, you've missed one of the greatest joys life has to offer.

Imagine waking up after 100 years of sleep, released from a curse, and finding your true love. You may feel inspired to attempt such superhuman feats as the one depicted in Figure 1-1 (after a good stretch, of course). In fact, you may even be exuberant enough to do it *three* times, like Princess Aurora and Prince Desiré in *Sleeping Beauty.* That's what we love most about ballet — above all, it can bring *ecstasy* into your life.

Figure 1-1:
The exuberance of ballet: Evelyn Cisneros and Anthony Randazzo in *Sleeping Beauty.*

In the Beginning . . .

The ballet moves in this book have a long tradition — longer than most things on earth. In ballet, an understanding of that tradition is extremely important. In this section, we acquaint you with the winding road that led to the beautiful art form you can experience today.

Just like music, dance has existed since prehistoric times. Rhythmic chanting — usually meant to appease the gods or to while away the time between woolly mammoth sightings — soon became accompanied by body movement. After all, what's more natural than swaying to the beat?

Some of the earliest organized dances took place in ancient Greek dramas, which sometimes incorporated a dancing chorus. Even then, it paid to know how to move your feet. The tradition made its way to Italy, where theatrical dancing became enhanced by manual gestures, or mime. (You can read more about mime in Chapter 16.) This tradition was kept alive for centuries by minstrels who sang, tumbled, juggled, and reveled their way through the Dark Ages.

Court dancing for fun and profit

It was during the High Renaissance in northern Italy that court ballroom dancing was born. (The words "ballet" and "ball" are both derived from the Italian word *ballare,* meaning "to dance".) Performed by the nobility, court dances became all the rage. They spread to France — where they reached their height at the court of King Louis XIV.

King Louis, the Sun King (or "Twinkle Toes," as he was almost certainly not known), was an accomplished dancer himself, as you can see in Figure 1-2. He established the first official school of ballet, known today as the Paris Opera Ballet. That's why, to this day, all ballet vocabulary is in French.

Figure 1-2:
King Louis XIV, the Sun King, in a ballet pose of his time.

Whereas the first performers were kings, noblemen, and other slackers dancing for their own enjoyment, ballet eventually became much more structured and elaborate, demanding strong legs, great balance, and increasingly virtuosic technique. Professional ballet was born.

If you were to suddenly wake up at a dance performance in the year 1680, two things would strike you: The dancers, as they accidentally slammed into your suddenly materialized body, and the fact that everyone onstage was a guy. Ballet was for athletes; it was unbecoming (so people thought) for women to participate in such bold and daring moves.

The first women didn't appear professionally until 1681 — and when they did, they wore big hoop skirts, high heels, and wigs. Eventually, someone got the idea that a ballerina could be much more effective with her legs visible. So beginning in the early 1700s, women began dancing in shorter and shorter skirts, and without hoops, heels, or wigs.

The Paris Opera and pointe work

The more of their bodies they revealed, the more popular ballerinas became. But in order to truly win the favor of the audience, one more element was needed. Something so strange, so masochistic, that you would never believe it in a million years. We're talking, of course, of dancing on the tips of their toes — *en pointe.*

The thought behind this bizarre concept was this: If a woman could point her feet unnaturally down at a 90-degree angle and stand *really* high off the ground, balancing on the very tips of two or three toes, she would appear to be floating.

And that was a good thing — this was the Romantic era, and most ballets of the time involved spirits, fairies, and supernatural creatures, like women whose day job involved being dead. Floating above the surface of the stage just seemed the right thing to do.

This feat of the feet was possible with the help of special shoes, known today as *pointe* shoes. And the first ballerina who pulled if off was Marie Taglioni (see Figure 1-3) — daughter of a famous choreographer at the Paris Opera.

Figure 1-3: Marie Taglioni, the first ballerina to dance *en pointe.*

Dancing *en pointe* did the trick — thereafter, women not only became the *equals* of the men onstage, but actually *dominated* ballet for well over a century.

As time passed, *pointe* shoes became stronger and more supportive, allowing ballerinas to stay up longer and dance more complicated steps. Today *pointe* work is a substantial area of any ballerina's training; she must be able to balance on the points of her toes, strong and secure, for longer than it took you to read this sentence.

After all these years, the Paris Opera remains one of the best ballet companies in the world, boasting some phenomenal dancers. If you ever visit Paris, make sure to stop by the Opera Garnier — where the first *pointe* shoes of Marie Taglioni are still on display.

Russia and America

After 1850, the center of the ballet world shifted from Paris to St. Petersburg, Russia. There the master choreographer Marius Petipa, working with the music of the great composer Peter Tchaikovsky, was beginning to draw the attention of the world. Their creations, such as *Swan Lake, Sleeping Beauty,* and *The Nutcracker*, remain immortal masterpieces of ballet.

Over time, the technical demands of Russian ballets continued to increase, and by the early 1900s, the Imperial Russian Ballet School was training the greatest dancers in the world. On a recent trip to Russia for the purposes of researching this book (at least that's what we told the IRS), we confirmed that it is still possible to see superb dancing in Russia.

But it wasn't long before some Russian dancers began to crave more artistic freedom, and a quiet exodus from Russia began. The so-called Ballets Russes, made up of some of Russia's greatest dancers, toured Europe and America in the early 1900s, reviving interest in classical ballet. The brilliant Russian ballerina named Anna Pavlova formed her own company and toured all over the world, bringing ballet to thousands who had never seen it before.

Several Russian dancers found a new home in America. One was George Balanchine, who established a major ballet school in the 1930s, which eventually supported the New York City Ballet. America's enthusiastic support of ballet continues to draw some of the best dancers and choreographers in the world.

Today's stage

Today you can find a ballet company, with magnificent dancers, in almost every major city on earth. Many companies have their own ballet schools — some for training future professionals, and others for interested amateurs.

After two hundred years of female domination, male dancers have regained ballet superstardom. Leading the movement were such geniuses as Rudolf Nureyev and Mikhail Baryshnikov — masters of clean lines, high jumps, and Olympian athleticism.

The technical demands on dancers still continue to increase. Dancers must excel in classical technique in order to master the old warhorses; yet they must also be ready to throw themselves — literally — into some of the newest choreography (see Figure 1-4). Ballet continues to be more and more diverse, fun to watch, and even more fun to do.

Figure 1-4:
Evelyn Cisneros and Anthony Randazzo in *Rubies* (choreographed by George Balanchine), a contemporary ballet that showcases the amazing possibilities of modern choreography.

© Marty Sohl

Watching Great Choreography for Inspiration

As you fine-tune your classical ballet technique — or even if you just like to *read* about it — you become better equipped to understand and fully enjoy the things that make choreography great. In this book, we hope to turn you on to many different styles of ballet. We take you from the classics of Marius Petipa and company to the more contemporary styles of George Balanchine, Jerome Robbins, Jiri Kylian, and Mark Morris — to name just a few.

Naturally, some styles of ballet are easier to understand than others. Some ballets immediately seem to sparkle like exquisite jewels, while others, at first glance, resemble a flurry of headless chickens. We're not here to torture you; we want to help you find out you what we love.

Does one style appeal to you more than all the others? If so, you can continue your exploration of ballet by delving into other works in that style or by that choreographer. Or if you like them all, fantastic! Our job just got a lot easier.

Gathering Your Ballet Materials

What equipment do you need to begin exploring ballet? To begin, not much. For example, any old workout clothes will do; if you want to get fancy, we suggest some special ballet clothing in Chapter 2.

Shoes are probably the most important and personal item you need (with the exception of the men's dance belt), and we point you in the direction of the right ballet slippers for you.

As for other equipment, you can do an impressive array of things with nothing more than a good-sized room and a solid piece of furniture. But there's plenty of optional equipment to choose from in Chapter 2.

Staying Healthy and Avoiding Injury

In ballet, you occasionally ask your body to do extraordinary things. Your body is your high-performance instrument — and it's essential to protect your body from injury any way you can. A healthy diet, good warm-ups, and adequate rest are essential. In Chapters 2 and 3 we show you some of the ways to keep your body healthy. And later, in Chapter 22, we show you how lifestyle can affect your performance.

We can't emphasize enough that ballet is *progressive*. Each exercise gives you the strength, balance, and confidence to prepare you for the next. And so, one of the best ways to avoid injury is to try the steps in the order that we present them. Do a good warm-up first (we show you how in Chapter 3); then go through the barre exercises in Part II, and the center floor exercises in Part III.

If you've exercised in the past, you know how important it is not to overstretch or strain your body. Note to self: Don't attempt anything in this book that feels painful or too difficult. There is a fine line between just enough and too much, and only you know where that line is.

Listen to your body: Nobody else can hear it. If they can, something is definitely wrong.

Getting Started: It's Easier Than You Think

As art forms go, ballet can get pretty intricate. Some of the most advanced moves in this book may take weeks or even months of practice. But you can do certain things right now, with almost no practice at all. Just to prove it to you, give this a try:

1. **Stand with your feet close together. Keeping your heels touching, turn your legs outward so that your toes point away from each other.**

2. **With a table or chair for support, rise up on your feet so that you are supporting yourself on the balls of your feet.**

3. **Now come back down and bend your knees, leaving your heels on the ground.**

Check it out — here you are, only a few paragraphs into Chapter 1, and you have already conquered first position, the *relevé,* and the *demi-plié!* You should be proud. (See Chapters 4 and 6 for more detailed information on these moves.)

Why Being a Ballet Novice Helps You Enjoy Ballet

You may not believe this, but it's true: You, O Novice, have a surprising advantage over many of the world's ballet fanatics. You cross the threshold of this astonishing creative realm unfettered by preconditioning or ballet prejudice. You're a veritable open book. A clean slate. An empty canvas on which the great choreographers can paint their visual landscapes. We can't *wait* to get started with you.

And that's what many "balletomanes" often forget: Ballet is not a purely intellectual pursuit. More than many other arts, ballet is about free, unencumbered expression.

In this book, we help you master that expression — and unlock your capacity to experience one of life's greatest highs.

Chapter 2

Stocking the Tools of the Trade

. . . .

. . . .

*R*eady to jump into the world of ballet? In this chapter we tell you everything you need to begin — the room, the floor, the barre, the outfit, the shoes, and more.

Finding the Right Practice Space

The right place to practice ballet is a place where you feel comfortable. And in order to feel comfortable, you need two different things — space and privacy.

When trying something foreign, like ballet, you need to feel totally at ease, with zero intimidation factor. So send away any snickering significant others, and consider locking out the dog as well.

Determining how much space you need

Regarding space: At first, you don't need much. If you can lie on the floor with your limbs outstretched, and then stand upright, arms above your head, without hitting the ceiling, you've got it made.

But later, as you attempt the turns and leaps of the so-called *center floor* work, the demands of the space increase. You need more unobstructed room around you in all directions. A 10-x-12-foot room can keep you happy for a little while; after you graduate to more advanced movements, you may want to rent a dance studio by the hour, join a beginner ballet class, or remodel your home.

At one time or another, all dancers deal with small spaces, even in the professional world. The backstage area of the City Center Theater in New York City is so small that the wings on the left side of the stage end literally a couple of feet from a brick wall. There is barely enough room for two skinny dancers to move around in the wings during a performance.

Other considerations

As you're looking for a place to practice, consider more than just the space of the room. The space you choose should also be warm, with no drafts. Your muscles need to get warm and *stay* warm, even as you strip off your outer layers of clothes.

Ideally, you should also have a mirror in the room. Ballet dancers are constantly checking their technique, adjusting their alignment, and admiring their great legs. With a mirror, you can compare your own work with the figures in this book.

Also, you definitely need a music system. The control (or remote control) should be close at hand, so you can start and stop the music as needed. You also need speakers good enough so that you hear the music, not the sound of your own heavy breathing.

For a "silent" art form, ballet sure makes a lot of noise. Your feet make swishing sounds as you brush them in straight lines or half-circles, rapping sounds as you tap the floor, or smacking sounds after a leap through the air. If you have downstairs neighbors, try to be considerate of their lives. See if you can practice while they're away. Better yet, tell them what you are up to, so they don't have you investigated for suspicious behavior. Who knows — they may get so inspired by your ballet quest that they'll want to come up and join you.

Practicing on a Ballet-Friendly Floor (or the Next-Best Thing)

Besides your shoes (see "Choosing Ballet Slippers," later in this chapter), the floor is the most important element that allows you to do your best. In ballet, you ask your body to do moves that stretch your boundaries a bit. A good floor helps you to be as kind to your body as possible.

Try to work on a wooden floor, or one which has wood under the surface layer. Wood gives your body a base that is solid, yet not rock-hard. Cement is very hard on your legs and back, and it's pretty unforgiving if you fall. Ballet is hard enough as it is — go for wood. Ideally, we recommend a "sprung floor." That means that the support beams beneath the floor are far enough apart to allow the surface to give and spring back, helping to ease the impact of jumping.

As a last resort, you can find portable floors online. These boast a foam backing to give you a soft surface, even if the portable floor lies over cement.

Besides the material, the surface of the floor is also all-important. The ideal floor surface is smooth, even, and a little springy, but not slippery. Uneven tiles are not a good choice. Neither is a shag carpet. On the other hand, kitchen floor linoleum can be quite good. (Just make sure you haven't waxed the linoleum too recently — you don't want to fly headfirst into the dishwasher.) A hardwood floor also works well. For some exercises, you can even work on a short pile carpet or large area rug, as long as the carpet or rug isn't likely to become suddenly mobile.

Of course, a dance linoleum — created specifically for ballet — is best. But you can improvise, especially in the first stages of your development.

The Barre Essentials

As you can find out in Chapter 6, the *barre* is the long horizontal cylinder that ballet dancers use every day of their lives. No matter how many years you study the art of classical ballet, you always start at the barre.

Barres can be either permanent or portable. A permanent barre, which is usually made of wood, is attached to a wall of a ballet studio. The cross-section is either circular (measuring 2 inches in diameter) or oblong, with a variety of heights to accommodate different ages and body types.

The ideal barre is somewhere between your waist and hip height. While holding on with one hand, you should be able to bend forward comfortably without having to let go.

If you don't have access to a ballet studio, a portable barre may be just the ticket. Today's portable barres may be covered aluminum (valued for its light weight), or covered steel (durable and preferred by professional ballet dancers for its solidity and stability).

Purchasing your own barre

If you're serious about buying your own barre, you can find permanent or portable barres at several Web sites online. Be warned, though — a barre is not cheap. At the very least, you're likely to pay $200 for the simplest barre.

The best Web site we have found belongs to Stagestep (www.stagestep.com). Their Modular Ballet Barres are available in various lengths. At this writing, Stagestep offers a "Dance Studio at Home" package, which includes a 4-x-6-foot mirror (not glass), their 4-foot long portable barre, and a 6-x-8-foot portable dance floor (with a foam backing designed to make even cement danceable), all at a big savings off the individual prices.

Another impressive Web site we found belongs to En pointe (www.enpointe.com/balletbarre.html). There you can find a 4½-foot portable barre made of covered aluminum of various colors, complete with a carrying case.

Finally, we recommend a British Web site, Ballet Barre (www.balletbarre.co.uk). This company offers the hardware and detailed instructions for installing permanent barres. The company also sells portable units, well-constructed with a steel frame and wooden oblong barre — the kind preferred by purists.

Setting up a barre substitute

At one time or another, every dancer has to find a makeshift barre. Although not absolutely ideal for ballet exercises, barre substitutes do have one advantage: They prevent you from getting spoiled. After you've tried a variety of barre substitutes, you won't be afraid to step out of your perfect ballet environment.

Going barreless

In the rare case where *nothing* in your vicinity makes a suitable barre substitute, then you might consider a last-ditch alternative. But be warned: This option is only for the very, very brave, those who are addicted to the adrenaline that pumps furiously through a slightly out-of-control body.

Your mission, if you choose to accept it, is to attempt any or all the barre exercises in this book free of the barre. Yes, that means free-standing.

If you do decide to take this challenge, you need to modify the exercises a bit. Work with your arms stretched out to the sides for balance. Substitute an easier foot position wherever you want to. (See Chapter 4 for much more on the positions of the feet.) And because the barre exercises usually involve raising just one leg, make sure to switch sides very often, so you build strength evenly without tiring out one leg too soon.

Going barreless is a great way to develop power and balance from the very beginning. It builds strength and coordination faster than regular exercises at the barre — and that's your greatest reward.

Almost any solid piece of furniture can be a barre substitute. A big dining table is ideal — and a heavy chair could work, too. But make sure your "barre" is immobile — you should *not* be able to lift it with one hand. (When you're about to tip over, you'd be surprised how much weight you can move.)

Whatever you choose, make sure that you have enough room on all sides, so that you won't whack anything in the midst of a difficult combination.

Dressed to Dance

Don't be fooled by what you see ballet dancers wearing onstage. Those are *costumes* — usually meant to set a specific mood or tell a specific story. The attire that ballet dancers wear to practice is usually very different from what they wear in performance.

Most dancers agree on a certain array of clothing to get them through their workouts and rehearsals. Let us, your trusty authors, steer you in the right direction.

Donning (and doffing) the right ballet clothes

In ballet practice, the key to sartorial success is to find something that allows you to warm up easily — and stay warm enough to move freely, easily, and unencumbered. We suggest that you wear extra layers to begin — that way, you can peel off each piece as the corresponding area of your body warms up.

According to long-standing ballet tradition, the "ideal" ballet body is very thin and well proportioned, with the legs longer than the torso, and well-arched feet at the end of those long legs. Of course, not everyone is built that way. You can help create the illusion of this form by wearing a *unitard*. Although this name sounds like an exotic mythical animal, it actually refers to a particular garment. The unitard consists of a *leotard* (a sort of stretchy one-piece bathing suit) attached to a pair of tights, which completely cover the legs. The unitard can be worn by anyone — men and women, boys, girls, and extraordinarily graceful household pets.

To help emphasize those beautiful body proportions, most professional dancers are convinced that black looks better than any other color — especially on the legs. Black is by far the color of choice among the pros, male and female, in the studio.

For men

Although we've been putting it off, we now find ourselves compelled to explore the sensitive, and sometimes controversial, topic of *dance belts*. All male dancers must wear dance belts.

A dance belt is a ballet-style athletic support girdle for men. Nobody likes wearing one, but male dancers must wear this garment for their own protection — the painful alternative being a hernia. (The compensation for men is that they never have to wear *pointe* shoes as long as they live.)

Men generally wear sweatpants, which should fit tightly enough to see whether the knees are straight, with a T-shirt tucked in at the waist with a waist elastic or belt. Alternately, they can wear unitards (tank style), tights, ¾-length tights, or biking-style shorts.

For more warmth, men often wear sweatshirts, sweaters, legwarmers, and socks over their ballet slippers. See "Other dancer-friendly clothes," later in this chapter for additional suggestions.

For women

In ballet, as in the rest of life, the clothing options for women are more varied than for men. Unitards, for example, come in long-sleeve, short-sleeve, tank, camisole, and two-tone styles, in a variety of materials. Capezio, M. Stevens, Mirella, Natalie, and Bloch are some of the most popular brands.

The most traditional female dancers prefer to wear separate leotards and tights. Like unitards, leotards come in a variety of sleeve lengths. Tights also come in different styles. You can find tights with "feet" attached, tights with stirrups, ankle-length tights, or the popular "convertible" tights (that may be worn with feet attached or with the feet rolled up to appear ankle length). Tights also come with or without seams. The most popular style today is the "hipster," which is cut lower to fit at the hip line. Keep in mind that hipsters make your legs look shorter, and your body longer — not ideal in ballet. Choose them if they're comfortable — but don't wear 'em to an audition!

If you want to take this ballet dressing thing to an extreme, then you can find all kinds of warm-up clothes to wear over the basics. For example, you can find legwarmers (see the next section), knit tights, sweaters that wrap, sweaters that are extra short in order not to cover the waist, longer sweaters that double as skirts when belted, and, of course, socks, worn over ballet slippers for warming up the toes on those really cold mornings. For these warm-up clothes, we recommend the Kd Dance brand, which uses cotton and silk-blended yarns that feel great and keep you very warm.

A visit to your local dance supply shop gives you the opportunities to try different styles. Or, if you are fairly sure of what you want, you can shop online at www.discountdance.com or www.capezio.com.

Other dancer-friendly clothes

If buying a whole new outfit doesn't appeal to you — or if you're not sure how far you want to go with ballet — not to worry. You can still find something in your current wardrobe to do the job.

For most ballet activities, a T-shirt and sweatpants can work just fine. And if you've ever taken a yoga class, you can use the same outfit for ballet.

However, you may want to make just a couple of alterations. If you decide to use sweatpants, we suggest adding a waistband of elastic, anywhere from half an inch to a full inch in width. This waistband can be tied, sewn, or pinned to the pants to help hold the pants up. If the sweatpants are baggy, we suggest adding additional bands of elastic around your legs just below the knees to ensure that you don't trip on the bottom of your pant legs.

If you're prone to feeling cold, you may also consider legwarmers. These are basically tubes of material worn at varying lengths around the legs to warm up the muscles. Usually these warmers are footless, but often a dancer adds socks to the mix. You can find legwarmers in just about any length.

Choosing Ballet Slippers

First, you may be asking, why wear ballet slippers at all? Why not just wear socks? Well, the danger with socks is that you can easily stub your toe. Your foot must be supported — but lightly, so that you have access to all the bones and muscles of your feet.

The quest for the perfect ballet slipper is like the search for the perfect *jalapeño* — it can take several years and give you an ulcer. Ballet dancers usually try out a wide variety of shoe makes, models, and materials before settling on a favorite. But your own taste and comfort are the perfect guide. To quote Dr. Spock: You know more than you think you do.

Looking at your options

The variety of shoes available is impressive (see Figure 2-1). Your options include:

- Leather full-sole slippers
- Canvas full-sole slippers
- Canvas split-sole slippers
- Dansneakers — split-sole dance sneakers in leather, canvas, or a combination of materials

Split-sole shoes have no sole between the ball of the foot and the heel. The added flexibility in the middle of the shoe helps the arch of your foot to look higher, requiring less effort to point fully. And that's a very good thing: In ballet, your arch can never be too high.

Ballet slippers range in price from approximately $16 to $25 a pair. How long they last depends on how often you wear them — and your tolerance for the smell of your feet.

Try wearing socks inside your ballet slippers. The slippers will remain April fresh a lot longer.

Figure 2-1:
The wide variety of ballet slipper options — including (left to right) Dansneakers, full-sole slippers, and split-sole slippers.

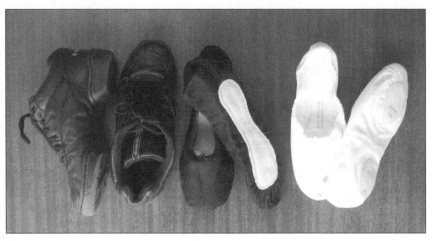

Getting the right size for your feet

All ballet slippers should fit snugly. At most, when you're standing up, a friend should be able to stick one finger into your shoe at the heel. (But ideally, there won't even be enough room for a whole finger in there.) However, your toes should be able to relax, without feeling squished.

If you live in any good-sized city, you're in luck. You can probably find at least one dance supply shop nearby. To find the right shoe, visit that local shop and try on several different styles, brands, and sizes of ballet slippers. Remember to bring along whatever socks you plan to wear.

Trust your local shoe-fitting person, but listen to your body as well. By trying on various widths and lengths, you can be assured that you have just the right shoe for your feet. Keep one overall rule in mind: If it feels good, buy it.

Different shoes for different floors

The material your slippers are made of should depend, at least partly, on the surface of the floor you're most likely to dance on. If you work primarily on a dance linoleum surface (created especially for ballet), then go with canvas slippers. They prevent you from accidentally stubbing your toes when you brush your feet.

On the other hand, if you primarily work on slippery surfaces, like marble, hardwood, kitchen linoleum, or motor oil, then leather may serve you better — it provides a stickier contact.

Customizing the fit of your shoes

Ballet dancers use elastic to hold their shoes securely on their foot. (You don't dance nearly as well when your shoes are falling off.) Most ballet dancers sew this elastic by themselves to fit the special characteristics of their own feet.

The salesperson who helps you to select ballet slippers can probably show you the traditional way to sew on the elastics — from one side of the shoe to the other just behind the side seam. But there are many other options:

- ✔ The single elastic option is the most traditional — but most ballet slippers come with a flimsy little half-inch wide elastic. If you want to use a single elastic, we highly recommend that you get a thicker (one-inch) elastic for more support. (At the left in Figure 2-2.)

- ✔ The most common *double* elastic support is crossed — starting just behind the side seam and attaching at the other side at the heel. (In the middle in Figure 2-2.)

- ✔ Another double elastic option consists of one large loop, which is attached at either side of the heel, and another elastic sewn straight across from one side seam to the other. (At the right in Figure 2-2.)

Some people prefer more than one piece of elastic — it gives them peace of mind. Using more elastic is okay, as long as you can still see your foot.

Traditionally, elastics are sewn on the inside of ballet slippers. But today, many dancers sew them elastics on the *outside*, preventing the elastics from irritating the skin and causing blisters.

After sewing the elastics on your shoes, make sure that you can bend your knees without cutting off the circulation in your ankle — which, in addition to being uncomfortable, can eventually lead to tendonitis.

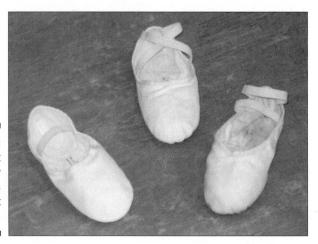

Figure 2-2:
Different ways to sew elastics onto ballet slippers.

All ballet slippers also come with a drawstring to tighten the top of the shoe. Pulling the drawstring, however, also tightens the heel at the back of the shoe — so start slow and increase incrementally. When you find that comfortable amount of tension in the drawstring, tie a knot and clip off the excess string.

Speaking of tension: If all this talk about elastics is giving you stress, don't worry. *Some* ballet slippers come with elastics already sewn in place. These give you less room for personal preference, but they're much less work.

Using Dansneakers

Dansneakers are basically tennis shoes with a split sole and a flat tip — making it easy to arch and point the foot. Dansneakers work especially well for floors that aren't very springy. They offer more support and cushion for the feet. In fact, if you work on a cement floor, we *strongly* suggest that you start with Dansneakers. Besides supporting and cushioning you from the punishing effects of repeatedly tenderizing your foot against cement, they also give your feet an enhanced arch. Looking good!

If you're feeling especially frisky, you can theoretically go *en pointe* (read on) in Dansneakers because of the flat tip — but don't tell anyone we said so.

Pointe shoes, and why you shouldn't wear them

Most women and girls dream of going *en pointe* — that is, up on the tips of a few toes. In order to achieve this feat, the dancer relies on specially crafted *pointe shoes.*

In order to get up *en pointe,* a dancer must develop tremendous strength in her legs and feet to support the entire weight of her body on the tips of a few toes. Developing this strength usually takes more than a year of intensive practice.

For much more on the mysterious *pointe* shoe, see Chapter 22. For now, suffice it to say that this shoe should remain, at least for the next year or so, in your dreams.

Keeping Your Hair in Its Place

The question of hairstyle is surprisingly relevant in ballet. Your hair should never distract you — or the audience — from your dance. If you have short hair, you can skip the rest of this section. If you have long hair, read on.

Ballet tradition is very strict. If you are a woman with long hair, and you plan to attend an actual ballet class, you should pull your hair back into a bun tightly secured to your head, with no hair flopping in your face, no matter what the style of the day may be.

Within this somewhat rigid framework, though, you have many options: The French Twist, the Low Bun, the High Bun, the French Braid, and other braid and twist combinations, to name just a few (see Figure 2-3 for inspiration).

For ballet at home, a bun works just as well — but you may feel more at ease with a ponytail.

A high ponytail makes a woman's neck look longer. A big plus in ballet. For guys: If you have long hair, put it in a ponytail.

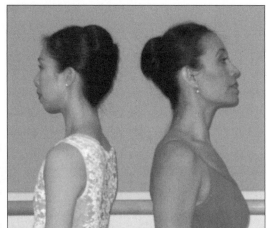

Figure 2-3:
Bunheads
made for
ballet.

More Ballet Paraphernalia

You often see professional dancers carrying around large bags containing an amazing array of attire, accessories, apparatus, and analgesics. And that's just the As.

At the minimum, a typical dancer needs to carry around these things:

- A unitard — or leotard plus tights
- Ballet slippers
- Warmers for your legs, back, and feet
- A T-shirt and dance belt for men

And here's some other stuff every dancer needs at times:

- A sewing kit (needles, white and black thread, scissors, and safety pins)
- A foot-care kit (band-aids, antibiotic cream, nail file and clippers, corn pads)
- For women: A hair kit (brush, comb, hairspray, hairpins, and rubber bands), a makeup kit (or at least lipstick), and a ballet skirt
- Advil for muscle aches
- A towel to absorb your sweat, a water bottle (preferably full!) to replenish it, and perfume or cologne to cover it up
- A bit of rosin (see the sidebar "Rosin: Turnout in a box")

No professional dancer is far from the following tools, essential for rolling out cramps:

- ✔ **A tennis ball.** While sitting on the floor, you roll the ball under your legs to ease tight muscles.

- ✔ **A foot roller.** Sitting in a chair, you roll this under the arches of your feet to relax them after a hard day's dance.

- ✔ **A golf ball.** Sitting in a chair, you can use this in place of a foot roller for those *really* resistant foot muscles.

- ✔ **A foam roller.** You can use this for tightness in your back and hips. For back muscles: Lying on the floor, drape your back over the roller and *relax,* allowing your muscles to succumb to the pressure. For hip muscles: Lie on your stomach and lift one leg with a bent knee, sliding the roller under that thigh. Then just try to relax.

All these items, of course, are great for your life *outside* the ballet studio. You can hardly ever be too flexible.

Rosin: Turnout in a box

Question: What white, powdery substance are dancers addicted to, sending them into fits of twitching ecstasy?

The answer is *rosin.* Rosin is a substance made from the sap of fir trees. As you might expect, it is very sticky stuff — and this stickiness makes dancers very happy.

As a solid, rosin is amber in color, but it appears white when crushed into a powder. The powder is put into in a container resembling a litterbox. Most dancers never go onstage without a trip and dip into this box.

Rosin prevents ballet shoes from slipping. Dancers use it on both the insides and outsides of their shoes. It keeps the heel of a ballet slipper or *pointe* shoe from slipping off a dancer's heel. A male dancer often puts rosin on his hands before dancing together with a female partner. The rosin helps prevent his hands from slipping off the ballerina's waist or back during lifts and turns.

Most of all, rosin helps the feet stick to the ground — creating the illusion that the hips are turned outward in a desirable way. (See Chapter 4 for much more on this phenomenon.) For this reason, rosin is often referred to as "Turnout in a box."

But we suggest that you go easy on the rosin in the early stages of ballet training. *Too much stickiness can trap your feet in positions that your body can't support* — causing deformities that you may never have dreamed of.

Chapter 3

Getting Toasty: Warming Up Your Body

....

In This Chapter

▶ St-r-r-r-r-r-e-t-c-h!!

▶ Supporting your body for life and dancing

▶ Strengthening the essential ballet muscles

....

Whether you're new to ballet or a seasoned pro, you must warm up your body every day before getting into the nitty-gritty of ballet work. Even if you're only *interested* in ballet, and you have no desire to master the awesome techniques in this book, you can still benefit from the warm-ups in this chapter.

Above all, remember: Be patient with yourself. It took you all those years to get all gnarled up, so allow yourself some time to unwind.

Getting Grounded: Floor Stretches

Every day of ballet begins with a good stretch of your body. In fact, we highly recommend doing all (or most) of the stretches in this chapter, in sequence. Both of your authors can testify that these stretches have been an enormous help in keeping injuries away.

Stretching can be fun, but we have to admit — it's always a bit of a challenge. Think about it — the whole point is to allow your muscles to stretch just a little farther than before. Naturally, they're going to put up a *touch* of resistance. Although your stretches should always be easy and gentle, we do acknowledge that not every stretch is pure pleasure.

If at any time you feel *sharp* pain during these exercises, stop. And that goes for every exercise in this book!

In order to maximize your enjoyment of this time, we suggest that you find some really wonderful music to inspire and distract you. Anything will do, as long as you love it.

The initial position

The best place to begin a stretching session is on the floor in what we call the *initial position* (see Figure 3-1). Place a mat (or a nice thick rug) on the floor to enhance your comfort level. Now lie on your back, knees bent and feet flat on the mat. Place your arms on the mat by your sides. Relax your back muscles and bring your lower back into contact with the mat, releasing any pressure on it. Relax your shoulders into the mat. Allow your neck to become as long as possible and look up at the ceiling. Breathe in and out a few times.

Figure 3-1:
The initial position gets your body ready to stretch.

The back

The back is the center of the body, and the back muscles provide support for all ballet activities. The first stretching exercises start by gently convincing your back to relax.

First stretch: Active relaxing

From the initial position, lift your bent knees up towards your chest and wrap your arms around your legs, grasping behind your knees (Figure 3-2a). Hold this position for the count of 20. Then release your legs and bring your feet back flat on the floor in the initial position.

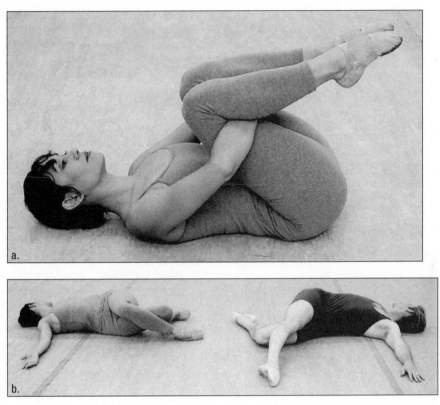

Figure 3-2: Stretching your back: active relaxing (a) and different versions of the lower back half-turn (b).

 If you don't yet have the flexibility to wrap your arms around your legs without strain, don't despair. That flexibility will come. For now, just hold your legs at whatever point gives you a comfortable back stretch. Try to find a position that you can live with for 20 seconds.

Feeling good? Time to move on.

Second stretch: Lower back half-turn

From your initial position, move your arms out along the floor, so that they stick directly out from your shoulders to your sides, palms facing upwards. Keeping your knees bent, rotate your legs as one unit gently down to the left, so that your legs rest on the mat on the left side of your body, with your knees pointing to the left, and *breathe*. (Note: If your body doesn't feel like cooperating, simply rotate your legs as far as you can *comfortably*, and hold.)

Keeping your shoulders in contact with the mat, gently turn your head to the right as far as you can comfortably. (If your neck is flexible, your chin eventually comes to rest somewhere over your right shoulder.) *Breathe* and feel the stretch in the lower back. Hold this position for 20 seconds. Then come back to the initial position and repeat this stretch on the other side.

If you're lucky enough to have built-in advanced flexibility, you may want to try an advanced variation of this maneuver. Starting in the initial position, *cross your right leg over your left* — and repeat the exercise to the left as before. (Refer to Figure 3-2b on the left.) For an *even deeper stretch* of the lower back, while your legs are on the floor, extend your right leg out straight (as shown on the right in Figure 3-2b).

Third stretch: The half push-up

Finally, we recommend a special back stretch called the "half push-up." Lie face down on the mat, arms bent at your sides, hands even with your ears at shoulder width — sphinx-style. Now push from your hands as if you were doing a push-up with your upper body, but leave your lower body (from the hips down) resting on the mat. When your arms are straight, hold for 30 to 40 seconds; then gently come down again. You can repeat this exercise as you like. It works wonders for mild lower back ailments and restores a healthy curve to the spine.

The glutes

Dancers have a love-hate relationship with their *gluteus* muscles, or *glutes*. According to the traditional ballet ideal, these rear-end muscles can never be small enough — at least on women. When this fact butts up against the realities of natural gluteal endowment, the result can be a dancer's biggest trauma.

Yet the strength of the glutes is responsible for some of the most awesome leaps in all of ballet. So good gluteal health is essential — and health begins with stretching.

Start in the initial position. Lift your right leg off the mat, keeping your knee bent, and begin to rotate the leg outward, so that your right knee points toward the right wall. Place your right ankle on your left leg, just above the left knee — this helps to continue the rotation. Notice that you have created a triangle with your legs.

Lift your left leg off the ground. Now reach your right hand through the center of the triangle. Take hold of your left leg with both hands (see Figure 3-3a). You should feel a stretch in your right buttock.

At first, most people have trouble grasping the left leg with both hands. If you fall into this category, you can solve the problem with a bath towel. Wrap the towel around your left thigh, and take the ends in both hands. In this way, you can stay relaxed as you draw your left leg into the stretch.

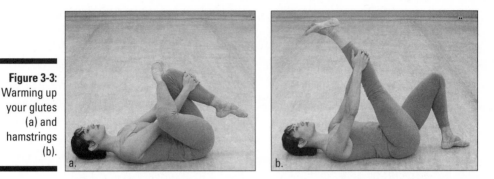

Figure 3-3:
Warming up
your glutes
(a) and
hamstrings
(b).

Another secret from the world of ballet: After you've begun to stretch, rocking your body gently from side to side allows you to stretch a little farther, with more comfort.

As you do this glute stretch, don't let your upper body stray from the initial position. Your shoulders should stay relaxed, pressing down into the mat; your neck should stay as long as possible, and your lower back should continue to touch the mat.

You're not done yet! Now repeat this exercise with the other leg.

The hamstrings

The *hamstrings* are the long muscles running down the back of your legs, from the hip joints to the back of the knees. Executing a convincing kick — or even a reasonably good forward bend — depends on the flexibility of the hamstrings.

But tight hamstrings are a feature of the modern world. A huge segment of the population spends long hours sitting every day. Every minute spent sitting is an opportunity for your hamstrings to tighten up.

Tight hamstrings make dancing extremely difficult. But even worse, tight hamstrings can eventually pull on the muscles of the glutes and back, causing severe back pain and other distasteful problems.

Whether you intend to make ballet a part of your life or not, flexible hamstrings are a major key to a happier life. Good thing that we have a stretch to help keep those hams as stringy as possible.

Assume the initial position (see "The initial position," earlier in this chapter) on the mat. Now lift your right leg up towards the ceiling, keeping your knee bent. Even in this position you get a hamstring stretch — albeit a minimal one.

For those hard-to-stretch hamstrings

If you'd like a simple alternative to the basic hamstring stretch — or if your hamstrings are *really* tight — try the following. Stand with a low chair in front of you. Holding onto something securely for balance, place your right leg up on the chair. Keep your right leg straight, but don't let it pull your right buttock forward; in fact, keep your buttock directed backward. Hold the stretch for 30 seconds, and then switch legs. After you become more flexible, you can use a taller chair or table — or graduate to the basic hamstring stretch.

Injury is a real risk in this exercise. When doing this stretch, don't put pressure into the back of your knee — you can easily overstretch this fragile joint. And be careful not to lose your balance.

We know, we know: Stretching the hamstrings is always painful. We wish we could let you in on a shortcut or secret, but we don't know any. Just take comfort in the knowledge that generations of ballet dancers feel your pain.

Now with both hands, take hold of your right leg — at the thigh, calf, or ankle, depending on your flexibility. Gently draw your right leg toward you with the leg in a relaxed position, and straighten the knee as much as possible (refer to Figure 3-3b).

If you can't reach your lifted leg, use a towel as an extension of your arms (see "The glutes," earlier in this chapter, for more on this technique).

Bend your right knee for a moment to take a break from the stretch, and flex the foot. Repeat this stretch three more times, staying in each position for a count of 10. Then release your leg and return to the initial position. Finally, repeat this stretch with the other leg.

As you stretch the hamstrings, keep the rest of your body in good form. Don't let your hip come off the mat — otherwise, your glutes get into the action, making the hamstring stretch much less effective. Keep your shoulders relaxed and resting on the mat, with your neck long and relaxed.

The calves

Moving down the back of the leg, you next come to the calf muscles. These tough muscles are responsible for some extraordinarily important ballet moves: lifting the weight of your body up onto the balls of your feet, pointing those same feet, and assisting your legs in running and jumping.

Stretching your calf muscles makes all these movements possible. Plus, it helps prevent ripping your Achilles tendon in your next pick-up game of basketball.

Start out in the initial position. Lift your right leg, keeping the leg bent with the knee reaching towards the chest, foot flexed. With both hands, grasp the toes of your right foot and gently draw the foot towards you (see Figure 3-4a). We guarantee that you'll feel a stretch in the right calf muscle.

To intensify the stretch, press the toes into your hands as you try to point your foot; then relax your foot and stretch out the calf again.

Repeat this stretch twice more, and then repeat it with the left leg.

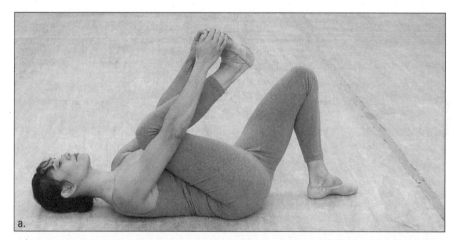

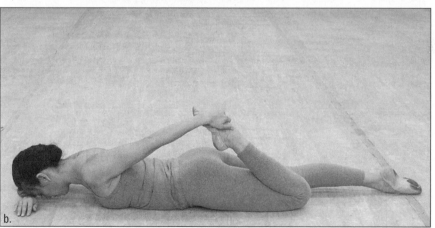

Figure 3-4:
Stretching
your calf
muscles (a)
and quadri-
ceps (b).

The quadriceps

Here's a little-known fact: The *quadriceps* (or *quads,* as they're affectionately known) are the largest muscles in the body. They cover the front of your thigh bones, which also happen to be your largest bones. Whenever you climb stairs, trudge up a hill, or bike a long distance, your quads are working overtime.

For this stretch, you are going to go floor snorkeling. Lie face down on the floor, using your bent forearms as a pillow. Rest both legs straight on the floor. Now bend your right leg and release your right arm to grasp your right foot, ankle, or whatever you can reach. Gently pull your right ankle toward the center of your right glute, without allowing your right thigh to come off the mat (refer to Figure 3-4b).

To avoid twisting your knee, make sure that your right foot stays in line with the middle of your right thigh at all times.

You should feel this stretch in the front of your right thigh. But take it easy — stretch only as far as you can comfortably, with a small but bearable amount of pain. *Breathe,* as always, and count to 10. When you feel long and loose, change legs and stretch your left quad.

Strengthening the Stabilizers

Oh, sure, ballet looks easy — that's the wonderful illusion of it. But much of this appearance of ease depends on the ability of the dancer to join the upper and lower portions of the body into one stable unit. This feat requires immense strength in the stomach, back, and inner thighs — the so-called *stabilizer* muscles in the middle of your body. (You'd never guess that underneath that frilly tutu, every delicate ballerina has abs of steel.)

Male dancers need even stronger stabilizer muscles than women: Not only do they have to jump higher, but they also have the added responsibility of lifting their partners, while maintaining aesthetically beautiful, "effortless" positions.

The abdominals

For the following abdominal exercise, pick some beautiful music with a steady beat — something that inspires you to do many more reps than you really want to.

First exercise: Slow half-sit-ups

To start, take the initial position (see "The initial position," earlier in this chapter). *Exhale* and pull your stomach in as much as you can.

Lift your upper body, while keeping your neck aligned and your lower back in contact with the floor. With your arms at your sides, lift them and reach forward along your sides as you lift your upper body. When you get as high as you can without bringing the lower back off the floor, bring your arms "rounded" in front of the body. Then *inhale* and return to the initial position.

The tempo for this exercise should be slow: Use four *counts* (that is, four beats of the music) to get to the lifted position and four more to return to the initial position.

Do seven more slow repetitions, and rest. If you'd like an added challenge, try doing this stretch in *double time* — that is, twice as fast.

Second exercise: Oblique abdominals

The oblique abdominal muscles are located at the lower sides of your abs. They come in handy when you have to lift your leg in just about any direction.

1. **From the initial position, open your knees and place the bottoms of your feet together. Bring your hands together behind your head, touching your fingertips to each other (Figure 3-5a).**

2. **As you lift your upper body, twist so that your shoulders face your right leg. Bring your arms together in front of your body in a rounded position and stay there for two counts (Figure 3-5b).**

3. **Without resting, twist your upper body back so that your shoulders are parallel to your hips — keeping your arms in that rounded position (Figure 3-5c).**

   Once again, stay here for two counts.

4. **Without resting, stay up and twist your upper body to face your left leg, maintaining the same position with your arms (Figure 3-5d).**

   Stay here for — you guessed it — two counts.

5. **Go back to the position in Figure 3-5a and rest for two counts.**

6. **Repeat this exercise three more times starting to the right; then do it four times starting to the left.**

Third exercise: Sit-ups with lifted knee

Start in the initial position. Place your hands behind your head, fingertips touching. Now do half-sit-ups (see "First exercise: Slow half-sit-ups," earlier in this chapter) facing forward. With the first sit-up, lift your right knee; lower your knees as you lower your upper body. Now repeat, lifting the *left* knee — and so on. Do a total of eight repetitions.

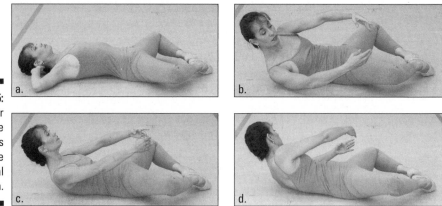

Figure 3-5:
Giving your oblique abdominals some special attention.

Don't pull your head with your hands — that move can injure an otherwise beautiful, swan-like neck. Let your abdominal muscles do all the work.

Fourth exercise: Putting it all together

Again, start in the initial position, but with elbows bent and fingertips gently touching the back of your head. Do one half-sit-up, lifting your right knee (see "First exercise: Slow half-sit-ups," earlier in this chapter). As you lower your body, straighten the right leg out just above and parallel to the floor, and open your arms to your sides (Figure 3-6a).

Now bend your right leg again, extending the knee about halfway out. As you do, again bring your fingertips to the back of your head, lift into another half sit-up, and bring your left elbow in to meet your right knee — engaging a whole *mess* o' abdominal muscles (Figure 3-6b). Then return all your various body parts back to the initial position. Now repeat the exercise with the left leg.

Figure 3-6:
Stretching every abdominal known to man.

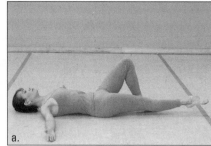

Try doing this combination a total of eight times without a break — if you dare.

To finish, relax your stomach completely. Bend your knees and wrap your arms about them in gratitude. You're done — with your abs!

"Why have we included so many abdominal exercises?" we hear you asking in agony. Well, each and every step in ballet engages the abs. You've just completed a five-minute ab workout. Imagine how strong they need be for a two-hour ballet!

The adductors

The *adductors* are the muscles of the inner thighs. In ballet, these muscles work whenever you rotate your legs outward from the hips, pointing your feet away from each other. As you can see throughout this book, you do this outward rotation *constantly* in ballet. You must have strong adductor muscles to promote good ballet technique.

From the initial position, lift both arms straight out from the shoulders along the floor. Bring your legs all the way up, legs over the hips, flexing your feet in the air so that they are directly over the bottom of your ribcage (see Figure 3-7). Alternately, if this position causes you leg pain, you can bend your knees — the workout will be almost as good.

Figure 3-7:
Working the
adductors.

If this position causes you any back pain — or if you'd just like a little more support — place your hands, palms down, under the two bones at either side of your spine at the lower portion of your back, and lift your hips slightly.

First exercise: basic adductor

From this starting position with your legs up over your body, press your inner thighs together as if you were holding a million dollar bill. Keep pressing the thighs together for four slow counts. Then, as you continue to press your legs together, rotate them outward so that your feet point away from each other. Hold this position for four counts, and then return your legs to their natural, nonspastic position.

Repeat this exercise seven more times.

Second exercise: opening and closing the legs

From the same starting position, point your toes outward and point your feet toward the ceiling. Open your legs so that your feet are the same distance apart as your hips. Now close your legs and press your heels together, holding for four slow counts. Repeat this exercise seven more times, for a total of eight times.

Third exercise: baby scissors

Maintaining the turned-out position of your legs (see the preceding section), separate them slightly. Now bring your legs together again, but this time cross your right leg in front of your left. Use two counts to press them together, and two more counts to open them. Do this move four times; then do it four times with the *left* leg in front — and repeat the entire exercise again.

To finish

Because you don't need your adductor muscles for many things in everyday life, these exercises may feel very weird, and even painful, at first. Make sure to stretch out your inner thighs after you finish to minimize soreness later. Relax your legs open to the side, with bent knees. For a little added support, feel free to hold onto your thighs with your hands.

More Strengthening: Floor Barre

Much of ballet takes place at the *barre,* that long, horizontal wooden pole that you find in every ballet studio. In Chapter 6 you can explore the exercises that dancers do when standing at this wondrous piece of equipment. In this section, you have the opportunity to try these barre exercises on the floor — without worrying about supporting the weight of your body.

These exercises are also good to have in your bag of tricks for those times when can't get to a studio. And if you ever injure your feet or legs, you may still be able to do some of these exercises.

Powering up your legs

Daily activities, such as going up stairs, may prepare your leg muscles for ordinary tasks. But the art of ballet is anything but ordinary.

When you put the weight of your body on one leg, and lift your other leg to hip or shoulder height, you engage *all* the muscles of your legs in a most intense way. Therefore, the best way to begin strengthening the leg muscles is to simulate these positions on the floor, *without* weight.

The following exercises help give your ballet technique a good foundation — literally.

First exercise: Bending and straightening the leg

Begin in the initial position on the floor and then follow these steps:

1. **Extend your arms out from the shoulders, palms up, and extend your right leg parallel to the floor (refer to Figure 3-6a).**

   Keep your abdominal muscles firm to support your lower back. And keep your hips strong — don't let them move around as you work the right leg.

2. **Bend your right knee and bring up your pointed right foot, passing the left ankle and knee. Gradually extend your right leg towards the ceiling (Figure 3-8a), eventually straightening your knee.**

   Your leg should end up perpendicular to the floor.

3. **When your knee is straight, flex your foot and rotate your leg out from your hip (Figure 3-8b). Then lower your leg to just off the floor; point your foot, and turn your leg parallel.**

Repeat Steps 2 and 3 for a total of four repetitions. Now it's time to reverse the exercise.

From the position in Figure 3-6a, flex your foot and turn it out. Now lift your foot up perpendicular to the floor with a straight knee (as shown in Figure 3-8b). Turn your leg to the parallel position, point the foot, bend the knee, and lower the leg, bringing the right foot past the left knee. Then straighten your right leg back to the starting position.

Repeat this reverse exercise for a total of four repetitions — and then repeat the entire exercise with the left leg, in both directions.

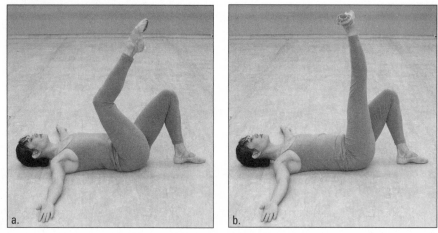

Figure 3-8:
Strengthen-
ing your leg
muscles.

Second exercise: Big kicks on the floor

This exercise helps to master the high kicks that come up later in this book:

1. **From the position in Figure 3-6a, point your right foot and turn out your leg.**

2. **Keeping both hips in contact with the ground, lift your right leg as high as you can, knee straight.**

3. **Lower the leg back to the starting position.**

Repeat this seven more times. As you bring your leg down the final time, bend your right knee and place your right foot on the floor, touching the floor with the toes first, then the ball of the foot and finally the heel — ending in the initial position.

Now do the entire exercise with your left leg.

Building up your back

For the back exercises in this section, you are once again going to perfect your floor snorkeling technique. Lie face down, arms folded and forehead resting your forearms, as we describe in "The quadriceps," earlier in this chapter.

For these exercises, you need to keep your gluteus and abdominal muscles engaged. If you have any doubt whether your glutes are engaged, touch your sides just below the hips. You should feel an indentation on the outside of the glutes. To engage the abdominals, pull your stomach in, as if you were trying to touch your belly button to your spine.

First exercise: Face-down leg lifts

From the face-down position, feel as though you are lengthening your right leg out of its hip joint. Slowly, over two counts, lift your leg up to the back, with a straight knee and pointed foot. (You only need to lift it a few inches, as shown in Figure 3-9a.) Over the next two counts, lower the leg back to the floor. Repeat with your left leg, and then do three more repetitions with each leg.

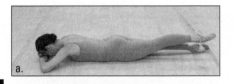

Figure 3-9:
Working up
your back
muscles.

Second exercise: Backward bends

During this exercise, you lift your upper back, while leaving your lower back on the floor, just as you did in "First exercise: Slow half-sit-ups," earlier in this chapter. But with one catch — now your back muscles are responsible for making the lift.

Start in the floor snorkeling position. Take two counts to lift your upper back up as high as possible (usually about six inches), leaving your arms touching your forehead (Figure 3-9b). Be careful not to lift your shoulders up toward the ears.

Now take two counts to lower your upper back to the starting position, forehead resting on the forearms. Repeat this exercise three more times.

Third exercise: The "angel"

Now that you've practiced lifting your legs (with pointed feet) and lifting your upper back, why not combine them?

Start in the floor snorkeling position (see "The quadriceps," earlier in this chapter). Over two counts, simultaneously lift both legs *and* your upper back, moving your arms overhead as shown in Figure 3-9c. Over two more counts, come back to the floor and rest. Repeat three more times.

For obvious reasons, this exercise is called the "angel," so cursing while you do it is frowned upon.

If you've actually done all the exercises in this chapter, your body is definitely warm by now. In fact, it may be both warm and sore. As always, be patient with yourself. As you practice these exercises more and more, you will be able to stand — and dance — with more strength and confidence.

Chapter 4

Leaping into Ballet Basics

· ·

In This Chapter

▶ Finding the correct ballet stance

▶ Walking like a duck

▶ Getting your feet and arms into position

▶ Forming a graceful ballet hand

· ·

*A*ll right, then! If you tried the warm-ups in Chapter 3, your body is toasty and you're ready to go. But before trying out any ballet step, you need to understand certain basic concepts. You wouldn't attempt brain surgery without a little training, would you? (Note to Mrs. Hallie Mae Beauregard of Galveston, Texas: Don't answer that.)

In this chapter you can encounter — possibly for the first time in your life — the strange ways that ballet dancers stand, balance, turn out, point their feet, and do all the things that make ballet what it is.

Finding the Correct Ballet Stance

Have you ever noticed the way a ballerina carries herself? Haughty, imperious, and unapproachable, right? She owns the world. She has utter self-confidence. She thinks very little of anyone else. Or so it seems.

Well, the truth is even stranger than that: She can't help looking this way. Most world-class ballet dancers, from the tender age of four or five, have been taught to hold themselves in a certain way. They practice and practice and practice their posture until it becomes second nature. This way of carrying themselves gets misinterpreted thousands of times a day, from fast-food joints to street corners worldwide.

The fact is, many ballet dancers are rather shy about what they do. (You would be too, if everyone mistook you for a snob.) But the ballet stance that inspires this misconception is a basic part of classical ballet technique, for men and women alike. Don't worry, though — if you're old enough to read this, you are in no danger of having this stance become permanent. You'll be able to turn it on and off at will.

One of the big goals of ballet is creating the illusion of elegance and poise. A certain confident ease of motion perpetuates this illusion. But that's exactly what it is — an illusion. Deep down, every ballet dancer is just as neurotic as you are.

Locating your center

If you were to videotape a world-class ballet dancer in action, and then stop the tape at any given frame, the ideal dancer will always appear graceful and balanced. This remarkable phenomenon applies to other pursuits as well — tai chi, for example, or thumb wrestling.

The key to this appearance is *centering.* As a potential ballet dancer, the first thing you need to do is *find your center* — the position in which you can rest in total balance. Here's how the pros do it:

1. **Stand at the mirror, facing sideways, with your feet parallel to each other.**

2. **Engaging your thigh muscles, straighten your knees — but without pushing back into your knee joints.**

3. **Lift your abdominal muscles upward and back towards your spine.**

   This is called *pulled-up position.* Imagine that you are placing your ribcage over your hips. Think of your neck as an upward extension of your spine. Your shoulders are relaxed downward, and your chin is slightly lifted — hence the haughty air.

4. **Curve your arms so that they are rounded and just in front of your thighs, and bring your weight forward into the balls of your feet.**

   You should be able to lift your heels slightly off the floor (see Figure 4-1). At first, you may feel as if you are about to fall forward onto your face. In fact, you have our permission to fall forward a few times. But with practice, this alignment becomes much more natural.

Now that you have found your *placement,* or *center,* you are ready for anything. All ballet movements begin from here, allowing the upper and lower sections of your body to work together as one.

TRY IT!

Keeping your spine in line

As you go through your daily routine — driving to work, sitting at the computer, flirting at the gym, scolding the kids — gravity has a way of causing your shoulders and head to slump. For aspiring ballet dancers, defying gravity is a good and healthy thing. Good posture is helpful for ballet — and for the rest of your life, as well.

Be aware of your posture during all the down times in your day, such as the time you spend standing at the bus stop or in the checkout line. Locate your center (see the preceding section)

during these activities and see how this posture differs from your "normal" stance.

Even as you sit reading this book, you can perfect your posture. Move to the edge of your chair and align your spine over your hips. Thanks to the chair, you don't need to hold any muscles to stay seated — instead, you can just rest your spine in-line over your hips. You and your back will be happier together for your efforts. And you're on the way to good ballet posture.

Figure 4-1:
Finding
good
placement
for ballet
technique.

Adjusting your posture for balance

In addition to aligning your spine, you need to be able to adjust your posture for different ballet positions. In order to maintain balance while your legs and hips move in a certain direction, your upper body moves *in opposition* to your lower body.

For example, say that you want to lift one leg behind you. In order to maintain balance, the weight of your upper body has to adjust slightly forward. When lifting your leg to one side, you adjust your body slightly to the other side to create balance. When lifting your leg to the front, you adjust your body slightly to the back. Got it?

Of course, these adjustments are very small. But the smallest adjustments make all the difference and lead to safe dancing.

Distributing and transferring your weight

When finding your center, you have to transfer your body weight a little forward, onto the balls of your feet. From this position, if you want to lift one leg off the ground, you must shift your weight more to the standing leg for solid balance.

Standing on one leg

Start with your heels together, toes pointing outward. Keep your arms at your sides, low and rounded, with your fingers almost touching your thighs. Now shift most of your body weight to the balls of your feet, while keeping your heels down.

Lift your left leg off the ground, bending your knee outward slightly. Now, pointing your left foot, place it in front of your right ankle (Figure 4-2a). Notice how much you must shift your weight to your right foot to maintain your balance.

Figure 4-2:
Shifting your
weight to
create
balance.

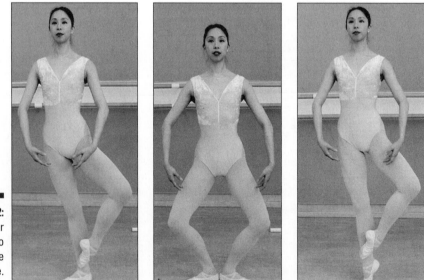

Now return your left leg to the starting position and repeat this exercise on the other leg.

Shifting onto one leg

Begin by bending your knees as far as you can while still keeping your heels on the floor (Figure 4-2b). Lift your left leg, just as you did in the preceding section, bending your knee outward. Point your left foot and let the toes touch your right ankle as you straighten your right knee. Bring your arms in front of you, rounded at the level of your ribcage. The goal — eventually — is to arrive in this position with your arms and legs at the same time. Notice that the weight shift to the ball of your right foot is more extreme than before. That's because your right leg has gone from bent to straight.

After you master this shift, do the movement on the other side. We wouldn't want you to develop a lopsided technique!

Balancing on the ball of your foot

Okay — we're getting advanced now. Here's the ultimate test in the transferring of weight. This exercise is similar to standing on one leg, but with a twist — this time, you balance not just on one foot, but on the *ball* of that foot.

Begin with your knees slightly bent, heels together, toes pointing outward. Keep your arms at your sides, low and rounded, with your fingers almost touching your thighs. Lift your left leg, with your left knee pressing outward, foot pointed, with the toes touching your right ankle. Meanwhile, rise up on your right leg, straightening the knee

Now here's the *really* tricky part: As you straighten your right leg, put your weight onto the ball of your right foot (Figure 4-2c). **Caution:** Don't fall! You may need to hold onto something as you practice this weight shift.

To balance in this position, you must send your weight way over to the right — but without leaning. Finding out exactly how much adjustment to make is a matter of practice. That, by the way, is one of those understatements that applies to the entire art of ballet.

Don't be dismayed if you don't get the hang of it right away — it takes a lot of practice. And don't worry if you find it much harder to balance on one foot than the other. *Everybody* has that problem.

Keep in mind that when you go to the ball of your foot, your balance must be very precise. After all, you're balancing the entire weight of your body on about 4 square inches. It's like trying to hold up a broomstick by balancing the end in your upturned palm. It may take a very long time to find the balance — with the help of strong abdominal muscles to keep yourself stabilized. But when you do find that balance, it feels effortless. And that's the most glorious feeling in the world.

What's my line?

Look closely at a good photo of any ballet dancer, and you can see that the positions of his or her body seem to create long, imaginary lines. In many positions, you can clearly draw a line from one end of the body to the other. Some lines are straight, others are curved — but all the lines look graceful and connected.

A recent ingenious advertising campaign for the San Francisco Ballet showed photographs of dancers in beautiful positions, superimposed with geometric designs that corresponded exactly to the lines created by their bodies. These designs helped everyone to experience one of the most beautiful aspects of ballet: the concept of *line*.

The entire body participates in the creation of a line — from pointed foot to leg to torso to arm to hand — with the head and neck enhancing the line, as well. Even a dancer's *eyes* can help, by gazing exactly in the direction that continues the line. Ideally, these lines seem to extend far beyond the body of the dancer, off into space. Even when the dancer stands still, you get a sense of motion and constant expansion. Achieving this feeling is the Holy Grail of classical ballet technique. And dancers work daily toward that goal.

The strange thing is, with the right adjustments, you can balance in *any* position. So here's the bad news — although you may find a balanced position, the position may not be "correct" in the classical sense. That's why every ballet studio is plastered with mirrors from floor to ceiling. Dancers are constantly checking their positions — *all* positions, all the time.

Walking Like a Duck: Proper Leg Alignment

If we've heard it once, we've heard it a thousand times — almost every ballet dancer walks like a duck. And the fact is, that's true. Not that it's a conscious choice or anything. But many dancers, after years of indoctrination into correct classical ballet posture, find the duckwalk to be a comfortable way of getting from one place to the other.

What could possibly cause such a phenomenon? Well, one basic principle behind ballet posture is an outward rotation in the hips, causing the feet to point away from each other, Charlie-Chaplin style. In fact, *all* ballet technique is based on this outward rotation.

We know what you're thinking: "Stop right there! If Chapter 4 of this book is going to make me look like a duck, then what will I look like by Chapter 22?"

Not to worry. Once again, unless you have practiced rotating your hips outward for at least four hours a day, several days a week, from the tender age of nine, you're in no danger of walking like a duck. Worst case scenario, you may temporarily take on some chickenlike tendencies. But it's worth practicing this technique a bit now, just to get the hang of it.

Turning out your legs

The rotation of the hips is known to the entire ballet world as *turnout*. Ballet dancers are judged by it, and they become very sensitive to the degree of turnout in their fellow dancers. Turnout envy, in fact, is a common phenomenon in the ballet studio.

Working on turnout on the floor

Follow these steps to develop turnout without injury:

1. **Lie on your back with your legs straight, resting on the ground.**

2. **Lift both legs over your hips, bending your knees if you like.**

   Your feet should end up directly over the bottom of your rib cage.

3. **Flex your feet.**

   This helps you see the difference between the parallel and turned-out positions.

4. **With your feet parallel, press your inner thighs together, as if you were holding up a $1,000 bill.**

   Or, if you prefer, use your thighs to hold up this book.

5. **Rotate your hips outward, causing your feet to point away from each other with your heels touching.**

   Naturally, your thighs may separate when you do this. (There goes the book!) But the trick is to keep your thighs *reaching for each other.* Stay in this position for a few seconds.

Repeat this exercise, alternating at least ten times between the two foot positions. You may want to do this exercise to music to make this experience more pleasant!

Aligning your body

The key to staying injury-free in ballet, and in everything you do, is to keep your body aligned. We know, we know — easier said than done. After all, ballet is all about complex movements. But whether you're standing, leaping, or spinning, you need to avoid *twisting* at all times. Here's an example: When you stand with your knees bent, you put a significant amount of stress on your knee joints and leg muscles. This stress can lead to injury if any part of your body is twisted. So plant each foot broadly on the floor. Keep your ankles relaxed, not gripping. Hold your knees directly over the center of your feet. Keep your pelvis directly over your heels, without sticking out your rear end. As you bend your knees, your hips move down without moving back and forth — like a horse on a merry-go-round. Now you're aligned.

Developing turnout on your feet

After you develop a flat-on-your-back mastery (or at least understanding) of turnout, you can give it a try on your feet.

Stand upright with your feet parallel. Now, keeping your heels together, and moving *from the hips,* rotate your legs and feet outward in one smooth motion. Don't overdo it — just go as far as you can without strain. This is your natural amount of turnout.

How much turnout do you have? Well, in the beginning, you may not have much. In fact, as you practice, you may not even notice the incremental improvements. Ballet dancers take years and years to improve their turnout. But because all ballet positions and movements start from the rotation of the hips, the time is well spent.

Point those feet!

We hear it all the time in the ballet studio: "She has such beautiful feet!" What on earth could cause a dancer to fixate on the second ugliest part of the body — let alone extol its virtues?

In actuality, this comment refers not to the feet themselves, but the way in which they can *bend.* Ballet dancers work for years — years! — on the concept of *pointing their feet.*

We know — foot-pointing is a bizarre choice for a life goal. But the fact is, ballet dancers have to point their feet almost every single time their feet leave the floor.

The secret is in the *instep* — the top of the foot between the ankle and toe. The higher that part of the foot sticks up when the foot is pointed — combined with a flexible ankle — the more beautiful it appears. If you have long feet, or thin ankles, the instep appears longer and more pronounced. And that's a good thing. Long toes don't hurt either.

Of course, a tiny percentage of dancers are blessed with an awesome capacity to point their feet without even trying. These lucky, lucky fools can immediately do things that take most people months or years of practice to perfect. That's an incredible advantage in ballet — an unfair head start.

The best way to start pointing your feet is by sitting down. This way, you can clearly observe the alignment of your feet, without worrying about falling:

1. **Sit on the floor with your back supported and your legs in front of you, with straight knees.**

   This may be a challenge in itself — if your hamstrings are tight, feel free to lean back a bit and support yourself with your arms.

2. **Flex your feet, drawing your toes toward you, so that your toes point to the ceiling (Figure 4-3a).**

   If your calves are well developed, the act of flexing your feet may cause your heels to lift off the floor a bit. That's perfectly okay.

3. **Bend your ankles so that your toes point towards the wall in front of you (Figure 4-3b).**

   Keep bending — within reason, or course — until you can't reach any farther. Make sure that your feet point as an extension of your shinbone, and that your feet don't curve to the inside or outside.

4. **Now reach your toes down toward the ground (Figure 4-3c).**

   Don't crunch your toes, but rather make them an extension of the curvature of the feet, creating the longest line possible. Need we say it? Don't hold this pose too long, or your feet will begin to cramp.

5. **Engaging the toes back towards the sky, follow through with the ankles until you return to the original flexed position.**

Just for fun, try this variation on the exercise. Point your feet as you did in Steps 3 and 4. Then, with your feet still pointed, rotate your legs out from the hips. *Voilà!* Turnout, plus pointed feet. You're a ballet dancer at last. Careful, though: In this position, you have to work extra hard to keep the feet pointing straight.

Figure 4-3:
Pointing
your feet.

Practicing the Positions of the Feet and Arms

We'd like to pause just a moment to give thanks for the fact that we have only two legs and arms. Just with these four basic limbs, the permutations for ballet seem almost unlimited.

But in reality, every ballet move has at its core one of the basic *positions*. There are six possible foot positions and five arm positions.

Because different schools of ballet developed simultaneously, there are three main schools of thought on the subject of arm and feet positions. Many ballet companies draw on elements from two or even three of these schools. But for consistency in this book, we demonstrate the positions as taught by the *Cecchetti method*.

If you master only one thing about ballet, it should be these positions. They form the basis for everything else.

First position

If you have practiced weight distribution and leg turnout (see the sections earlier in this chapter), you have already discovered *first position*.

Stand straight, your heels touching, your toes pointed outward — like Charlie Chaplin. Keep your arms rounded, to the sides of your body, with your finger-tips just off the thighs at the middle of your legs. Keep your shoulders down, neck long, and chin slightly lifted (Figure 4-4a).

Figure 4-4:
First (a),
second (b),
and third (c)
positions.

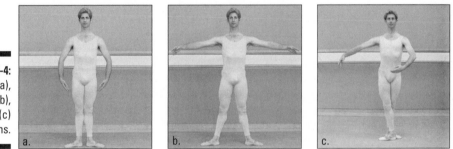

First position is so fundamental, so common, and so important in ballet, that we use it as a point of departure for many steps.

Second position

Starting in first position, slide one foot straight out to the side, and point your foot. Now lower your heel so that it lines up with the other. Redistribute your weight evenly on both feet. Your knees are straight, and your toes remain pointed outward. This is *second position* — basically a spread-out version of first position.

Now for the arms. From first position, lift them to the side, while keeping them slightly rounded. The palms of your hands should be visible from the front, with your elbows slightly lower than your shoulders, and your wrists slightly lower than your elbows. Your shoulders are down with your neck long and your chin slightly lifted (Figure 4-4b).

Third position

Unlike first and second positions, which are symmetrical, third position involves putting one foot in front of the other. For that reason, you can do third position in either direction. Start off by going to the right.

From second position, bring your right foot in front of your left foot, so that your right heel touches the middle of your left foot, just below the bunion joint. Your toes still point outward, and your knees are still straight. Keep your stomach lifted. This is *third position.*

Careful — when you do this motion, make sure that your hips don't twist to the left. They should face forward, directly under your shoulders, which again are down, with your neck long and your chin slightly lifted.

In this position, the arms work *in opposition* to the legs. If your right foot is in front, your left arm should be in front. In this case your left arm is rounded, with the fingertips lifted to about belly button height. Meanwhile, your right arm is rounded to the side, with the palm of your hand forward, also at about belly button height (refer to Figure 4-4c).

Third position can be done in reverse — to the left — simply by reversing your legs and arms.

Fourth position

From third position, slide your right foot forward, away from your left, so that your right heel is directly in front of the left big toe joint, by about the length of one foot (not 12 inches, but the actual length of your own foot).

Keep your toes pointed away from each other, ideally in opposite directions.

You are now in *fourth position* — the most challenging of all the positions. Keep your knees straight and your hips facing forward as much as possible, with your stomach lifted.

As in third position, your arms work opposite from your legs. Bring your left arm forward, rounded, with your fingertips the height of your breast bone. Your right arm is to the side, slightly rounded, with the palm forward (Figure 4-5a, the dancer on the left).

From here you can create another, alternate arm position. Lift your left arm, rounded, over your head and slightly forward. Be careful not to lift your shoulder when you lift your arm. This is the *high fourth position*, as shown in Figure 4-5a, the dancer on the right.

Figure 4-5:
Fourth position: low and high (a); fifth position: arms low, middle, and high (b).

a.

b.

Fifth position

From fourth position, close your right foot in front of your left foot — so that your right heel is directly in front of and touching your left big toe, with your toes pointing outward. Keep your knees straight and try to keep your hips facing forward without twisting, with your thighs, stomach, and the gluteus engaged, lifted and firm.

There are three positions of the arms in fifth position, each one named after its height in relation to the body. You often hear ballet dancers and choreographers talking about *low fifth, middle fifth,* and *high fifth.*

First, with your arms rounded and your palms facing you, bring your arms together so that your fingertips are approximately six inches apart and in front of your thighs. This is *low fifth position* (refer to Figure 4-5b, the dancer on the left) or in French, *en bas* — "ahn BAH" — which simply means "below".

From this position, bring your arms up, rounded, in front of your breastbone, creating a downward diagonal line from shoulders to elbows to wrists (refer to Figure 4-5b, the dancer in the middle). This is *middle fifth position* (*en avant* — "ahn a-VAHN" — literally, "ahead").

Finally, lift your arms up, over, and in front of your head, still rounded, with your hands approximately six inches apart, your palms facing inward (refer to Figure 4-5b, the dancer on the right). How high should your arms go? Without moving your head, look up — you should be able to see your hands. This is *high fifth position* (*en haut* — "ahn OH" — meaning "on high"). This is the position every child copies when imitating a ballerina; it's been used on more music boxes than any other position.

It's all French to me

We had to bring it up sometime — the uncomfortable topic of French. If you eavesdrop on any ballet studio on earth, you hear a lot of French words. Because so much of classical ballet technique was developed in France, the French names for things stuck. So when ballet dancers talk about a particular move, they almost always use the French name for it.

We don't use *much* French in this book, but we have to use some. We're not yielding to ingrained snobbery, or blind adherence to the past, or even a preference. It's just convenience. Very often, a French term serves as an incredibly handy abbreviation, or shorthand, for a concept that would take much longer to describe in English.

Here's an example: In describing a particular move, we could say, "Stand with your legs turned out, heels together, toes pointing outward, knees bent as far as you can while keeping your heels on the floor, without allowing your rear end to stick out, keeping your spine straight, shoulders down, neck long with your chin slightly lifted and your arms rounded to the sides of your midthighs."

Or we could say: "*Demi plié* in first position."

So in the interest of avoiding a 12,000 page volume, we introduce you to some French terms, bit by bit, throughout this book. But not to worry: All of the French terms we use are fully explained, with pronunciations, in the handy glossary at the back of this book.

And we promise to be gentle. After all, French is the language of love.

Sixth position

In the old days, five positions were enough. They sufficed for centuries, in fact. But with the recent turn of classical technique toward contemporary style, *sixth position* was born. For that reason, sixth isn't usually considered part of the basic classical ballet positions. But sixth position appears so frequently today in choreography that you should be familiar with it.

Sixth position is the easiest of all. It's the closest position to the way non-dancers stand. Your feet are parallel, your toes pointing straight ahead, and your knees are straight. Your upper body is lifted, with your chin slightly raised. No arm movements to worry about. We *knew* you'd like sixth position!

The Graceful Ballet Hand

If you think *feet* are beautiful, let's talk *hands*. There is so much beauty in the hand of a ballerina: delicate and fragile as a flower, airy as a spacious sky, fluid as an amber wave of grain. Hands have a life of their own, but they also exist as extensions of the arms, continuing their lines smoothly, just as this final clause gracefully brings this sentence to a close.

In classical ballet, the key to a beautiful hand is relaxation. But the technique varies slightly depending on what gender you happen to be.

For male dancers, the hand should accentuate a feeling of *strength with ease.* Therefore, the hand must be relaxed, but shouldn't become limp, flaccid, or otherwise dysfunctional. (See the upper hand in Figure 4-6.)

For ballerinas, old-fashioned, politically incorrect feminine grace is the goal. To practice this, shake your hand out in front of you; then let your hand go limp. Extend your index finger to elongate it slightly; now do the same with your little finger. Next, gently draw in your thumb so that it is directly under your index finger. None of the fingers should be straight (which would look stiff) or curled under (which would shorten the all-important long line). Your fingers should neither appear glued together nor spread far apart from each other. (See the lower hand in Figure 4-6.)

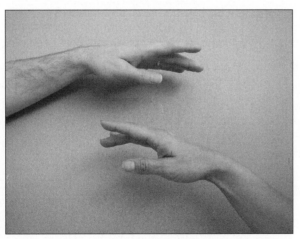

Figure 4-6:
The graceful ballet hand — male and female.

Having said all that, there are infinite variations to the shape of a dancer's hand. And that's a good thing, because the hand can be a huge help in portraying a character. For example, in the ballet *Swan Lake,* the ballerina dancing Odette the Swan Queen may consciously choose to keep her fingers aligned in a row, giving the appearance of feathers.

Yes, it's true — duck feet, swan hands.

Chapter 5

Music, Maestro!

. . . .

In This Chapter

▶ Choosing music for dancing

▶ Moving to the music

▶ Counting out the music

. . . .

*W*e've lost track of the number of times we've heard dancers say, "I was so inspired by the music! It made me dance at my best." Music is one of the most glorious things about ballet.

It would be hard to imagine the gorgeous steps of a ballet such as *Swan Lake,* for example, without the music. First of all, the boredom factor would multiply by about a thousand. But second, and more important, the specific music of that ballet serves as a guideline for its choreography. When the music is grand, the steps are grand. When the music is graceful, the steps are graceful. When the music is triumphant, so is the dance. And when the music is mournful, the characters onstage seem to cry.

All the ballet steps you practice in this book can be danced to music. And furthermore, they *should* be. Music adds an importance, a flow, and an extra measure of beauty to every move you make. It connects the moves together into a fluid whole. That's why a ballet set to music is much more than a collection of graceful moves: It's art.

In this chapter we help you understand the music you hear — and put all your future dance to music.

Finding Musical Options for Each Exercise

Throughout this book you can find many ballet exercises that combine one kind of step with another. For obvious reasons, these exercises are known as *combinations.*

For every combination in this book, we suggest a piece of music to inspire you. If you want, you can find that music at your local library or record store. Alternately, you can listen to these pieces (or download them) *online,* at www.byronhoyt.com. Or you are welcome to substitute something you already have. For any given combination, you can find several pieces of music that are equally appropriate — when you know what to listen for.

The Seven Habits of Highly Effective Ballet Music

In order to work for a ballet combination, a piece of music should fulfill all the following criteria.

The beats are easy to hear

All music has rhythm. For ballet dancers, rhythm is the most essential characteristic of any piece of music. When you dance ballet steps, you need a strong rhythm to respond to.

All rhythm is made up of *beats.* Simply stated, a beat is the length of time it takes you to tap your foot once. When you dance ballet steps, you often have to *count* the beats — and so they must be easy to hear.

Many kinds of music have a very clear beat. (Disco probably has the clearest of all, but we don't recommend listening to it for more than five hours at a time). In fact, *most* of today's popular music has a very clear beat. (For more on that concept, see "Finding contemporary alternatives," later in this chapter.) In classical music, the beat-audibility quotient varies widely — peaking in music that was composed specifically for ballet.

The tempo is steady

The second most important characteristic is *tempo.* In some European countries, the word *tempo* is used to describe automobile speed, in kilometers per hour. In music, *tempo* refers to the speed at which the beats (or counts) come flying at you. If you tap your foot to the music, and your foot is going really fast, then you're dealing with a fast tempo.

When you dance an exercise or a combination, you can negotiate the steps more easily if the tempo stays steady. A piece of music that seems to lurch forward and then screech to a halt — like a car jumping a curb — isn't recommended for beginners.

To prove it, just sit in on any ballet class. In the corner you're likely to see a rehearsal pianist, dutifully (and sometimes brilliantly) playing away in a very steady tempo. In fact, in the rare cases where the rehearsal pianist doesn't play in a steady tempo, that pianist may not be around for much longer.

All ballets have tempo changes, of course. But even then, during the course of any *particular* dance movement, the tempo usually stays basically the same. When a dancer leaps across the stage in a *grand jeté,* a sudden change in tempo can throw him off. Similarly, if a ballerina is attempting to do 32 *fouetté* turns in a row, a tempo change can actually make her fall over. So keep the tempo steady.

The tempo is appropriate

A great ballet conductor we once knew used to joke that there are only two tempos in ballet: "Too fast" and "Too slow."

One of your trusty authors has conducted for many a ballet, and he can attest that there's some truth to that joke. It's tricky to find the tempo that is *exactly* right for a particular dance. Different dancers feel more comfortable with different tempos — and they feel differently about them on different days, or different times of day. In fact, a conductor can take the same tempo every single day, and the same dancer may find it too fast on one day and too slow the next.

But that difference in perception happens for a reason. Your body reacts differently on different days. Sometimes you're really warmed up and ready to rock. Sometimes you have a slight injury that slows down your dancing. Sometimes a particular move is new to you (and therefore trickier to do, requiring a slower tempo); sometimes it's old hat (and easy, requiring a quicker tempo).

Within reason, though, the best dancers can adjust their movements to fit whatever tempo is going on at the moment. They understand that in ballet, the tempo exists not just to fit their own private motions and emotions, but also to create a certain mood, or allow a certain musical phrase to happen.

Of course, most of the time — especially if you're a beginner — this question never even comes up. You work with recorded music in a set tempo, and that's that. In that case, you can decide to *take* the music (and simplify your steps) or *leave* it, finding another piece of music to work with.

The piece of music is long enough for the exercise

Obviously, it's no fun to stop in mid-*plié* and waddle over to your CD player to start the music over. Pick a piece of music that keeps your desired tempo for at least as long as the exercise you're doing — even with a couple of false starts.

The music is appropriately "heavy" or "light"

Some exercises — especially for women — involve feeling lighter than air. The best ballerinas look like they can reach escape velocity at any moment. For moments like these, the music should be light.

But by "light," we don't mean "not serious." We mean that it should sound like little elves touching down with tiny steps. "The Dance of the Sugar Plum Fairy" from Tchaikovsky's *Nutcracker* is a perfect example. So is Aurora's solo in *Sleeping Beauty,* Odette's Act II variation in *Swan Lake,* and the quick, fast variation for the ballerina in Balanchine's ballet *Divertimento no.15,* set to music of Mozart.

But for other moments — especially moments when the male dancer has a chance to shine — the steps are big, brazen, and yes, even heavy. A huge leap off the ground, with a big turn in the air and a landing down on one knee with outstretched arms — as if to say, "Ta-DAAAAAH" — demands strong steps.

For strong steps, the music should sound strong as well. Loud and heavy beats are the key, especially for the *first* note in any group of counted beats. Listen to the Cavalier's *tarantella* in *Nutcracker,* Prince Desiré's third act variation in *Sleeping Beauty*, and Siegfried's variation in the Black Swan *pas de deux* of *Swan Lake,* and you'll get the idea.

The music is fun to listen to

If you don't enjoy the music, you won't have too much fun dancing to it. Pick something that gives you pleasure.

Even better: The music is inspiring

Try to find music that inspires and energizes every fiber of your being. The most inspiring music takes you to new places, gives you a lump in your throat, makes your heart sing, and encourages you to aim for greater heights.

We've found that a couple of ballet pieces in particular seem to send musicians, dancers, and audiences alike into fits of twitching ecstasy. Specifically, we're referring to the ballet music of Tchaikovsky, Prokofiev, and Stravinsky. For more on these composers and their masterful creations, read on.

Using traditional classical music

If you decide to do your ballet exercises to traditional classical music, we guarantee you that the whole experience will be extremely fulfilling. We're talking about great masterpieces here!

Of all the classical music you can use, music written specifically for ballet is the easiest to dance to. Because the composers had ballet dancers in mind when they wrote their music, they took into account most of the criteria we mention in the preceding sections. Most classical ballet music has beats that are easy to hear and count, a steady tempo, appropriate length, and intentional emphasis on lightness or heaviness.

However, *some* ballet composers went a little overboard in getting all these production values right — often to the detriment of the music itself. The music that tried too hard to be easy to count and dance to ended up sounding boring and repetitive.

You see, in the olden days of ballet, the dance was the only important thing. The composer's job was to write music that let the dancers show off. Musical considerations such as drama, pacing, and even beauty of sound were secondary to the spectacle of the dance: young men and women with fabulous legs and buns of steel. Accordingly, early composers didn't put much effort into their compositions for ballet — after all, it was just "background music."

But then Peter Tchaikovsky came along. Tchaikovsky (1840-1893) wrote such stunning music for his ballets *Swan Lake, Sleeping Beauty*, and *The Nutcracker* that people could no longer take the "background" music for granted. Starting with Tchaikovsky's ballets, people began to pay attention to the music in its own right.

Thanks largely to Tchaikovsky's music, his three ballets are still among the most popular and beloved in the history of ballet. Soon, other composers began to take a cue from him. Two other Russian composers in particular, Sergei Prokofiev (1891-1953) and Igor Stravinsky (1882-1971), got into ballet composing in an equally big way.

Much of this ballet music became popular even without the dancing. You've heard Tchaikovsky's masterpieces everywhere, especially music from *The Nutcracker* at Christmastime. Prokofiev's ballets *Romeo and Juliet* and *Cinderella* are regulars in the ballet world, but their musical scores are also popular with orchestras on the concert stage. And although not all the ballets of Stravinsky are regularly performed by dancers today, orchestras around the world are constantly playing *The Firebird, Petrushka, The Rite of Spring,* and a host of his other compositions.

We can't possibly do justice to all the magnificent composers who followed in the footsteps of these masters, writing great ballet music in the twentieth century and beyond. Classical music is an enormous, awe-inspiring world. If you find that it turns you on — and if you have a hankering to know more about the music itself — then we gently nudge you in the direction of *Classical Music For Dummies* (published by Wiley).

Finding contemporary alternatives

Even if you love classical music, you may have days when you'd like to dance to something different — especially if you do the same exercises day after day.

What kind of music gives you pleasure and makes you *want* to move around? If that music fits the Seven Habits of Highly Effective Ballet Music, it will work for ballet. It may be your favorite rock or soul artist, the Bulgarian Women's chorus, or even Dixieland jazz. Someone we know used the soundtrack to *The Patsy Cline Story* as an alternative for her private barre work. It had the perfect tempos for all her barre exercises — all played, miraculously, in the right order.

Whatever music you pick, we suggest that you listen to it once before you begin to dance, so that you won't suddenly be surprised in practice by the wrong tempo or inaudible beats.

Working to ballet class CDs

Anticipating the needs of ballet students, many teachers and musicians have created CDs, tapes, and videos of their own ballet class music for your dancing pleasure. Of these choices, we have found that CDs work best because you never have to guess where each track begins, and you can use a remote control to skip ahead.

World-renowned ballet teacher David Howard has created several excellent ballet recordings, using various rehearsal pianists. Another excellent teacher, Finis Jhung, has made recordings of his own. Pianists Lynn Stanford, Douglas Corbin, Josu Gallastegui, Lisa Harris, and Nina Pinzarrone all have high-quality recordings available. And even some famous dancers — like Natalia Makarova, Suki Shorer, and Kristine Elliott — have produced recordings of ballet music.

You can find ballet music online in many places, including http:// barryscapezio.com, www.finisjhung.com, and www.discountdance.com (which has the best prices).

Counting It Out

In this section, we tell you all about counting beats — so that you can set your dance combinations and exercises to music.

After you find the beats in a piece of music, the next step is to organize these beats into groups. (If you have any trouble finding the beat, we respectfully refer you to disco music.)

Grouping beats in sets of eight

Given that you have a steady stream of beats, and that you have to dance a particular step on each beat, how do you count in order to refer to these beats?

The answer, as anyone who has seen *A Chorus Line* knows, is that the beats are usually grouped in bunches of eight. (The choreographer/dance master in that show is always shouting, "One, two, three, four, five, six, seven, eight!" and then starting over.) Without too much cerebral trauma, then, you can figure out this fictitious direction, which you may find in a dance combination someday:

> "Count this music in groups of 8 counts, where each count lasts about one second."
>
> **On count 1, do a *demi-plié*.**
>
> **On count 2, come back up.**
>
> **On count 3, do another *demi-plié*.**
>
> **On count 4, come back up.**
>
> **On count 5, do another *demi-plié*.**
>
> **On count 6, come back up.**
>
> **On count 7, do another *demi-plié*.**
>
> **On count 8, come back up.**

Of course, some moves take more than one count to perform — either because the music flows more quickly; or because the moves themselves are more complicated; or both. Take a look at this combination:

> "Count this music in groups of 8 counts, where each count lasts about one second."
>
> **Over counts 1 through 4, do nothing.**
>
> **Over counts 5 through 8, bring the right arm up in front of your body, and then open it out to the side.**
>
> **Over counts 1 through 4, do a *demi-plié* and come back up.**
>
> **Over counts 5 through 8, do another *demi-plié* and come back up.**

Not exactly particle physics, is it?

Notice that in the preceding exercise, you count from 1 to 8 and then start over again. That counting system is extremely common in ballet.

But sometimes in this book, we ask you to count the music in groups of four, and then start over. Why on earth would we do that? Because sometimes, the steps are shorter and less complicated, and it takes fewer counts to complete them.

Double (or triple) your fun: subdivisions

Often, the music you dance to doesn't just have beats. The beats themselves can be divided up into mini-beats, or *subdivisions*. If this sounds strange, don't worry — you already understand this concept.

Say that you're dancing to a quick waltz. All over the world, people understand that a waltz in is three beats, grouped like this: STRONG, weak, weak.

Put this another way, and you get the tuba sound from any Waltz band world-wide: "OOM-pah-pah."

Now most of the time, when you count out a waltz, you count the "OOMs." Every time you hear an "OOM," you go to the next number. Like this:

OOM-pah-pah   **OOM**-pah-pah   **OOM**-pah-pah   **OOM**-pah-pah

1   **2**   **3**   **4**

Every beat in this example has *three* subdivisions. The first subdivision is the "OOM." The second subdivision is "pah." And the third subdivision is the other "pah."

Why is this concept important? Because very often in ballet, you're called upon to do complicated steps that involve motions not only *on* the beats, but also *between* the beats.

For example, you may want to try this dance combination:

> **On BEAT 1: Hop forward, wiggle your hips; then flap your arms like a chicken.**

> **On BEAT 2: Hop forward, wiggle your hips; then flap your arms like a chicken.**

On BEAT 3: Hop forward, wiggle your hips; then flap your arms like a chicken.

On BEAT 4: Hop forward, wiggle your hips; then flap your arms like a chicken.

(By the way, it can happen — a combination very similar to this one comes up in Sir Frederick Ashton's ballet *La fille mal gardée.*)

Notice that you do the same motions over and over again on each beat. In fact, it's the same *three* motions over and over: (1) hop, (2) wiggle, and (3) flap. And as you have three motions per beat, it's very helpful to use music that has three *subdivisions* to each beat.

This dance step would be very easy to do, in other words, with music that goes "OOM-pah-pah." But it would be almost *impossible* to do with polka music (which has two subdivisions to the beat), marching music (also two subdivisions to the beat), or other kinds of music (four or more subdivisions to the beat).

Now that you understand counts, and subdivisions, you're ready to put this music to the test — by dancing to it.

Part II
Belly Up to
the Barre

The 5th Wave

By Rich Tennant

In this part . . .

Although we've been putting it off, now we're going to have to get a little technical. Please lower the safety rail and keep hands and feet inside the tram at all times.

If you've read Part I, you now know what ballet is and how it works. You know a little bit about the history of ballet, and the choreographers who shaped it. Now you're ready to start exploring it yourself — up close and personal.

This part is all about the barre, a dancer's best friend. The barre is always there for you, offering unending support without a complaint. This is where all ballet technique begins.

Chapter 6

Basic Barre-Tending

*Q*uestion: What three things can you find in every single ballet studio, all over the world?

Answer: Dancers, ibuprofen, and a barre.

The barre — French for "bar" — is a horizontal wooden cylinder fixed to the wall of a ballet studio, about one foot away from the wall. And it is about to become your world.

Traditionally, every day of ballet begins with a warm-up class, and every class begins at the barre. One of your faithful authors enjoyed a 23-year career as a dancer with the San Francisco Ballet, and she attributes much of this longevity to the discipline of daily work at the barre.

The use of the barre makes perfect sense. At first, even the simplest movements work best when you hold on to something stable. And because all ballet motions are founded on the outward rotation of the hips — and hardly anyone was born in a turned out position — you must first develop strength in the muscles and tendons to execute these required positions. The barre is perfect for this purpose. We designed this chapter — and the two that follow — to let you start at the beginning, activating your muscles in the traditional sequence that thousands before you have used.

Because all dancers begin each day at the barre, it becomes a trusted old friend. There is a comfort in the ritual of warming up — whether for a rehearsal day or for your first performance as Aurora or the Prince in *Sleeping Beauty*. Sometimes the barre can become *such* a secure place for dancers that they hesitate to leave their "safety zone."

Standing at the Barre: Starting Position

Before beginning any exercises, you must find the correct placement at the barre. If you have a bona fide barre available, try this yourself. If not, you can easily simulate the experience with a strong table, chair, stool, kitchen counter, or extremely sedentary spouse. From now on, when we use the word "barre," we refer either to the real thing or your own reasonable substitute.

Stand with your left side to the barre, about an arm's length away. Now step about six inches to the left, toward the barre. Place your left hand on the barre, making sure that your hand rests slightly in front of your shoulder. Drop your left elbow and keep it slightly bent. Your arm should create a downward and forward diagonal arc, from your shoulder to the hand resting on the barre. Your right arm is low and rounded with your fingertips just to the side of your right leg (otherwise known as first arm position). Bring your feet to fifth position. (See Chapter 4 for more on fifth position.) We call this stance the *starting position*.

As a poised and elegant ballet dancer, you should try not to grip the barre for dear life — except in the most extreme situations, of course. Instead, rest your hand comfortably on the barre, keeping your thumb alongside your index finger. The barre is there to offer you balance — not to hold up your body weight!

After you master the individual positions of the feet and arms, you can have enormous fun mixing them up in different concoctions at the barre. Ballet dancers have been known to mix up concoctions until well after midnight.

As you experiment, remember one thing: Every exercise in ballet can be danced in different directions. For now, try all the exercises in this chapter while facing in one direction — with your left side to the barre. Then, of course, you should try them in the other direction, as well, to avoid becoming Quasimodesque.

Small Knee Bends: Demi-Pliés

The first exercise at the barre is the small knee bend, or *demi-plié* ("duh-MEE plee-AY"). The word *plié* means "bent," and *demi* means half — just as *demitasse* means half a cup, *demi monde* means half a world, and Demi Moore is half a Moore.

When you do a *demi-plié,* you bend your knees as far as you can *while still keeping both heels planted on the ground.* That little caveat is the key. It means that the depth of a *demi-plié* varies a little for every single dancer — as you're about to find out. Your challenge now is to execute a *demi-plié* in four of the basic positions.

Demi-plié in first position

Stand at the barre in the starting position (see the preceding section) — but with one exception: Bring your legs into first position. (See Chapter 4 for more information about first position.) Turn your feet out only as far as is comfortable.

From here, slowly bend your knees as far as possible, while keeping your heels on the ground, with your knees directly over the middle of your feet. While you descend, your lower right arm (from wrist to elbow) moves outward and slightly up, no higher than the level of your hips. This beautiful motion gives you the illusion of floating (Figure 6-1a).

Now unbend your knees, moving back up to the starting position — and bring your right arm back down to its starting position as well.

Your arms and legs should always arrive at their finishing positions together.

Congratulations — you have executed a bona fide *demi-plié*. Repeat it four times. And now, as much fun as this is, it's time to move on.

Figure 6-1:
Demi-pliés
in first and
second
positions.

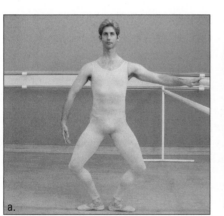 

Demi-plié in second position

From first position, transfer your weight to your left leg and slide your right foot sideways along the floor. As you do this, allow your right heel to lift up, until your right foot is fully pointed, with your right knee straight. Your right foot should remain turned out during this motion — that is, your right heel should stay forward, just as in first position. While you point your right foot, bring your right arm up *through* middle fifth position, and then open it up to second position. (See Chapter 4 for more information about arm positions.)

Can we pause to ponder the importance of this moment? In switching from one leg position to the next, you have unwittingly accomplished a very tricky, yet essential, ballet move, called a *battement tendu* ("bat-MAHN ton-DUE" — literally: "stretched out"). You can read much more about this move later in this chapter.

Now lower your right heel and transfer your weight evenly to both legs. Your heels should be in line with one another. Ideally, the distance between them should equal the length of your own foot; but the move is a little easier with the feet a bit farther apart than that.

Now that your legs are in second position, do a *demi-plié*.

Bend your knees slowly, keeping your upper body straight, and lower your hips halfway down to knee level (refer to Figure 6-1b). Don't stick your rear end out. As you descend this first time, lower your right arm. Now straighten your knees, but continue to lower your arm.

Now repeat this *demi-plié* any number of times, moving your right arm just as you did for first (leg) position.

Demi-plié in fourth position

You may have noticed that we skip third position, and there's a reason for that. It's safe to say that nobody ever does *demi-pliés* in third — except by accident.

From second position, begin by pointing your right foot. This time, draw a quarter circle on the ground, from the side to the front, without moving your hips. This is called a *demi rond de jambe* ("duh-MEE ROND duh JAHMB") — literally, a "half round of the leg." (Yeah, yeah, we know — we call it a quarter circle, the French call it a half. It's *art.* Give us a break.)

Keep your right heel turned out as much as you can, within the realm of possibility. Lower your right heel in front of your left, about a foot in front. (Again, the distance ideally equals the length of your own foot.) Meanwhile, bring your right arm up through middle fifth position and open it out to second position. Check to make sure that the weight of your body is evenly distributed over your legs. You are now in fourth position.

Now for the *demi-plié.* Once again, bend your knees as far as possible with your heels firmly on the ground. Make sure that your knees are pointing out-ward and are placed over the middle of your feet. Move your right arm as you do in the *demi-pliés* in second position (Figure 6-2a).

Concentrate on keeping your hips parallel to the front, without twisting — easier said than done.

Figure 6-2:
Demi-pliés
in fourth
and fifth
positions.

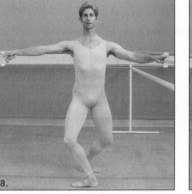

a.   b.

Demi-plié in fifth position

To go from fourth to fifth position, begin by pointing your right foot, keeping it turned out as far as you can. Now close your right foot directly in front of the left, gently touching toe to heel. Lift your right arm through middle fifth position, and open it out to second. There you have it — fifth position.

Even in the unlikely event that you were born with mega-turnout, don't try to press your right foot flat against your left. A move like that can damage something important — your knees, for example.

In fact, your fifth position may stay "open" for years. It takes a long time for a dancer's hips to loosen up enough, and the muscles to strengthen enough, to hold the ideal position. Patience, young grasshopper.

While your right leg moves from fourth to fifth position, your right arm has something to do as well. Lift your right arm through middle fifth (arm) position, into second position.

Okay now — time for the *demi-plié*. All the same rules apply, and the arm movements are the same in second position (refer to Figure 6-2b). Because of the strange contortions involved, the *demi-plié* in fifth position is the shallowest bend of them all. But perseverance pays off.

A combination for demi-pliés

When you can comfortably move through *demi-pliés* in all the positions (see the preceding sections), you can put them all together into a continuous exercise. Logically enough, this is known in the world of dance as a *combination.*

All combinations benefit from the use of music. Throughout this book, we suggest particular pieces of music that you can find in your local library, CD store, or online at sites like byronhoyt.com. By using your newfound musical knowledge from Chapter 5, you should feel free to make substitutions.

For this combination, we suggest the slow section of "Polovtsian Dances" from Alexander Borodin's opera *Prince Igor.* (You may recognize this music as the song "Stranger in Paradise," from the musical *Kismet.*) Count this music in groups of four beats.

1. **Take the starting position, with the exception that your legs are in first position. During the first 4 counts, just listen and do nothing.**

2. **Over the next 4 counts, move your right arm through middle fifth position, then out to second position, and then lower your arm into first position.**

3. **Over the next 2 counts, do a *demi-plié* in first position, moving your right arm out to the side as you descend. Over the next 2 counts, straighten back up, and bring your right arm back down to low fifth position.**

   Repeat this step twice more.

4. **Over the next 4 counts, do the famous *battement tendu* with your right leg, bringing it out to second position. Meanwhile, bring your right arm up through middle fifth (arm) position, and open it out to second (arm) position. As you lower your right heel, lower your right arm into first (arm) position.**

   See the section "Demi-plié in second position" for more on the *battement tendu.*

5. **Over the next 2 counts, do a *demi-plié* in second position. Over the next 2 counts, straighten back up. Move your arms just as you did for the first position *demi-plié.***

   Repeat this step twice more.

6. **Over the next 4 counts, do a *battement tendu* with your right leg to the side, bringing your right arm to middle fifth position. Do a *demi rond de jambe* to the front, opening your right arm to second position, and lower your right heel into fourth position.**

   See the section "Demi-plié in fourth position" for more information on the *demi rond de jambe.*

7. Over the next 2 counts, do a *demi-plié* in fourth position. Over the next 2, straighten back up. (Repeat the arm movements from first position.)

   Repeat this step twice more.

8. Over the next 4 counts, do a *battement tendu* with your right leg to the front. As before, move your right arm up through middle fifth position to second, and lower it to first (arm) position just as your front foot closes into fifth (leg) position.

9. Over the next 2 counts, do a *demi-plié* in fifth position. Over the next 2, straighten back up. (Repeat the arm movements from first position.)

   Repeat this step twice more.

10. Now for the big finish. Bring both arms into high fifth position, lifting your head as well, and gaze innocently in the direction of your right elbow.

Bravo! If you have completed your first combination without reinventing the game of Twister, pat yourself on the back. By now, you can probably pat yourself on the back with your right *foot.*

Adding Bends — The Port de Bras

Demi-pliés are great for building strength and warming up your thighs and calves, but they also involve muscle contraction. To stretch out some of those muscles, we now proudly introduce upper-body bends — forward, back, and to the side. The combination of strength building and stretching makes classical ballet dancers both strong and supple, and can add years to a dancer's career.

Because these bends involve broad arm movement from one position to another, we use the term *port de bras* ("POR duh BRAH") — literally, "carriage of the arms." You can do these movements in all the different leg positions, but for now, start with the simplest.

Forward bends

Begin in first position at the barre, with your left hand resting on the barre, and your right arm in second position. Engage your leg muscles to stabilize yourself and support your knees.

Now slowly bend forward from your hips, keeping your back, neck, and head aligned. Stretch with your torso, making it feel as long as possible.

After years of hamstring stretches, most ballet dancers can easily touch their palms to the floor without bending their knees. Therefore, they have the flexibility to do a forward bend quite deeply. But this flexibility can take a very long time to achieve. So don't despair! For now, just bend as far as you can, comfortably, while keeping your legs straight.

As you bend forward, move your right arm gradually into high fifth position. The word "high," of course, is relative. In high fifth position, your arm stretches overhead — or more accurately, in the direction your head is pointing. So if your hamstrings allow a total forward bend, then "high fifth" actually means "toward the floor" (Figure 6-3a).

Figure 6-3:
Port de bras — a forward bend in first position (a); a side bend in second position (b); and a back bend in fifth position (c).

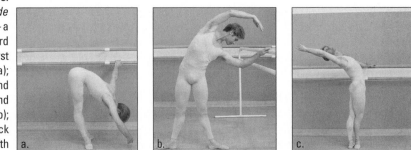

To come up from a forward bend, initiate the movement from your head, and reverse the motion, until you're back where you started.

Keep your abdominal muscles engaged the entire time to support your back and reduce the strain on the discs of your spine. Remember all those ab exercises from Chapter 3 that you considered skipping? After doing a forward *port de bras,* you'll know why you need 'em.

Side bends

Stand at the barre in second position, left hand on the barre, and right arm in second position. To begin, lift your upper body and stomach (while keeping your shoulders down), and lean to the left, toward the barre, keeping your weight evenly distributed between both legs. Make sure that you bend directly to the side, without twisting forward or back.

As you bend, lift your right arm over your head, into high fifth position. Turn your head toward the barre (refer to Figure 6-3b). Return to the upright position by reversing the bend, and return your right arm to second position.

Back bends

Ah, the sacrifices we make for beauty! In our opinion, the backward *port de bras* is the most beautiful of them all. But it's also the most treacherous. So take extra care when doing this one. Support yourself well with your leg muscles, keep your knees straight, and keep your abdominal muscles engaged.

Begin in fifth position at the barre, with your right arm in high fifth. Tilt your head slightly to the right, toward your right elbow, and keep it there throughout the entire movement.

Now, keeping your shoulders down, lift from your ribcage and begin to bend backward from your head, working your way down through the middle of your back, until you have bent as far as you can *safely* go (refer to Figure 6-3c).

To come up from a back bend, initiate the motion from your upper back, following through with your neck and head, returning your arm to second position.

A combination for port de bras

This handy combination allows you to review your *pliés,* plus all the *port de bras* bends. For your music, we recommend the Waltz from Tchaikovsky's great ballet, *Sleeping Beauty.* This music is in three beats to the bar: think "*OOM*-pah-pah, *OOM*-pah-pah. . . ." Each complete *OOM*-pah-pah gets one count, giving you a moderate tempo to work with. (See Chapter 5 for more information on counting music.)

For each position, follow this combination: do two *demi-pliés* (see "Small Knee Bends: *Demi-Pliés*," earlier in this chapter), taking two counts for each *demi-plié.* Now add a *port de bras* in the direction of your choice, taking two counts to reach the full bend, and two counts to return.

Rises to the Balls of the Feet (Relevés)

The *relevé* ("ruh-luh-VAY") which is done in every position, is crucial to the strength of your legs. It gives you the strength to support the weight of your body, especially during the really fun steps, like jumps and pirouettes. And it's the best calf exercise we've ever seen.

The word *relevé* means, literally, "raised up again." Specifically, it refers to moves in which you go up on the balls of your feet. The French term for this is *demi pointe,* or half-point. The French are very optimistic in their terminology.

It wouldn't be a bad idea to sit down right now, take off any slippers, high-heeled shoes, or jackboots you may be wearing, and identify the *exact* spot we're referring to. Take a look at the bottom of one foot. Just behind the spot where your toes connect to your feet, there's a soft pad. Eureka! You've found it. The aim of each *relevé* is to rise and support yourself, for a second or two, on that precise spot.

Relevé in first position

For your very first *relevé* practice, face the barre, in first position, with both hands resting on the barre. Using your hands for balance, but not for support, try rising up to the balls of your feet (Figure 6-4a). Keep your knees straight and your ankles well supported. Keep your stomach muscles engaged. Keep your back strong. Keep *everything* strong.

Does this motion feel strange? If so, you're not alone. But after a few dozen tries, you may begin to enjoy this step. And after a few more, it may become addictive. We certainly hope so — every ballet dancer does it hundreds of times every day.

Figure 6-4:
Relevés in first and fifth positions.

Relevé in fifth position

Just for fun, we thought we'd show you this masochistic little number. In practice, however, you should wait until you feel comfortable — however long that may be.

When you do a *relevé* in fifth position, you may see space between your feet. (In purist ballet technique, space between the feet here is a definite *faux pas.*) To remedy this shocking situation, ballet dancers release the front foot and slide it sideways until it completely obscures the back foot. What the viewer sees, therefore, is a single foot — with two heels (refer to Figure 6-4b)! Weird, we know. But beautiful by ballet standards.

After practicing *relevés,* we strongly recommend this thorough calf stretch for a happier tomorrow: Stand facing the barre, holding on with both hands. Place your feet parallel to each other. Now slide your right leg straight back, allowing your heel to lift off the floor, and gently bend your left knee. Keep your back upright. Now reach your right heel down toward the floor, slowly and with control. Hold for about 20 seconds — or less if you begin to feel a cramp. Then switch legs.

Never bounce your heel up and down when doing this stretch. Slowly, evenly, and with control — now *that's* how to stretch.

Big Knee Bends (Grands Pliés)

The *grand plié* ("GRAHN plee-AY") is simply extension of the *demi-plié* (see "Small Knee Bends: Demi-Pliés," earlier in this chapter). In a *demi-plié* you bend your knees only as far as possible *while keeping your heels on the ground;* in a *grand plié* you can allow your heels to lift — and bend even farther.

During the bend in a *grand plié,* your heels should lift only out of necessity. Keep them down as long as you can, lift them when you need to, and bring them back down again as soon as you can. This technique not only adheres to the venerable ballet tradition, it also builds strength in your thigh muscles and stretches out your calf muscles.

Keep your knees directly over your feet — and be careful never to sit, or rest, at the bottom of the motion. Your knees will thank you.

Grand plié in first position

Begin in the starting position, with the exception that your legs are in first position. Bring your right arm up through middle fifth position, and open it to second position. Now start downward, just as you do for a *demi-plié*. When you can no longer keep your heels down, allow them to lift (as needed) off the ground. At the bottom of the motion, your hips should still be higher than your knees — giving your legs a diamond shape. Start upwards again without hesitation, reaching for the ground with your heels as soon as possible, and continue back up to first position with straight legs.

As your body descends, your right arm does as well, in a graceful swooping motion, arriving in low fifth position at the bottom of the *plié* (Figure 6-5a). As you ascend, lift your arm, so that it reaches middle fifth position halfway through the motion (which is the *demi-plié* you know so well); then open your arm to second position to finish.

Figure 6-5:
Grands pliés
in first and
second
position.

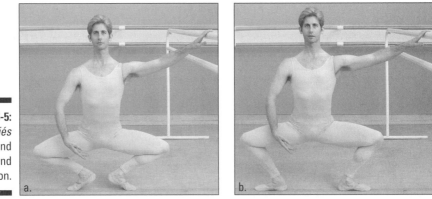

Grand plié in second position

Second position is the easiest for executing a *grand plié* — and also the safest position to avoid injury.

Begin with your legs and right arm in second position, and lower your body as you do for a *grand plié* in first position. As you do, be especially careful to keep your upper body aligned, without sticking out your rear end. At the bottom of the motion, make sure that your hips never go lower than your knees (refer to Figure 6-5b). Come up as before, with the same motion of your right arm.

A grand plié combination

This combination includes many of the movements in this chapter. The centerpiece, of course, is the *grand plié*.

Our suggested music for this combination could hardly be more beautiful. It's "Alla tedesca" from *Symphony no. 3* by Tchaikovsky, used in George Balanchine's ballet entitled — appropriately enough — *Diamonds*.

Count this piece in groups of eight beats as you follow these steps:

1. **Start in the starting position, with the exception that your legs are in first position. For the first four counts of the music, just listen and do nothing.**

2. **On counts 5 through 8, bring your right arm from first position, through middle fifth, to second position.**

3. **Over the next 8 counts, execute two *grands pliés* in first position.**

   Use two counts to go down and two counts to come up.

4. **On counts 1 through 3, do a forward bend (*port de bras*); over counts 4 through 6, return to the starting position.**

5. **On counts 7 and 8, do a *battement tendu* to the right with the right leg, and bring your heel down into second position.**

6. **Over the next 8 counts, execute two *grands pliés* in second position.**

7. **On counts 1 through 3, do a side bend (*port de bras*); over counts 4 through 6, return to second position.**

8. **On counts 7 and 8, do a *battement tendu* to the right with the right leg, and then close your right leg into first position.**

9. **Over the next 8 counts, do a *relevé,* take your left arm off the barre, and balance with the arms and legs in first position.**

10. **To finish, lower your heels, and lower your arms to low fifth (arm) position.**

Extending the Legs (Battements Tendus)

It you hang around a ballet studio, you're bound to hear the French words *battement tendu* ("bat-MAHN tahn-DUE") — or *tendu* for short — at least 50 times a day. This is the name for a very common kind of leg extension that is essential to ballet. And, in fact, a very simple *battement tendu* comes up earlier in this chapter.

Battement tendu extensions come in many different heights and looks, but their origin is very basic. They are used not only to warm up the feet, but also as the driving force behind the biggest jumps in ballet. They are the focal point for the slow dance — known as *adagio* — that begins nearly every classical *pas de deux* (dance for two). In the *grand pas de deux* in Act II of *Swan Lake*, when the ballerina lifts one leg slowly into the air and holds it, that's a form of *battement tendu*. Then, during the final section of the third act "Black Swan *pas de deux*," when the Prince comes bounding across the stage, his huge leaps begin with a *battement* to hurl him into the air. There is a lot of force in those legs — and it all comes from the ground up.

Battements tendus from first position

The *battement tendu* is easiest from first position, and that's where we start. There are three directions — to the front, side, and back.

A *battement tendu* is a brushing action. In all these exercises, the right leg never loses contact with the floor.

To the front

Follow these easy steps to do a *battement tendu* forward:

1. **Begin standing sideways to the barre, with your left hand resting on the barre and your right arm in second (arm) position.**

   Your right arm stays in this position throughout this exercise.

2. **Brush your right foot forward along the floor and transfer all your weight to your left leg. As soon as possible during this motion, lift your right heel and point your foot (Figure 6-6a).**

   Keep your foot turned out while you do this.

3. **Flex your right foot back and draw it back to first position by brushing it along the floor. Meanwhile, bend your right ankle (and un-point the toes), to return your weight evenly to both feet.**

Figure 6-6:
The battement tendu from first position to the front, side, and back.

To the side

For the *battement tendu* to the side — or *à la seconde* ("ah la se-COND") — the process is the same as for the *tendu* forward. But in this case, you brush your foot *sideways* instead of forward (refer to Figure 6-6b).

To the back

The motion backwards — or *en arrière* ("ahn ar-YAIR") — is a little harder to do because it involves keeping your right leg turned out and your upper back stationary during the exercise (refer to Figure 6-6c). Obviously, this movement improves with time, practice, and flexibility. But don't be frustrated if you have trouble at first.

If you look into a mirror at your side while doing a *battement tendu en arrière,* theoretically you would not see your right heel at all. We know: idealistic. That's the goal, anyway; that is one of the many brass rings that ballet dancers reach for every day.

Battements tendus from fifth position

From fifth position of the legs, the *battement tendu* follows the same basic procedure as from first position. The difference, of course, lies in the crossed position of the legs. Normally this crossed position would complicate everything. But the fifth position makes one thing easier: the transfer of weight to the standing leg.

For the *battement tendu* from fifth position to the front, side, and back, keep in mind that the steps are exactly the same as from first position. The only difference is that you *begin* and *end* in fifth position.

A battement tendu combination

If your body is warm, limber, and ready for more, here's an exercise combination to practice the *battements tendus* that we tell you about in the preceding sections.

For music, we recommend the wonderful pizzicato movement from Act I of Glazunov's ballet *Raymonda.*

Count the music in groups of four beats as you follow these steps:

1. **Begin in the starting position. For four counts, do absolutely nothing but ponder how impressive it is that you understood the previous sentence.**

2. **Over the next counts 1 through 4, move your right arm (*port de bras*) through middle fifth position to second position, and keep it there throughout the rest of the combination.**

3. **Over the next counts 1 through 4, with the right leg, do a *battement tendu* to the front and return.**

   Repeat Step 3 three more times.

4. **Over the next counts 1 through 4, do a *battement tendu* to the side and return to fifth position with your right foot in front.**

   Repeat Step 4 three more times. But each time, when you close your right foot, alternate between back and front. That is, one time your right foot closes behind your left foot, and the next time it closes in front.

5. **Over the next counts 1 through 4, do a *battement tendu* to the rear *(arrière)* and return to fifth position with your right foot in back.**

   Repeat three more times.

6. **Over the next counts 1 through 4, do a *battement tendu* to the side and close to fifth position with your right foot in back.**

   Repeat three more times. But each time, as in Step 4, when you close your right foot back in, alternate between front and back.

For a greater challenge, try doing this combination twice as fast!

And you're finished. Congratulations — ballet immortality awaits.

Battements tendus at 45 degrees (dégagé)

In the *battement tendu dégagé* ("day-gah-JAY"), you can think of your right foot as an airplane, rushing down the runway. At a certain point your foot reaches the requisite speed and takes off. Then, in midair, it pauses, as if connected to the ground by an enormous bungee cord — and returns gracefully back to the runway, touching down smoothly in reverse. Or something like that.

1. **Take the starting position. Lift your right arm through middle fifth position into second position.**

   Don't forget to keep your head slightly tilted toward your right arm, as in the original *battement tendu*.

2. **Brush your right foot toward the front, as in a *battement tendu*. As you brush, lift your right leg up to nearly a 45-degree angle (Figure 6-7a).**

3. **Return your right leg back to fifth position, right leg in front.**

   As you do this, imagine that the left leg is lifted upwards, without actually leaving the floor — allowing the weight to distribute evenly over both legs in fifth position.

There you have it — the *dégagé*.

For the motion to the side (Figure 6-7b) and to the back (Figure 6-7c), the rules remain the same. Do the same brush that you did for the simple *battement tendu,* but just add the lift.

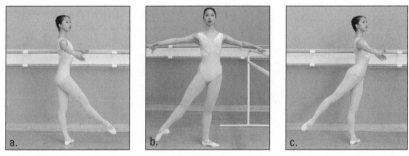

Figure 6-7:
Dégagés
from fifth
position to
the front,
side, and
back.

a. b. c.

A dégagé combination

For the music to this combination, we suggest the *Valse in A-flat, opus 64, no. 3,* by Fréderic Chopin. In this music, each beat has three subdivisions: so think "*OOM*-pah-pah, *OOM*-pah-pah . . ." as you count the music. Each complete *OOM*-pah-pah gets one count, giving you a moderate tempo to work with. (See Chapter 5 for more info on counting beats in music.) Count this music in groups of eight beats as you follow these steps:

1. **Take your starting position. On the first 4 counts of the music, contemplate the dinner you will soon deserve.**

2. **Over counts 5 through 8, bring your right arm in a *port de bras* through middle fifth (arm) position, out to second (arm) position.**

   Your right arm stays here throughout the entire combination.

3. **Over the next counts 1 and 2, with your right leg, do a *dégagé* to the front and return.**

4. **Over counts 3 through 8, repeat this front *dégagé* three times.**

5. **Over the next counts 1 and 2, do a *dégagé* to the side and return to fifth position with your right leg in front.**

6. **Over counts 3 through 8, repeat this side *dégagé* three more times, closing your right foot in back the first time, in front the second time, and in back the third time.**

7. **Over the next counts 1 and 2, do a *dégagé* to the back (*arrière*) and return to fifth position with your right leg in back.**

8. **Over counts 3 through 8, repeat this back *dégagé* three more times.**

9. On the next counts 1 and 2, do a *dégagé* to the side and return to fifth position with your right leg in back.

10. Over counts 3 through 8, repeat this side *dégagé* three more times, closing your right foot in front the first time, in back the second time, and in front the third time.

11. Finish by lowering your right arm to first position.

Ready for a bigger challenge? Try doing this baby in double time — or add a *demi-plié* after three *dégagés* in each direction.

Drawing Circles on the Floor (Rond de Jambe à Terre)

Earlier in this chapter (see "*Demi-plié* in fourth position") we introduce you to the concept of the *demi rond de jambe,* which is a quarter circle drawn with the foot. Now we bring you the bigger, bolder concept of the *rond de jambe* ("RON duh JAHMB") itself. As the absence of the word *demi* in the name might imply, this move is larger than the last. Twice as large, to be exact.

Connecting your tendus

The *rond de jambe* consists of a half circle drawn with the foot. This move can be done either on the ground (*à terre*) or in the air (*en l'air*); for now we stick to the ground.

Sounds complicated, no? Actually, no! What if we told you that all the moves necessary to dance a beautiful *rond de jambe à terre* can be found in previous sections of this chapter?

If you connect all the simple *battements tendus* from first position, described earlier in this chapter, you have a perfect *rond de jambe* from front to back. Here's how to do it:

1. Begin in the starting position, with the exception that your feet are in first position. Bring your right arm through middle fifth to second (arm) position.

   Your arm remains in second position throughout the exercise.

2. With your right leg, do a *battement tendu* to the front.

3. **Keeping your toes touching the floor, draw your right leg around to the side, with the heel forward.**

4. **Keep drawing your right leg around to the back — keeping your heel forward as long as possible.**

There's a great temptation to let your hips swing in rhythm with these leg circles. But try to resist — and save the hula for Hawaii.

5. **To finish, simply close your right leg back into first position.**

Because the motion initially goes from the front out to the side, this is known as the "round of the leg outside" (*rond de jambe en dehors* — "RON duh JAHMB ahn duh-OR"). Can you see where this is heading? Time to do the motion in reverse; that is, moving from the back around to the front — the "round of the leg inside" (*rond de jambe en dedans* — "RON duh JAHMB ahn duh-DAHN").

Usually, you do these two motions, "outside" and "inside," one after another in quick succession. After you finish the "outside step" and you find yourself in first position, don't linger there for a nightcap. Instead, just stop in for a quickie, all toes briefly touching the ground in first position, and move on.

A rond de jambe à terre combination

To accompany this combination, we suggest the beautiful *Pavane,* opus 50, of Gabriel Fauré. This is a slow, stately dance, and each slow beat gets one count. Count the music in groups of four as you do this combination:

1. **Begin in the starting position, with the exception that your legs are in first position. Over counts 1 through 4, do nothing.**

2. **Over the next counts 1 through 4, move your right arm through middle fifth position, to second position.**

3. **Over the next counts 1 through 4, do a *rond de jambe en dehors* — that is, to the "outside." Repeat seven more times and end with a *battement tendu* in front.**

4. **Over the next counts 1 through 4, do a *rond de jambe en dedans* (to the "inside"). Repeat seven more times, and end in first position.**

5. **Over the next 8 counts, do a forward *port de bras*.**

Make sure to hold your abs, glutes, and legs strongly.

6. **On the next 8 counts, do a *port de bras* to the back, and return to the position in Step 1.**

7. **Over the next 8 counts, rise to the balls of the feet (*relevé*), sliding the legs into fifth position, with the right foot in front. (Your legs should be tightly pressed together — from top to bottom.) As you rise, bring the right arm through middle fifth to high fifth (arm) position.**

8. **After you find your balance, release the barre with your left hand, allowing the left arm to join the right in high fifth position.**

   Your face should gaze lovingly in the direction of your right arm.

Whenever you get tired, bored, or cramped — or run out of music — do a *demi-plié* in fifth position, bringing your arms down through second position to arrive in low fifth position when you straighten your legs.

Practicing Your One-Legged Balance (Retiré and Relevé)

Barre work prepares you to stand unsupported. One exercise that helps you stand on your own is the *retiré* ("ruh-tee-RAY"). As you can discover in Chapter 10, the *retiré* is the position used for *pirouettes*, so finding your balance is very important.

1. **From the starting position, transfer your weight to your left leg.**

2. **Lift your right foot off the floor, bending your knee and pointing your foot. Draw the right baby toe up your left ankle and shin, toward the left knee.**

3. **Touch your pointed right foot to your left leg, just below the kneecap.**

   Your right knee should be reaching outward toward the wall to your right, and your hips and shoulders should stay down.

4. **Bring your right arm into middle fifth position. Then, letting go of the barre with your left hand, join both arms in middle fifth (arm) position (Figure 6-8a). Try to balance there!**

Keeping your abs engaged and lifted as you do this exercise helps you to balance.

Now for an even greater challenge: balancing while you are up on the ball of one foot. (This is *retiré relevé*.) This time, try moving your arms overhead in high fifth position (refer to Figure 6-8b)!

If you successfully balanced without the barre, even for a second or two, you're in great shape. It's just a short step (and a couple of chapters) from here to the world-famous *pirouette*. Congratulations — you deserve a drink.

Figure 6-8:
The *retiré*, arms in middle fifth position, and the *retiré relevé*, arms in high fifth position.

a.

b.

Chapter 7

Stepping It Up at the Barre

In This Chapter

▶ Coordinating one leg on the floor with one in the air

▶ Cooking up *fondus* and *frappés*

▶ Horsing around

Chapter 6 introduces you to the basic warm-up exercises at the barre. This chapter picks up where that one left off — and makes up the middle group of barre exercises that most ballet dancers do in sequence every day.

In this chapter you pick your legs up off the ground (one at a time, that is) and sustain a higher lift than before. Don't worry — you can start very slowly. You'll soon be amazed at what you can accomplish with your two lower appendages.

Melting into a One-Leg Knee Bend (Fondu)

Although this exercise is called the *fondu* ("fon-DUE"), it bears very little resemblance to melted cheese. It is so named because, after you master this exercise, you get to eat whatever you want.

Actually, the French word *fondu* does indeed mean "melted," and it's a good description of this step. To do a *fondu,* you start from two legs, and — by gradually bending both legs and transferring all your weight to one leg — you lower yourself closer and closer to the floor, like a Gruyère that has gotten a bit runny.

As you are about to discover, the best way to master this exercise is in the so-called *cou-de-pied* position.

The so-called cou-de-pied position

Simply put, the *cou-de-pied* ("KOO de peeAY") *position* is a pose in which one foot is slightly raised off the ground. You can do the *cou-de-pied* position to the front and to the back.

Begin in the position that's probably oh-so-familiar to you by now. Stand with the barre at the left side of your body and place your left hand on the barre. Bring your feet to fifth position with your right foot in front, and bring your right arm to low fifth position (*low fifth*). For the rest of this chapter, we call this the *starting position*.

Cou-de-pied position in front

To do the *cou-de-pied* to the front, follow these steps:

1. **Supporting yourself well with your left leg, lift your right foot off the floor. As you do, bend your right knee slightly and turn it outward.**

2. **Touch your pointed right foot to your left ankle at the bone that sticks out on the inside of your ankle.**

   Because your feet are turned out, that bone is facing *forward.* The heel of your right foot should be just forward of your right toes.

There you have it — the *cou-de-pied* front position. (See Figure 7-1a, the dancer on the right.)

Figure 7-1:
The *cou-de-pied* position in front (a) — with and without a *fondu* added — and in back (b) — with and without a *fondu.*

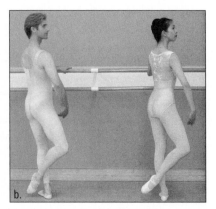

Now for the *fondu.*

1. **Begin in the starting position and repeat the *cou-de-pied* front motion. But this time, as you lift your right foot, do a *demi-plié* with your left leg.**

   By the time you are in the *cou-de-pied* position, you have reached the deepest point of the *demi-plié*. That is the *fondu* to the front (refer to Figure 7-1a, the dancer on the left).

   Time to come up.

2. **Bring your right foot back into fifth position as you straighten both knees simultaneously.**

Cou-de-pied position in back

Well done. Next, try the *cou-de-pied* back position. Once again, begin in the starting position, but this time with your right foot behind your left.

1. **Lift your right foot into *cou-de-pied* back position, as shown in Figure 7-1b, the dancer on the right.**

   Make sure that the toes of your right foot are pointing back, and the heel of your right foot is touching your left leg at the lower attachment of the calf muscle.

2. **Now return to the starting position, right foot in back.**

   Fondu time.

   From this starting position, do the same motion again — but add the *demi-plié* (refer to Figure 7-1b, the dancer on the right).

That's the *fondu* in back.

When you feel comfortable with these motions, try them with your legs reversed. Begin in the mirror image of the starting position: the barre at your right side, right hand on the barre, feet in fifth position with your left foot in front, left arm in low fifth position.

Mixing the fondu with the battement tendu

You can combine the *fondu* with just about any of the motions from Chapter 6. To begin, try a *fondu* followed by a *battement tendu* to the front.

1. **Stand in the starting position, with one slight change: Bring your right arm into second (arm) position.**

   See Chapter 4 for more information on arm and leg positions.

2. **Do the famous *fondu* with your right foot in *cou-de-pied* front position.**

3. **As you straighten your left leg to come up again, extend your right leg in front of you — into the forward *battement tendu* position that we show you in Chapter 6.**

   Your right leg should arrive in the forward position, with a straight knee, just as you straighten your left knee.

   Need another challenge? It's time to involve your right arm.

4. **Do another *fondu*. This time, as you reach the lowest point, bring your right arm to middle fifth position. Then, as you straighten your left knee and move your right foot forward into the *battement tendu*, open your right arm, arriving in second (arm) position at the same moment that your leg arrives at its final destination (Figure 7-2).**

   That's it!

Figure 7-2: Coming out of the *fondu* from *cou-de-pied* front position, ending in a *battement tendu* to the front.

Of course, you can do this motion to the side — everything, even your arms, is the same, except that your foot does the *battement tendu* to the side instead of the front. But on the return, bring your right foot in front and in back alternately. This means that when doing several *fondus* to *battement tendus* to the side, you are alternating the *cou-de-pied* position: front, back, front, back.

Now try the *fondu* again, followed by a *battement tendu* to the back, with your right foot in back. Move your right arm exactly as you do for the *battement tendu* to the front.

Finally, repeat the *battement tendu* to the side and finish by closing in fifth position with your right foot in front, just as you began.

The sequence you just performed— front, side, back, side — is the most common in ballet. It's called *en croix* — "in a cross"— because your foot moves in the shape of a cross, as drawn by, say, Klingons.

Don't skimp on this or any other exercise: Do this exercise to the front, side, and back. Then, get into the mirror image of the starting position (turn so that the barre is to your right) and repeat the whole exercise using your *left* leg.

Try the following combination to get some practice mixing the *fondu* and the *battement tendu.* For this combination, go out and find yourself a tango recording. Either that, or you can use the instantly recognizable *Habanera* from Georges Bizet's opera *Carmen.* Count this music in groups of eight, where each count lasts about two seconds. (See Chapter 5 for more info on counting music.)

1. **Stand in the starting position. For the first 4 counts, do nothing.**

2. **Over counts 5 through 8, bring your right arm up from low fifth to middle fifth position and open it to second position.**

3. **Over counts 1 through 4, do a *fondu* in the *cou-de-pied* front position, going to a *battement tendu* in front.**

   Meanwhile, bring your right arm up through low fifth to middle fifth position (for the *fondu*) and open to second position (on the *tendu*).

4. **Over counts 5 through 8, and then again over the next counts 1 through 4, repeat Step 3 twice more.**

5. **Over counts 5 and 6, do a *fondu* in the *cou-de-pied* front position. Over counts 7 and 8, close to fifth position with your right foot in front and the right arm in second position.**

6. **Over counts 1 through 4, do a *fondu* in the *cou-de-pied* front position, going to a *battement tendu* to the side.**

   Meanwhile, bring your right arm up through low fifth to middle fifth position (for the *fondu)* and open to second position (on the *tendu).*

7. **Over counts 5 through 8, do a *fondu* in the *cou-de-pied* back position, going to a *battement tendu* to the side.**

   The right arm follows the same path and timing as in the *fondu* to *battement tendu* exercise earlier in this chapter.

8. **Over counts 1 through 4, repeat Step 6.**

9. **Over counts 5 and 6, do a *fondu* in the *cou-de-pied* back position. Over counts 7 and 8, close to fifth position with your right foot in back, and the right arm in second position.**

10. **Over counts 1 through 4, do a *fondu* in the *cou-de-pied* back position, going to a *battement tendu* to the back.**

    Meanwhile, bring your right arm up through low fifth to middle fifth position (for the *fondu*) and open to second position (on the *tendu*).

11. **Over counts 5 through 8, and then again over the next count 1 through 4, repeat Step 10 twice more.**

12. **Over counts 5 and 6, do a *fondu* in the *cou-de-pied* back position. Over counts 7 and 8, close to fifth position with your right foot in back, and the right arm in second position.**

13. **Over counts 1 through 4, repeat Step 7.**

14. **Over counts 5 through 8, repeat Step 6.**

15. **Over counts 1 through 4, repeat Step 7.**

16. **Over counts 5 and 6, repeat Step 9, and close to fifth position with your right foot in front.**

17. **To finish, lower your right arm to low fifth position.**

Switch sides and do this exercise in the opposite direction; that is, with the barre to your right.

Combining the fondu with the dégagé

Up to this point you have done the *fondu* in the *cou-de-pied* position, and you have done it adding *battement tendus.* Now, following the traditional ballet sequence that has been in place for centuries, the next step is to do the *fondu* adding the *dégagé* positions from Chapter 6.

If you're worried about adding the *dégagé,* have no fear! This is one of the easy steps. It's just a matter of extending your leg a few inches off the floor — to just a little under a 45-degree angle.

Stand in the starting position.

1. **Do a fondu with your right leg in the *cou-de-pied* front position. Meanwhile, bring your right arm through middle fifth position.**

2. **As you come back up from the *fondu*, extend your right leg out in front to the *dégagé* position, and bring your arm out to second position, just as you did in the previous exercise.**

Don't forget to straighten both knees at the same time!

In opposition

In the ballet world, you often hear the term *opposition*. In order to achieve the balance needed in many ballet moves, your muscles often have to work in opposite directions at the same time.

A classic example of opposition is the *fondu relevé*. As your standing leg raises up on the ball of your foot while the other leg is in the *cou-de-pied* position, your body invariably wants to turn in toward your standing leg. In order to coun-teract this, you must keep the knee of the *cou-de-pied* leg pressing outward.

For this reason, we would never describe any ballet position as static, or motionless. There is *always* motion, even when your audience (or your dog) can't see it. In ballet, work is being done at all times throughout your body.

If you don't have a split personality already, your body soon will.

After this move feels comfortable, try the motion to the side. Start with another *fondu* — but while straightening up, do a *dégagé* to the side.

Bring your leg in for another *fondu*, but this time in the *cou-de-pied* back position. Repeat the step a few times more — always alternating where your right foot returns to *cou-de-pied*. Front, back, front. Finish by closing in fifth position with your right foot in *back*.

Now try a *fondu* opening to *dégagé* to the back, and return to the *cou-de-pied* back position. Repeat that motion at least twice more, and on the last repetition, close to fifth position with your right foot in back.

Next, try a *fondu* opening to *dégagé* to the side, and return to the *cou-de-pied* front position. Finally, do this move two more times, alternating *cou-de-pied* back and front, and close to fifth position with your right foot in front.

You may have noticed that when you repeat these exercises, your foot doesn't necessarily close into the fifth position "resting place" for each *fondu.* Of course, repeating the exercise without stopping is much harder on your muscles — and that's a good thing. These repetitions work to develop long muscles, great strength in your legs, and that "Ballet Butt" you keep hearing about.

To practice combining the fondu with the *dégagé,* just repeat the exercise you do in "Mixing the fondu with the battement tendu," earlier in this section — same music and all. But in every step, you substitute the word *dégagé* for *battement tendu*. In other words, instead of extending your leg straight to the floor (*tendu*) as you straighten your knees, you extend it out to the 45-degree position off the floor (*dégagé*).

After working your legs — as in the previous exercises — it is always a good idea to stretch your back and hamstrings. (For more on stretches, refer to Chapter 3.) Remember to take your time with each stretch.

When you're this warm from exercise, stretching suddenly becomes easier, and you may be tempted to stretch farther than your body can really handle. Don't go for the gold medal just yet — or a strain could follow.

Adding rises to the ball of the foot (relevé)

Time to ratchet up the challenge just one notch. This exercise includes all the elements of the previous *fondu* exercise in this section — plus one more: the *relevé*. As you may remember from Chapter 6, *relevé* means "lifted up again." In this exercise, you add a little rise onto the ball of your foot.

The so-called *fondu relevé* is the ultimate antigravity exercise. It lifts you at the very top of your hamstrings — just where they attach to the base of the glutes. As a result, your legs and glutes become much firmer. And as you develop the control needed to execute this move well, you build a tremendous amount of strength.

Stand in the starting position, but with your right arm in second position.

1. **Do a *fondu* on your left leg, with your right foot in the *cou-de-pied* front position. Meanwhile, bring your right arm through low fifth position.**

2. **Straighten your left knee and rise up on the ball of your left foot.**

   Your trusty authors shall now attempt to lower you down.

3. **As you lower your left leg from *relevé*, touch your left heel down to the floor, and then bend your knee into a *fondu*.**

   See sidebar "Hiding the seams" for tips on how to do this gracefully.

When you do this exercise, the *cou-de-pied* position doesn't change — even when you go up on the ball of your foot (*relevé*) or down into the bent-knee position (*fondu*).

Of course, this move can be done in all the same directions as the other *fondus*. We suggest you repeat all the *fondu* positions, enabling you to concentrate on the addition of the *relevé* each time. The art of ballet is nothing if not thorough.

Stretch out your hamstrings and back after you finish this exercise for a more salubrious mañana.

Adding the retiré

In the _retiré_ (see Chapter 6), your standing leg is straight and turned out, while your other leg is lifted, knee bent outward, with your toes touching your standing leg just below the kneecap.

The _retiré_ is often combined with _fondu_ exercises at the barre. From any _fondu_ in _cou-de-pied_ front position, straighten your standing leg, bringing the toes of the working leg (that is, the leg you're not standing on) up your shinbone to your knee. There you have it — a _fondu_ to _retiré_ front.

As you can find out in Chapter 10, the _relevé_ in _retiré_ is the position used in ballet turns, or _pirouettes._ Of course, everyone seems to want to do pirouettes, and for good reason — they're _fun!_ But they take a lot of work to master, and this is the first step.

When you do a _relevé_ with one leg lifted in _retiré,_ your lifted leg always wants to turn in. Just as in the _fondu relevé_ that we describe in the previous section, you have to work consciously against this tendency.

A complete fondu combination

Time to pick your favorite moves and put them together. To create the ultimate fondu combination, you can include _different_ moves from earlier in this section. The constant is the _fondu_ — you melt into a one-legged knee bend again and again. But every time you come up out of the _fondu,_ try alternating between _battements tendus, dégagés_ and _retirés._ And to add a little spice, occasionally go up on the ball of your standing foot as well (_relevé_).

Hiding the seams

Within any given minute of ballet performance, the average dancer may go through 100 different moves. Of course, to the average viewer, the performance is one long, fluid, beautiful motion. The secret? Not showing the seams.

For example, in a typical _relevé,_ the standing leg has at least two things to do: straighten the knee, and rise up onto the ball of the foot. These motions follow a specific sequence — the dancer always straightens his standing knee completely before rising onto the ball of his foot. However, these movements follow in such quick succession that they appear to be a single motion.

For the reverse motion, the same concept applies: As the dancer comes down from the _relevé_ into the melting _fondu,_ the standing heel touches the floor _just before_ the knee begins to bend.

Seamless, man, seamless!

For music, we recommend any tango music. Count the music in groups of 8 counts, where each count lasts about one second.

Because you count the music in groups of 8, try to create 8-count groupings of steps. (See other combinations in this chapter for inspiration.)

The Pas de Cheval (Horse Step)

Horses hold a special fascination for ballet dancers, and ballet dancers are often compared to thoroughbred racehorses. Perhaps the reason is the beauty of dancers' musculature, the leanness in their legs and long necks, or the perception that, like horses, they were simply created for graceful movement. Or perhaps the reason is that like horses, ballet dancers drink a lot of water, love to herd together, and tend to kick when provoked.

Whatever the essence of this fascination, it must be a long-standing one, because someone long ago named a step in the classical ballet vocabulary the "horse step," or *pas de cheval* ("PAH duh shuh-VAHL").

To understand the inspiration for this step, think about how a horse walks. As each hoof lifts off the ground, the ankle bends so that the hoof remains a little behind the rest of the leg. Then, as the leg extends towards the next step, the hoof comes forward to meet the ground. This is the motion used in the *pas de cheval*.

To do this step, stand in the starting position.

1. **Lift your right foot into the regular *cou-de-pied* front position.**

2. **Extend your foot to the front as if you are going to the *dégagé*, and place your toes on the ground in the *battement tendu* front position.**

   There you have it — the *pas de cheval.*

3. **Now bring your right foot back to close in front of your left, in fifth position.**

It does look an awful like the action a horse makes; aren't you glad you don't walk like that?

Now you know the drill — repeat the step in all directions. Starting from fifth position with your right foot in front, do a *pas de cheval* to the side; then close in fifth position with your right foot in back. Now horse-step to the back and close. Then complete the shape of the "cross" by repeating the step to the side;and finish in fifth position with your right foot in front.

To practice the *pas de cheval,* try a brilliant dance from Tchaikovsky's immortal *Nutcracker:* the Waltz of the Flowers.

Wait until about a minute into the music, after the harp plays a showy little solo. Then the orchestra starts to play an "OOM-pah-pah" rhythm, and from here the beat stays steady. Count this music in groups of eight.

1. **Stand in the starting position. For the first four counts, do nothing.**

2. **Over counts 5 through 8, do a *port de bras* with your right arm, from low fifth, through middle fifth, to second position.**

3. **Over the next 16 counts, do four *pas de cheval* to the front.**

   Coupé on one, lift your right leg toward the *tendu* on two, reach the final *tendu* position with a straight leg on three, and close in fifth position with your right foot front on four.

4. **Over the next 16 counts, do four *pas de cheval* to the side. Close in fifth position with your right foot in front the first time, and alternate thereafter.**

5. **Over the next 16 counts, do four *pas de cheval* back.**

6. **Over the next 16 counts, do four *pas de cheval* to the side. Close in fifth position with your right foot in back the first time, and alternate thereafter.**

Repeat the exercise on the other side.

Striking the Floor with Your Foot (Battement Tendu Frappé)

If you've ever wondered how ballet dancers can move their feet so quickly and point their feet so sharply, you're about to find out. The ballet world has devised an exercise to hone the feet like the toughest steel: the *battement frappé*.

As you may gather from the name — *frappe* ("frah-PAY") is French for "struck" — this step is all about striking the floor with your foot. Beginning ballet students are sometimes encouraged to strike with an extra measure of aggressiveness.

The purpose of this exercise is twofold — first, to build strength; and second, to sharpen the reflexes in your lower legs and feet. When this move becomes second nature, you can point your feet faster than you can *think* about pointing them.

Every dancer works to achieve this instinctive ability — along with the satisfaction that your feet are pointing, even without conscious effort, every time they leave the floor.

Getting in position

Before doing the *battement frappé* itself, you need to get in position.

The starting position for the *frappé* is similar to the *cou-de-pied* position (see "The so-called *cou-de-pied* position") — but imagine wrapping your right foot around your left leg like a snake. The French term for this is also quite similar: *sur le cou-de-pied* ("seur luh KOO de peeAY") — literally, "on the neck of the foot." If you didn't think ballet was weird already, this may be the time to start.

Specifically, your right foot is wrapped about your left leg where the calf muscle lowers towards the heel (Figure 7-3, on the right). The position of the right foot on the left ankle stays the same whether the left foot is flat on the floor or raised up (in *relevé*). Try it at the barre.

Figure 7-3:
The *sur le cou-de-pied* position.

As you've probably guessed, this move has a back version as well — the *sur le cou-de-pied* position in back. In that position, your right foot is in the exact same shape as when it is wrapped around your ankle, just move it to the back of your left leg (refer to Figure 7-3, on the left).

Remember to keep your right knee turned out.

To the battement tendu

Before you add the striking motion that gives the *battement frappé* its fearsome moniker, see if you can do a few of the old familiar *tendus,* coming back to the *sur le cou-de-pied* position between them.

Stand in the starting position.

1. **Brush your right foot to the side (*battement tendu*), and bring your right foot into the front *sur le cou-de-pied* position on your left ankle.**

2. **From here, do a *battement tendu* forward with your right foot, and then return to the *sur le cou-de-pied* position. Easy enough.**

3. **Next, try a *battement tendu* out to the side. When you return, bring your right foot to the *sur le cou-de-pied* position in *back*.**

4. **Now, of course, comes the *battement tendu* to the back. Return again to the *sur le cou-de-pied* position in *back*.**

5. **Finally, do another *battement tendu* to the side. Return your right foot to the *sur le cou-de-pied* position in *front*.**

If you held a pencil firmly between the toes of your right foot while moving from the *sur le cou-de-pied* position to any of the *battement tendu* positions, you'd draw an absolutely straight line on the floor.

To the dégagé

Having mastered the preceding like a pro, you're now ready for something a little more challenging. Time to ease into the *frappé* to the *dégagé* position, and strike the floor en route to your final destination.

For this exercise, your legs need a new "ready" position — and this one is called *cou-de-pied flexed.* It's very similar to the original *cou-de-pied* position you tried at the beginning of this chapter, with a twist. Literally.

Try getting into the old familiar *cou-de-pied.* Feel where your right pinkie toe touches the inside of your left shinbone. Now *flex* your right foot and touch your right heel to the same spot on the flat inner side of the left shinbone (Figure 7-4a).

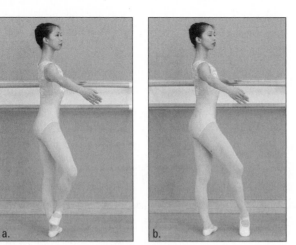

Figure 7-4:
The *cou-de-pied* flexed position for striking your foot in *frappé,* and the strike in the *frappé.*

a.   b.

This position is not very balletic-looking, is it? That's because, for practically the first time in your ballet career, you're *not* trying to point your foot as it leaves the floor. The most challenging part of the *frappé* to *dégagé* is the coordination involved in alternately flexing and pointing your foot.

To do this exercise from the beginning, stand in the starting position. Now brush your right foot to the side (*battement tendu*), and bring your right foot into the front *cou-de-pied flexed* position on your left ankle.

Now for some action! From the *cou-de-pied flexed* position, move your right leg out in front, as if doing a *battement tendu dégagé,* but a little closer to the floor. Halfway through the motion, suddenly and without warning, strike the ball of your right foot against the floor (refer to Figure 7-4b). Try to do this motion so suddenly that you surprise even yourself. Well, almost.

Actually, there is no need to use an excessive amount of force in this action — just enough to tap the floor, in an outward brushing motion. Your toes then point fully in the *dégagé* position.

Then return your right foot to the *cou-de-pied flexed* position without any floor contact — and repeat the exercise.

Now try the *frappé* to the side, going out to the *dégagé* as we show you in Chapter 6. Once again, strike the floor on the way out.

Just like the *sur le cou-de-pied* position, you can use the *cou-de-pied flexed* positions in front and in back. Whichever one you use, though, the endpoint to the side is exactly the same.

When you do a *frappé* to the *dégagé* back, the contact point of the "strike" is a little different. In order to maintain the correct turned out position of your foot, you have to strike with the pad at the inside and slightly under the big toe joint. Using the whole ball of the foot would be physically impossible. Unless, of course, you are put together quite uniquely.

As you practice *frappés,* keep few important rules in mind:

✔ Between the *cou-de-pied flexed* and the *dégagé* positions exists an imaginary straight line, which is the path your foot must take in arriving at the end point. We hope this image will keep you out of the common trap of dipping your leg downward in the foot's path. A dip in the middle of the motion gives the *frappé* a sluggish look.

✔ You should execute the *frappé* with an "accent" — a sudden speeding up of the motion as your foot strikes the floor. Therefore, don't perform this motion with a constant speed. If you were to divide the *frappé* into three counts, you would brush out and strike the floor on count 1, maintain the *dégagé* position on count 2, and close your leg back to the *cou-de-pied flexed* position on count 3.

✔ Don't forget — you are trying to develop a quicker response time for your *lower* legs. Your upper leg and knee remain serenely quiet and turned out as the striking takes place.

A chocolate frappé combination

Here is a combination for practicing the famous *frappé* out to the *dégagé* positions (front, side, and back). For music, we suggest the Spanish Chocolate movement from Act II of Tchaikovsky's *Nutcracker.*

This music is a very fast waltz: "OOM-pah-pah, OOM-pah-pah." Give one count to each complete "OOM-pah-pah." (In other words, every time you hear an "OOM," count to the next number.) Count the music in groups of eight. After reaching 8, start over with 1 again.

1. **Stand in the starting position. Over counts 1 through 4, do nothing.**

2. **Over counts 5 through 8, bring your right arm up through middle fifth to second position. At the same time, point your right foot and do a *battement tendu* to the side. Now close your right foot in the *cou-de-pied flexed* front position, ready to strike.**

   Your arm stays where it is, in second position.

3. **Over the next counts 1 through 4, counts, do four *frappés* to the front.**

   Throughout rest of this combination, always reach the fullest extended *dégagé* position on each count, and always close back into cou de pied flexed between the counts.

4. **Over counts 5 through 8, do four *frappés* to the side.**

   The first time, close your right foot in front, and alternate each time after that.

5. **Over counts 1 through 4, do four *frappés* to the back.**

6. **Over counts 5 through 8, do four *frappés* to the side — alternating back and front.**

7. **To finish, close to fifth position with your right foot in front.**

   Or, if you're feeling frisky, repeat the combination all around (*en croix*).

Throughout this exercise, remember to maintain a turned-out position from the hip to the knee, so that most of the *frappé* movement is from the knee down.

Now it's time to do the exercise in reverse. Turn so that the barre is to your right, with your right hand on the barre, and repeat the whole exercise using your left foot.

Finishing with little beats (petits battements sur le cou-de-pied)

As is so often the case with ballet movements in isolation, you may find yourself asking, "Why the heck am I trying to do this?" The answer is that each exercise works as a building block for something much greater.

So it is with the little beats — *petits battements sur le cou-de-pied* ("puh-TEE bat-MAHN seur luh KOO duh peeAY"). The purpose of this exercise is to build up the strength and coordination needed to "beat" your legs while jumping, as if they were the wings of a hummingbird. These big jumps, usually performed by men, can make the audience gasp.

You've probably seen it — the Cavalier or Prince leaps into the air, flaps his legs back and forth innumerable times, and lands. Then, incredibly, he repeats that jump again and again.

To do this exercise, stand in the starting position.

1. **Lift your right foot into the front *sur le cou-de-pied* position.**

   See "Getting in position," earlier in this chapter.

2. **Open your right leg to the side, from the knee down, so your foot just clears your left ankle.**

3. **Close your right foot into the back *sur le cou-de-pied* position.**

4. **Open your foot again to the side, and close it onto your left ankle in the front *sur le cou-de-pied* position.**

If you held a pencil between the toes of your right foot during this motion, you'd scratch yourself something fierce. With enough practice, though, you could draw a narrow "V" on the floor: from the front of the ankle, to the side, and then to the back of the ankle. Then the pattern would reverse exactly, as if on a track. There you have it: *Petits battements sur le cou-de-pied.*

This sounds too easy to be true, doesn't it? But the greatest challenge is not the exercise itself — it's the speed. After ballet dancers get really revved up, they can do millions of repetitions per second. Well, at least two.

As always in ballet, pitfalls abound here. The first pitfall is the movement of your upper leg. While your lower leg is beating away, your upper leg must remain absolutely still with your knee pressed outward. Ideally, the movement takes place only in the *lower* leg, from knee to foot. Your upper body must also remain still, as must your head.

In fact, the only other body part that may legally move is your arm. And even then, your arm must have a mind of its own. While your leg moves quickly, your arm takes the slow road, most often using 8 counts to complete one full *port de bras*. It then takes another 8 counts to reverse the *port de bras* movement.

These *petits battements* work very well at the end of another combination. Feel free to add some to the end of your *frappé* combination — if you dare.

Little beats, big heart

The little beats (*petits battements sur le cou-de-pied*) may *look* easy, but they take enormous control. And to add even more to the challenge, they usually take place at exactly the point where the dancer would rather go lie down — the very end of a long combination.

An extreme example of this is the *Grand pas de deux* in Act II of Tchaikovsky's *Swan Lake*. Odette, the Swan Queen, has just danced an enormously difficult set of *adagio* movements with Prince Siegfried. Now, as he strolls slowly around her, she must keep her entire body still — except for those quick beats of her right foot against the left leg.

We can tell you from personal experience that if you were in Odette's shoes, the last thing you would choose to do is these little beats. You're exhausted. Your muscles are screaming. And your left foot feels like it's grinding a hole in the floor. To do these beats — and make them look as if you are a graceful swan shaking water from the tips of your wings — requires a fortitude not easily summoned.

Next time you go to *Swan Lake*, don't forget to watch for this most special moment — and take pity on the ballerina and her left foot.

Chapter 8

Getting a Leg Up

· ·

In This Chapter

▶ Lifting and sustaining with the barre

▶ Kicking like a Rockette

▶ Stretching it out

▶ Rising to new levels

· ·

*T*he three chapters in this part make up a complete barre routine that you can do in sequence every day as an essential part of your ballet training. Chapters 6 and 7 help you with some basic barre moves, awakening and strengthening the muscles and skills that you need for ballet.

If you have already attempted all the moves in Chapters 6 and 7, you may develop a nervous eye tic on merely hearing the word "barre." But stick with us for one more chapter — the payoff is straight ahead.

In this chapter you explore your newfound strength in order to hold one leg up higher and higher, accessing the proper muscles with impressive control — just like the pros. And when you can do *that*, you'll be ready for anything.

Extending Your Leg Slowly into the Air (Grand Battement Développé)

If you chose your all-time favorite ballet moves, we bet the *grand battement développé* would be among them. This step, known as the *développé* ("DAVE-low-PAY") for short, is one of the most beautiful elements in classical ballet. It is usually performed by the ballerina in a slow (so-called *adagio*) tempo, often held up by her partner.

In fact, the *pas de deux* movements from the great ballets are positively *riddled* with *développés*. You've got yer *Nutcracker pas de deux*. You've got yer *Sleeping Beauty pas de deux*. And you've even got yer *Othello pas de deux*. Every one of them depends heavily on *développés*.

The look of a *développé* should be absolutely smooth and seamless, exactly as if performed underwater. With the exception that you can still breathe. And you don't get drenched or tied up in seaweed. But otherwise it's *exactly* the same.

The movement involves lifting your leg and sustaining it with seemingly no effort. As you might guess, this illusion requires a lot of muscle control and strength. And as you know by now, the best way to develop the strength and control you need is at the barre. So back to the barre with you.

Développé to the front

Stand in the famous starting position (see Chapter 6). This time, bring your right arm to second position (see Chapter 4 for more information on all the arm and leg positions).

Keeping in mind that this exercise forms part of the set of movements called *adagio* (very slow and at ease), take your time doing it.

1. **Pick up your right foot and place it into the *cou-de-pied* front position (remembering to keep your right heel forward of your right toes), and lower your right arm to low fifth position.**

2. **Continue lifting your right foot up your left shin to the level of your knee; you are now in the *retiré* position. As you do this, lift your right arm to middle fifth position.**

   Still with us? Of course you are.

3. **Extend your right leg toward the front, leading the motion with your pointed foot. As you continue straightening your right knee, lift your right arm to high fifth position (Figure 8-1a).**

Don't forget to keep your hips turned out during this motion. We bet your right hip really, *really* wants to turn in, doesn't it? *Bad* hip! Don't let it cheat.

Depending on the flexibility of your hamstrings, the angle between your leg and the floor may vary. The great ballerinas of the world can point their legs almost straight up. But for now, if you can lift your leg to 90 degrees — parallel to the floor — you are doing great. Even 45 degrees is fine to start. Don't push it.

Figure 8-1:
Développé
to the front,
side, and
back, with
port de bras.

4. **When your leg is straight, feel it rising for one second more, to enhance the illusion of endless lift and ease. Now lower it back down, keeping your knee straight, and close it into fifth position with your right foot in front. Your right arm opens into second position.**

Ladies and Gentlemen of the Jury — a *développé* to the front.

Développé to the side

For most of us mortals, the *développé* is much easier to do out to the side than to the front. Why? Because with your legs starting in fifth position and hips turned out, your leg is much less constricted when it goes to the side.

Inhale, exhale . . .

Breathing correctly is essential to dancing well — especially once you begin to dance more aerobic and strenuous combinations, like the one in this chapter.

The most important thing to remember is this: *Never hold your breath*. At any point in any motion, you are either breathing in or breathing out.

In any *développé* exercise, as you lift your leg to the highest point, inhale. Then, as you lower your leg back to fifth position, exhale. And for bends of the body, exhale as you bend over, and inhale as you return upright.

Stand in the starting position, but with your right arm in second position.

1. **Draw your right foot up to the *cou-de-pied* position front as you bring your right arm to low fifth position.**

2. **Continue to bring your right foot up your left shin until your pointed toes are even with your left knee, simultaneously bringing your right arm up to middle fifth position.**

   Now this is where it gets interesting.

3. **With your right leg turned out, start to lift your right knee. As you straighten your right knee, open your right arm into second position, in front of your right leg.**

4. **When your leg is straight, lift it for one second, remembering to breathe. Then, keeping your right knee straight, close it into fifth position, this time with your right foot in *back*.**

If you look into a mirror in front of you when you have reached the full extension, you should be able to see the bottom of your right foot (refer to Figure 8-1b). Don't be discouraged if you can't get this unusual view right away. For now, the goal is grace and control. The extension comes with practice.

Here's a general rule: When both your arm and leg are out to the side (the so-called *à la seconde*), your arm should *always* be in front of your leg.

Développé to the back

The *développé* to the back is the most difficult of all — thanks not only to the aforementioned hip joint, but also to the stubborn (and often uncooperative) bones and muscles of the back.

Of course there are exceptions to every rule, and there do exist exceptionally limber and gifted dancers (read: freaks of nature) who can lift their legs even higher to the back than to the side. These dancers are few, which is a good thing for the rest of us. The gift of exceptionally loose hip and back joints often draws oohs and aahs from the audience, as well as the occasional snicker of "You've got to be kidding!"

So don't be discouraged if you lack the flexibility of an acrobat when doing this exercise. The key in ballet is *not* to look acrobatic, but to appear natural and flowing at all times. You can do this.

Start in fifth position with your right foot in *back,* right arm in second position.

1. **Lift your right foot into the *cou-de-pied back* position, remembering to keep your toes farther back than your heel. Meanwhile, lower your right arm to low fifth position.**

2. **Bring your right foot up the back of your left leg, touching your right heel along the leg and slowly moving the foot sideways until the toes of your right foot are touching the back of your left knee. (This is known as *retiré* back.) Bring your right arm to middle fifth position.**

   Now it's time to put the "back" in *développé back.*

3. **Start straightening your right leg out in back of you. *Slo-o-o-o-owly,* now, keeping your knee lifted and pressed out, allow your foot to follow your knee's lead into the full extension backward. Meanwhile, bring your right arm to middle fifth position, then straighten the elbow and reach forward with the right side of your torso.**

   This is known as a *second position arabesque.* Your entire torso, in fact, should appear calm and in balance — blissfully unaware of that appendage sticking out behind you (Figure 8-1c). This is a momentous achievement.

4. **After your leg is completely straight, lift your leg for one second more with a fully straight knee, remembering to breath the entire time (see the sidebar "Inhale, exhale . . ."). Then lower your leg down into fifth position with your right foot in back, and open your right arm into second position.**

For maximum photogenic potential, try to coordinate your arms and your legs so that they arrive at their final positions at exactly the same time. This little trick makes all your *développés* appear seamless, and gets you one step closer to the cover of *Dance Magazine.*

Kicking Your Leg Up, Controlling It Down (Grands Battements)

You *gotta* love this step; it's one of the catchiest, most recognizable, beloved steps of all time. If that's because the Rockettes made it famous, then so be it.

In ballet lingo, the straight-legged trademark kick of these multitalented ladies is called a *grand battement* ("GRAHN bat-MAHN"), and it has many uses in ballet. Alone, of course, it makes quite an impact: Kicking so high, and so often, and in unison with so many other people, never fails to impress.

But the *grand battement* also works well in combination with other steps. For example, if you were to leap off the ground, with the intent of splitting your legs in the midair, the first part of the jump would be a *grand battement*. Just think of the potential: Your legs are approximately half of your body length, so if you manage to throw *that* half up in the air, getting the *other* half up is that much easier.

Kicking with attitude

Before you book your ticket to Rockefeller Center, though, it's time to explore a *grand battement* on training wheels. In this kick, your lifted leg is bent at an angle of slightly less then 90 degrees. Technically, this angle is known as *attitude*.

Starting this way enables you to lift your legs with the same energy and "attack" as in the straight-legged kick, but with much less strain on the ol' hamstrings. Plus, let's face it — a bent leg can go much higher than a straight leg. You might as well have some fun while you can.

To the front

Stand in the starting position, but with your right arm in second position.

1. **Brush your right foot forward as if you were doing a *dégagé* to the front, and lift your leg up as high as you can. (Don't forget to keep your leg turned out.) While you do, bend your right knee to almost 90 degrees, and keep your *left* knee straight (Figure 8-2a).**

   The motion of your right leg should feel more like a kick than a lift. Imagine throwing your leg up into the air underhanded, as if it were a softball.

2. **Control the descent of your right leg, pushing gently against the force of gravity, as your leg floats back down into fifth position like a balloon.**

Figure 8-2:
Grand battement en attitude to the front, side, and back.

There you have it — a complete *grand battement en attitude.*

After you get a feel for this motion, you can access the feeling for jumps. And that comes in very handy in future chapters.

To the side

Standing in the starting position, but with your right arm in second position:

1. **Brush your right foot to the side as if you were doing a *dégagé* to the side, and lift your leg, bending your right knee to almost 90 degrees.**

   Just as in the *développé* to the side, the sole of your right foot should be visible when you look in a mirror in front of you — and from your perspective, your right heel should be in front of your right knee. Remember to keep your left knee straight (refer to Figure 8-2b).

2. **Control your return to fifth position, with your right leg behind your left.**

   Your return to fifth position needs the same control as you used with the forward kick. But this time, in preparation for the *grand battement en attitude* to the rear, close your right leg behind your left.

To the back

Just one more attitude adjustment, and you'll be in the big kick business. From fifth position, with your right leg behind your left and your right arm in second position, brush your right foot to the back as if you were doing a *dégagé* to the back, and lift your leg, bending your right knee to about 45 degrees (refer to Figure 8-2c).

In this move, your foot automatically wants to lift higher than your knee. That's a good thing, as long as you maintain the turnout in your hip joint.

Remember to allow your upper body to adjust forward in this *battement* to the back, keeping your shoulders parallel to the front wall, and return your leg, back, and hips to an aligned fifth position with grace and control.

Aging ballerinas, in the twilight of their careers, often choose to use this *grand battement en attitude* to the back as a substitute for the straight-legged *arabesque.* (See the following section.) Even young and healthy dancers who are suffering from temporary back pain are grateful for the alternative. And you're welcome to use it throughout this book, as well.

Kicking with straight legs

Your brilliance with the *grand battement en attitude* has inspired us to challenge you with something more brazen — the Rockette kick itself. The concept is exactly the same, but both knees are straight — giving your legs enormous power and momentum.

One of your authors found out about this power during a performance. While kicking away in the finale of Balanchine's ballet *Symphony in C*, she kicked so high that her standing leg, which had been *en pointe,* came right off the ground. Your author found herself with both legs in the air in front of her, in a tutu, knowing that she was going down in a big way for the whole theater to see. There is nothing quite like hearing 3,000 people gasp at once.

To the front

Stand in the starting position, but with your right arm in second position. (Keep the right arm here throughout these *grand battement* exercises.)

1. **Brush your right leg forward as if you were doing a *dégagé* forward.**

2. **Continue to lift your right leg as high as possible while keeping your stomach and back lifted, both knees straight, and your hips turned out.**

   This motion should feel more like a kick than a lifting of your leg (Figure 8-3a).

3. **Control your straight right leg as it comes back down to the fifth position.**

   Notice that with a straight right knee, your leg feels significantly heavier than when you did this kick in *attitude* (see the previous section).

Figure 8-3:
Grand battement to the front, side, and back.

To the side

Now for a *grand battement* to the side.

1. **From the starting position with your right arm in second position, brush your right leg out to the right.**

2. **Continue to lift your right leg out to the right.**

   The toes of your pointed right foot should be the very last thing to leave the floor. Keep both knees straight, and your hips turned out. At the top of the kick, you should see the sole of your right foot in the mirror in front of you. Your right leg is behind your right arm (refer to Figure 8-3b).

3. **As you lower your leg back into fifth position, touch the ground first with your toes, and then brush your foot along the ground. Finish by closing your right foot *behind* the left into fifth position.**

To the back

Ready for a kick to the back? From fifth position, with your right foot in back, brush your right foot to the back, just as if you were doing a *dégagé* to the back. Make sure your toes are the first to brush the floor; then bring your leg up to 90 degrees behind you, keeping your foot pointed and your hip rotated out. If this position looks familiar, that's because it comes up in a million ballets. It's called *arabesque*.

At the full height of this motion, if you look in the mirror on your right side, your right heel should be completely hidden, in line with your leg in its most turned-out position.

Meanwhile, as you lift your leg to the back, counterbalance this motion by bringing your upper body forward. There's a great reason for this — it allows the maximum freedom of the leg in back, and prevents the vertebrae of your spine from crowding together and causing injury. Make sure that your torso adjusts forward in a straight line, parallel with the front wall of the room, with no tilting or twisting. Keep your arm in second position (refer to Figure 8-3c).

A Combination for Développés and Grands Battements

ALLLLL-righty then. You can't imagine how much fun you can have performing *développés* and *grands battements,* one after the other, in a combination. This exercise does wonders for warming up your legs, hips, and back, and developing great strength.

For music, we suggest the Valse from Act I of Tchaikovsky's *Sleeping Beauty*. Count the music in groups of 8 counts, with each "OOM-pah-pah" getting a single count. (Chapter 5 tells you all about counting beats in music.)

1. **Stand in the starting position. Over counts 1 through 4, do nothing.**

2. **Over counts 5 through 8, move your right arm through middle fifth position and out to second (arm) position.**

3. **On the next count 1, bring your right foot to the *cou-de-pied* position in front, and bring your right arm to low fifth position. Then, over counts 2 and 3, bring your right leg up to *retiré* and bring your right arm to middle fifth position.**

4. **Over counts 4 through 6, do a *développé* to the front, simultaneously lifting your right arm up to high fifth position.**

    After reaching the extended position, lift your leg slightly.

5. **Over counts 7 and 8, lower your right leg, passing through the *battement tendu* position in front, to reach fifth position with the right leg in front.**

6. **Over counts 1 through 6, do three *grands battements* to the front (one count up, one count down), with *straight* knees.**

    After each kick, return your legs to fifth position, maintaining your arm in high fifth position.

7. **Over counts 7 and 8, bring your right arm to second position.**

8. **On the next count 1, bring your right foot to the *cou-de-pied* position in front, and move your right arm to low fifth position. Then, over counts 2 and 3, bring your right leg up to *retiré* and bring your right arm to middle fifth position.**

9. **Over counts 4 through 6, do a *développé* to the side, simultaneously opening your right arm to second position slightly in front of your leg.**

    After reaching the extended position, lift your leg slightly.

10. **Over counts 7 and 8, lower your right leg , passing through the *battement tendu* position at the side, to fifth position with your right foot in front.**

    Your right arm stays in second position.

11. **Over counts 1 through 6, do three *grands battements* to the side with straight legs.**

    Return to fifth position each time, alternating the right leg back, front, and back.

12. **On counts 7 and 8, bring your right arm to low fifth position.**

13. On count 1, bring your right foot to the *cou-de-pied* position in back, right arm in low fifth position. Over counts 2 and 3, bring your right foot up to *retiré* in back, while lifting your right arm to middle fifth position.

14. Over counts 4 through 6, do a *développé* to the back, simultaneously extending your right arm in front of your shoulder into second position *arabesque* (as defined in the previous section).

15. Over counts 7 and 8, lower your right leg, passing through the *battement tendu* position in back, to close in fifth position, with your right foot in back.

   Leave your right arm where it is.

16. Over counts 1 through 6, do three *grands battements* to the back with straight legs.

   Each time, return to fifth position with your right foot in *back* of the left.

17. On count 7, round your right arm in middle fifth position. On count 8, open it to second position.

18. On count 1, bring your right foot to the *cou-de-pied* position in back, while bringing your right arm into low fifth position. Over counts 2 and 3, lift your right leg into the *retiré* position in back, while lifting your right arm to middle fifth position.

19. Over counts 4 through 6, do a *développé* to the side, simultaneously opening your right arm to second position slightly in front of your leg.

   After reaching the extended position, lift your leg slightly.

20. Over counts 7 and 8, close your right leg into fifth position, with your right foot in back.

   Your right arm stays in second position.

21. Over counts 1 through 6, do three *grands battements* to the side with straight legs.

   Return to fifth position each time, alternating your right leg front, back, front.

22. Over counts 7 and 8, lower your right arm to low fifth position.

Repeat the exercise with your left leg. Why should your right leg have all the fun?

The *développé* and *grand battement* exercises in this chapter can be very stressful on your muscles. Beware of cramps — nature's way of punishing you for trying to defy gravity. If you sense a cramp coming on, *stop immediately,* and stretch out whatever muscles are crying out for attention (see Chapter 3 for suggestions).

Watch where you're going!

In Chapter 2 we show you how to go *barreless* — practicing ballet barre exercises in the comfort of your own home, using solid furniture for balance in place of a barre.

If you opt for this alternative, make sure that you can lift your legs in all directions without hitting anything. Nothing stops the flow of the barre exercises more abruptly than a fractured fibula.

One of your present authors, unfortunately, learned this lesson the hard way. Before a performance many years ago, while warming up on *grands battements* backstage, she kicked her leg to the side just as a violinist from the balletorchestra was walking by. The top of her foot

slammed into his violin case. Recovering from the crash, she was relieved to discover that the violin was safe inside its steel case. We wish we could say the same thing about her right foot, which was broken in three places.

Over the years, your author's foot has also had unfortunate contact with other dancers, unsuspecting balletomanes, light booms, cocktail glasses, and even the family cat, which for a brief moment became a flying feline. (For more on the *pas de chat,* see Chapter 12.)

The lesson is clear: Watch where your legs are going.

Stretching Out Your Legs on the Barre

Now that all your muscles are warm — perhaps a little *too* warm — the time has come to *re-e-e-e-ally* stretch out your legs. Stretching is a very slow process, and you may need weeks to see true progress. But be patient. Every muscle can stretch, given the time.

Although acceptable barre substitutes abound, an actual barre is ideal for supporting these stretches. When you first start to stretch, look for a barre at hip level, or a little lower. Then, as your flexibility increases, try a higher barre.

The positions in the following stretching exercises are the same positions you need for lifting your legs in center-floor exercises (the subject of Part III) — unaided by the friendly barre. By stretching your legs at the barre now, you will eventually be able to lift your legs to these new heights by yourself.

The ideal position in front

Stand in the starting position. Now turn halfway towards the barre, so that you are facing it at a 45-degree angle.

Place your left hand on the barre and bring your right arm to second position. Lift your right leg up to rest on the barre just above the heel. (That's where the Achilles tendon lives.) Make sure that your shoulders and hips are aligned perpendicular to your right leg. Keep both knees straight, both legs turned out, your right foot pointed, your back straight, and your stomach pulled up. Got it? Take a look at Figure 8-4a, just to be sure.

If you're just starting out in ballet, this position itself gives you plenty of stretch. But if you can still move and breathe comfortably, it's time to ratchet up the level a little — with the famous *forward bend.*

Figure 8-4:
Stretching
at the barre
to the front,
side, and
back.

Leave your left hand on the barre, and right arm in second position. Keeping your torso in the same alignment with your right leg, *inhale* — and simultaneously lift your torso a little bit.

Now *exhale* — and while keeping your back straight, bend forward at the hips toward your right leg. When you reach your maximum stretch, bring your right arm to high fifth position. Stay there for about three seconds.

Return upright, with your back straight. Meanwhile, bring your right arm back out to second position. Then repeat the forward bend and return.

The ideal position to the side

From the front stretch of your right leg at the barre (see the previous section), turn to face the barre, maintaining the turnout of your left leg as you turn. Place both hands on the barre and line up your hips and shoulders with the barre.

With both legs fully turned out, point your right foot fully, as shown in Figure 8-4b. Keep your right hand on the barre, and lift your left arm to second position. Now *inhale,* and bring your left arm to high fifth position. *Exhale,* and bend your torso to the right. Make sure to bend only to the side — don't let your body pull you forward or back. After you have reached the maximum stretch, hold it for about three seconds.

Now *inhale* as you slowly return upright — and lower your left arm to second position, ready to repeat this stretch.

The ideal position in back

From the side stretch position, with your right leg still on the barre, turn to your left, until your right leg is behind you in *arabesque.* (Support your turn by sliding the right hand forward along the barre to just in front of the right shoulder, as you open the left arm to second position.) Meanwhile, turn out your left leg farther, with a straight knee, and align your shoulders in front of your hips. The right side of your upper torso should be well forward in opposition to your right hip — which is open to allow your leg to turn out in *arabesque.*

This may be plenty of stretch, so just stay there and breathe for an few moments, with your left arm in second position (refer to Figure 8-4c). Ahhhhhhh. Masochism.

If we've somehow underestimated you, and that's not enough stretch, try a little back bend. *Inhale,* and bring your left arm to high fifth position. Now *exhale,* and bend back from your upper torso. This is a *very* difficult stretch — so don't push it. Go only as far as you can. Some things in ballet are worth waiting for.

To get out of this contortion, lower your leg from the barre into fifth position. Careful here — your right leg will almost certainly want to slam down into the left like a slingshot. Keep the motion slow and controlled.

Now repeat the entire sequence of stretches with your left leg.

Focusing on Relevés

After you warm up all your muscles, and stretch out your legs and back, it's time to do one final set of *barre* exercises — *relevés.* These exercises involve lifting your body up to the balls of your feet, and back down again, in repetition.

Relevés are crucial to the mastery of nearly *all* ballet steps — from slow (*adagio*) movements, to pirouettes, to big jumps. Muscular control in the ankles, calves, and knees allows ballet dancers to point their feet every time their feet leave the floor — and acts as a shock absorber on the way down.

If you need some help on how to do *relevés* (as well as the *demi-pliés* between them), refer to Chapter 6.

When you are in *relevé* position at the barre, make sure that you don't use the barre to help you lift your body up and down on the supporting leg. The barre is only there for balance, in case you need it. To ensure a light touch, try placing only your index and middle fingers on the barre. As you practice, it might *feel* better to lean on the barre. But no cheating!

For music, we suggest the Street Dancers' Scene from Act II of Prokofiev's *Romeo and Juliet.* This music has an "OOM-pah-pah" rhythm like a waltz. For each *relevé,* go *up* on one "OOM-pah-pah" and *down* on the next. That speed allows you to do these *relevés* smoothly and at an even pace — like a piston.

In first position at the barre

This is not only the first *relevé* that a dancer masters, but it is also the first exercise that most experienced ballerinas do whenever they put on their pointe shoes — regardless of how many years they have been dancing.

1. **Face the barre and place your hands on the barre at about shoulder width apart. Stand in first position.**

    Your elbows should be slightly bent and pointing downwards, placing you at a comfortable distance away from the barre.

2. **Do a *demi-plié*.**

3. **Straighten back up and do a *relevé* in first position.**

    When you rise up, finish straightening your knees before beginning the *relevé* — but try to make this coordination seamless.

4. **Lower your feet from the *relevé*. When your heels touch the floor, do another *demi-plié*.**

Repeat Steps 3 and 4 until you have completed six *relevés*. End with a *demi-pli*é in first position; then straighten your knees to finish.

In second position

From first position, sweep your right foot to the side in a *battement tendu,* and lower your heel down, placing your heel in line with your left foot. You are now in second position.

When getting into position, be careful not to place your heels too far apart. Ideally, the distance between them should equal the length of one of your feet. If your heels end up too far apart, the pressure of the *relevé* can cause some knee pain and your ankles may have difficulty in doing a *relevé* all the way up to the balls of your feet.

1. **Face the barre and place your hands on the barre about shoulder width apart. Stand in second position.**

    Your elbows should be slightly bent and pointing downwards, placing you at a comfortable distance away from the barre.

2. **Do a *demi-plié*.**

3. **Straighten back up and do a *relevé* in second position, remembering to finish straightening your knees just before starting the *relevé*.**

4. **Lower your feet from the *relevé*. When your heels touch the floor, do another *demi-plié*.**

Repeat Steps 3 and 4 until you have completed six *relevés*. Finish with a *demi-pli*é in second position; then straighten your knees, bring your right foot to the side in *tendu,* and lower your heel to first position. This completes the first and second-position *relevés.*

In sous-sus position

As you have probably noticed, when you rise up from a fifth position *demi-plié* and do a *relevé,* your heels are no longer in line with one another. The so-called *sous-sus* ("soo-SUE"), meaning "down-up," alleviates this dilemma.

To accomplish the *sous-sus,* as you do the *relevé,* slide both feet together to meet, one directly behind the other (Figure 8-5). From the front, you seem to have one foot with two heels. (Why this is considered ideal is beyond us.) To reverse the motion, slide your feet apart and bring them into a *demi-plié* in fifth position.

Try a few, alternating your forward foot.

Figure 8-5:
The *sous-sus* position.

Escaping from fifth to second position (échappés)

In the following exercise, you use the *relevé* and *demi-plié* motions in another active combination. The French word *échappé* ("ay-shah-PAY") means "escaped" — an appropriate word for this move, in which your feet "escape" from the cramped confines of fifth position out into the wide open spaces of second.

1. **Face the barre and place your hands on the barre at about shoulder width apart. Stand in fifth position with your right foot in front.**

   Your elbows should be only slightly bent and pointing downwards, placing you at a comfortable distance away from the barre.

2. Do a *demi-plié*.

3. **Straighten your legs with enough force to be able to slide your legs out into second position** *relevé.*

   Make sure your feet maintain contact with the floor the whole way out.

   Be careful to not jump into the *relevé*, because that would put a lot of pressure into the joints of your hips, knees, and ankles, and can cause injury. Also, be careful not to go into a second position that is too wide.

4. **From the** *relevé* **position, use your inner thigh muscles to pull your legs back together. Then close to fifth position with your left foot in front, and immediately do a** *demi-plié.*

Repeat Steps 3 and 4 seven more times, ending with *demi-plié* in fifth position. (Each time you reach fifth position, alternate the forward foot.) Straighten your knees. Repeat until your legs feel too weak to continue.

In the cou-de-pied position

This type of *relevé* is absolutely *pregnant* with meaning and possibility.

The *relevé* on one leg, with the other leg in the *cou-de-pied* back position, is an essential building block for some of the most beautiful steps in ballet. After you can do *that,* the next logical step is to do a *relevé* on one leg while lifting the other — to the front, side, back, or in *retiré.*

Don't try this at home!

While we're on the subject of *relevés,* it would be downright unballetic not to mention *pointe* work.

Of course, you've seen ballerinas go *en pointe* time and time again. They do it hundreds of times in every performance. But did you know that going *en pointe* is nothing more than an extension of the very same *relevé* you're practicing here?

When you do a *relevé* in first position, you're transferring all your body weight up onto the balls of your feet. Now if you were to continue transferring that weight farther, through the toes

themselves, all the way out to the very *ends* of the toes, you'd be *en pointe.* (There are other ways to get there, too — for example, the *sous-sus* position.)

But going *en pointe* is an advanced technique. Women usually need a year or more to discover the necessary balance. As for men, they never go *en pointe* at all — except in highly unusual moments of satirical choreography.

For more on *pointe* work — and the shoes that make it all possible — we gently nudge you toward Chapters 1 and 22.

1. **Face the barre and stand in first position.**

2. **Do a _demi-plié_.**

3. **Rising up, do a _relevé_ onto your left foot. Meanwhile, lift your right foot into the _cou-de-pied_ back position.**

In the _cou-de-pied_ back position, your right heel is just in back of your left lower calf muscle, with the toes of your right foot pointing backward, away from your left leg. Check out Chapter 7 for more information on _cou-de-pied_ positions.

4. **Do a _demi-plié_ on your left leg, while maintaining the _cou-de-pied_ position of your right leg. (Don't let that right foot wander.)**

Repeat Steps 3 and 4 six more times. After the final _relevé,_ bend both knees into a first position _demi-plié,_ and then straighten your knees. Burn, baby, burn!

Passing the barre

Still with us? If so, congratulations — you have completed your first "barre"! Truly an achievement worth celebrating.

But before we release your brain to a well-deserved hour of intellectually devoid TV-watching or bathtub soaking, we're obligated to point out that these last three chapters, when done in succession, form the complete barre sequence that professional ballet dancers go through _nearly every day._

The strength and control that you can develop in these chapters will serve you very well in the future, especially on the so-called "center floor" — where you dance across the length of the room, bowling alley, or parking lot, _without_ the aid of the barre.

Never thought you'd accomplish _that,_ did you?

Part III

Center Floor, Anyone?

The 5th Wave   By Rich Tennant

PICKUP BALLET AT A VACANT LOT

In this part . . .

*E*ven before you learned to walk, you were bouncing to music. In this part, we show you how to bounce with style and grace, away from the barre — in Center Floor.

This part has it all — balancing, turning, lifting your legs, transferring your weight quickly, using your arms, and yes, even bouncing.

But wait, there's more! This part shows you how an *arabesque* works. It describes the art of landing gracefully. And it even quotes *The Teachings of Buddha*.

"Suppose a donkey, with no nice shape, no voice, and no horns like those of the cow, was following a herd of cows and proclaiming, 'Look, I am also a cow.' Would anyone believe him?"

— The Teachings of Buddha

Behold, the mysteries of Center Floor.

Chapter 9

Getting to Center Floor

. . . .

In This Chapter

▶ Leaving the barre and finding your way around the room

▶ Crossing, opening, and unfolding your legs — not necessarily in that order

▶ Attitude adjustment

. . . .

*I*f you enjoy dancing at the barre, you'll love *center floor*. You get to take the steps you dance at the barre and place them in an open space — preferably in front of a mirror.

Of course, the center floor does present a whole new challenge. In the exercises at the barre, you only had to be worried about one arm at a time. Now, you've got *two* to worry about. Plus, you now have to consider the angles of your body and head, which are important parts of each position.

So away from the barre with you — and proudly take your place at the very center of the room.

Ahhhhhh. The fresh salt air of freedom.

Mapping Out the Room

In the days of yore (yore great-great-great-great-grandparents, that is), choreographers had a hard time telling their dancers exactly where to dance. "Stand facing the wall," they would say. "*Which* wall?" was invariably the reply.

So the ancient choreographers, in their wisdom, devised a system to solve that problem. They divided the room into eight parts, numbering each wall and each corner (see Figure 9-1). That way they could easily specify the direction in which the dancers' various body parts should point or face.

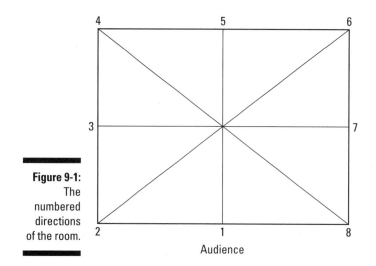

4   5   6

3   7

2   1   8

Audience

Figure 9-1:
The
numbered
directions
of the room.

Due to the indisputable fact that ballet was created to be seen from the front, they called the front *Direction 1*, or *D-1* for short. This number can refer to either the front wall of the room, or the open front of a stage.

To find it yourself, stand in the center of your space and face forward, with shoulders parallel to the front wall. There you have it — *D-1*.

Now turn your whole body to the right and face the first corner you get to. That's *Direction 2*, or *D-2*.

Continue to turn to the right until you're facing the next wall (which used to be on your right side). That's *D-3*.

Surely you're beginning to see a pattern here? If so, you know what's next: the next corner, which we call *D-4*.

Keep turning your body until you face the back wall, which is of course *D-5*, and the following corner is *D-6*. The last wall in this particular tour is *D-7*, and the final corner in your directional quest is *D-8*.

The directional numbering is actually such a good idea that several different systems have been invented. The one we use comes from the so-called *Vaganova Method*, which sounds like a bizarre form of birth control but is actually a perfectly respectable school of ballet.

All this fuss may seem very eccentric. But for the purposes of center floor work, these numbers turn out to be extraordinarily helpful. *So* helpful, in fact, that you may be tempted to mark 'em on the walls with a big thick magic marker. You have our blessing.

Positioning Your Body in Battement Tendu

If you wonder why we obsess over *battements tendus* in Part III at the barre, you're gonna find out now. When you get to the center floor, *battements tendus* take on a spectacular, even mythic importance.

One of our favorite moments in a ballet performance depends heavily on *battements tendus*. This special moment comes in the finale of George Balanchine's ballet *Symphony in C*, set to music by Georges Bizet.

Picture this: All 30 women from the *corps de ballet* stand along the sides and back of the stage, in white tutus, all doing *battement tendus* to the front and side, with *port de bras*, in perfect unison. Even after a hundred viewings, it's a thrilling sight.

In this section, you get to discover for yourself all the different directions in which you can do a *battement tendu* onstage — or at home. And you'll be happy to know that these same directions apply in lifting your leg to any height, in preparation for turns, and even in jumps.

We conveniently list the directions in an order that lets you go smoothly from one to the other. In all the following directions, your right leg is the working leg. After you complete the entire sequence, make sure to do the mirror image too — working with your left leg.

You are about to practice away from the barre. Although these exercises are not very difficult, be careful not to throw yourself off balance. Work slowly and deliberately at first — no sudden moves

Crossed and to the corner (croisé devant)

For the *battement tendu croisé devant* ("kwah-ZAY duh-VAHN"), stand facing corner D-8 in fifth position with your right foot in front, your arms in low fifth position.

With your right foot, do a *battement tendu* to the front to D-8. Meanwhile, bring your right arm to second position and your left arm overhead. Your head faces D-2 (Figure 9-2a).

Figure 9-2:
The positions of the body in *battement tendu: croisé devant* (a); *quatrième devant* (b); *effacé devant* (c); *écarté devant* (d); *à la seconde* (e); *écarté derrière* (f); *effacé derrière* (g); *quatrième derrière* (h); *croisé derrière* (i).

Flat front to the front (quatrième devant)

Stand facing D-1, in fifth position with your right foot in front, arms in low fifth position.

With your right foot, do a *battement tendu* to the front, lifting your arms through middle fifth position into second position. Your head faces forward with your chin slightly lifted (refer to Figure 9-2b). This is *quatrième devant* ("kah-tree-EM duh-VAHN").

To the corner in front, open (effacé devant)

Stand facing D-2, in fifth position with your right foot in front, arms in low fifth position.

With your right foot, do a *battement tendu* to the front, toward D-2. Meanwhile, bring your arms through middle fifth position, and lift your right arm into second position as your left arm comes over your head. Your head faces D-8 with your chin slightly lifted (refer to Figure 9-2c). Voilà! *Effacé devant* ("ef-fah-SAY duh-VAHN").

To the corner, open side (écarté devant)

Stand facing D-8, in fifth position with your right foot in front, arms in low fifth position.

With your right foot, do a *battement tendu* to the side, toward D-2. Meanwhile, bring your arms through middle fifth position, and lift your right arm overhead as your left arm opens to second position. Your head faces D-2 with your chin slightly lifted (refer to Figure 9-2d). This is *écarté devant* ("ay-car-TAY duh-VAHN").

Flat front to the side (à la seconde)

For the *battement tendu à la seconde* ("ah la se-COND"), stand facing D-1, in fifth position with your right foot in front, arms in low fifth position.

With your right foot, do a *battement tendu* to the side, toward D-3. Meanwhile, bring your arms through middle fifth position, and open them into second position. Your head faces front (D-1) with your chin slightly lifted (refer to Figure 9-2e).

Open and back to the side (écarté derrière)

Stand facing D-2, in fifth position with your right foot in front, arms in low fifth position.

With your right foot, do a *battement tendu* to the side toward D-4. Meanwhile, bring your arms through middle fifth position, and lift your right arm overhead as you open your left arm to second position. Your head is facing corner D-8 with your chin slightly lifted and your eyes lowered looking over your left arm (refer to Figure 9-2f). This is *écarté derrière* ("ay-car-TAY duh-ree-AIR").

To the back corner in back (effacé derrière)

For the *effacé derrière* ("ef-fah-SAY duh-ree-AIR"), stand facing D-2, in fifth position with your right foot in back, arms in low fifth position.

With your right foot, do a *battement tendu* to the back toward D-4. Meanwhile, bring your arms through middle fifth position, and lift your right arm overhead as you open your left arm to second position. Your head is facing corner D-2 with your chin slightly lifted (refer to Figure 9-2g).

Flat front to the back (quatrième derrière)

Stand facing D-1, in fifth position with your right foot in back, arms in low fifth position.

With your right foot, do a *battement tendu* to the back toward D-5. Meanwhile, bring your arms through middle fifth position, and open them into second position. Your head faces front (D-1), with your chin slightly lifted (refer to Figure 9-2h). That's the *quatrième derrière* ("kah-tree-EM duh-ree-AIR").

Crossed and to the back (croisé derrière)

To do the *battement tendu croisé derrière* ("kwah-ZAY duh-ree-AIR"), stand facing D-2, in fifth position with your right foot in back, arms in low fifth position.

With your right foot, do a *battement tendu* to the back toward D-6. Meanwhile, bring your arms through middle fifth position, and lift your right arm overhead as you open your left arm into second position. Your head is facing corner D-8 with your chin slightly lifted (refer to Figure 9-2i).

The nine positions of battement tendu together again

Try putting all the *battement tendu* positions in center floor together in this combination. For music, we suggest the beginning of Tchaikovsky's *Suite no. 3,* finale. The legendary choreographer George Balanchine used this movement for his brilliant ballet *Theme and Variations.* Count this music in groups of 8 counts, where each count lasts a little more than a second.

Start facing D-8 in fifth position with your right foot in front, arms in low fifth position.

Listen carefully, now — the first note of the music is your only preparation. After that, begin to move.

1. **On counts 1 through 6, do three *battements tendus croisé devant,* with your arms opening through middle fifth position into the proper arm position. Close to a *demi-plié* in fifth position, as your arms come around and down to low fifth position.**

2. **On count 7, do a *sous-sus* ("soo-SUE"): *relevé* and simultaneously slide both feet even closer together, to meet in the middle, as you change to face the next direction.**

   See Chapter 8 for more information on the *sous-sus relevé*. Meanwhile, lift your arms through middle fifth to high fifth position.

3. **On count 8, do a *demi-plié*, as you open your arms to second position; as you come back up, bring your arms to low fifth position; then through middle fifth position to the next arm position.**

   In all subsequent *sous-sus* movements, repeat the above arm movements.

4. **Over counts 1 through 8, repeat Steps 1-3 in *quatrième devant* position.**

5. **Over counts 1 through 8, repeat Steps 1-3 in *effacé devant* position.**

6. **Over counts 1 through 8, repeat Steps 1-3 *à la seconde* (in second position).**

7. **Over counts 1 through 8, repeat Steps 1-3 in *effacé derrière* position.**

8. **Over counts 1 through 8, repeat Steps 1-3 in *quatrième derrière* position.**

9. **Over counts 1 through 8, repeat Steps 1-3 in *croisé derrière* position.**

10. **Over counts 1 and 2, do a *demi-plié*, and lower your arms to low fifth position.**

11. **Over counts 3 through 5, do a *sous-sus* to fifth position and lift your arms to high fifth position.**

12. **Over counts 7 and 8, do a *demi-plié* and straighten, as you open your arms through second position and lower them to low fifth position.**

Now you are ready to do the exercise in the opposition direction. Start facing D-2, in fifth position with your *left* foot in front, arms in low fifth position.

Lifting Your Leg Slowly (Développé — Adagio)

After you practice the nine positions of the *battement tendu* in the center floor, you're ready to try those same positions with one leg lifted in the air. This is none other than the *développé (adagio)* from Chapter 8 — where one leg unfolds seamlessly into the full extension, as if underwater, creating the illusion of relaxation.

Of course, doing this move without that little wooden barre may come as a bit of a shock at first. As you start lifting one leg without the help of the barre, your supporting foot and ankle suddenly seem way too small and unsteady to support and balance your entire body. We know the feeling.

But you can achieve amazing things with constant practice. Keep at it — *slowly* — and success will be yours. Just be glad you're not wearing pointe shoes!

Your five-step développé program

It takes five different positions combined to create any *développé* in center floor. As an example, here's how to do the *développé croisé devant* — literally, "crossed in front."

1. **Stand facing D-8, in fifth position with your right foot in front, arms in low fifth position.**

2. **Lift your right foot into *cou-de-pied* front position (Figure 9-3a).**

3. **Continue to lift your right foot into the *retiré* position, as you lift your arms into the middle fifth position (Figure 9-3b).**

   Your foot and arms should arrive in position at the same time.

4. **With your right foot, begin reaching out to the *développé* position. Meanwhile, begin to bring your left arm to high fourth position, and begin bringing your right arm out to second position (Figure 9-3c).**

   When your right leg has unfolded halfway, you're in the so-called *attitude croisé devant.*

   Make sure that your arms don't yet arrive in full position — they're *halfway* there, just like your leg.

5. **Finish the motion by straightening your right knee all the way, into the *développé croisé devant* position. Simultaneously, keep moving your arms — the left to high fourth position, the right to second position.**

   When you reach the full *développé*, you should look something like Figure 9-3d.

Don't forget to breathe! As you reach the full extension of the *développé*, inhale. When you reach full extension, lift your right leg for one second more, and then close it in front of your left, into fifth position.

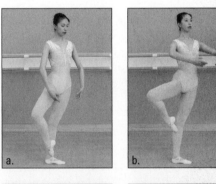

Figure 9-3:
The various stages of the *développé croisé devant* position.

a.

b.

c.

d.

Développés in all the positions

After you get the hang of the five-step *développé* sequence, you can (and should) use the same five steps to do the *développés* in *all* the directions and positions described earlier in this chapter — from *croisé devant* to *croisé derrière.*

Although each *développé* may differ from the others, the initiation is always the same. Start in fifth position with your arms in low fifth position. Bring your working leg through the *cou-de-pied* position into *retiré,* and bring both arms to middle fifth position.

From there, open your arms and working leg toward whichever position you're aiming for. (The leg always goes through *attitude* before it becomes straight.) And you're there!

Lifting Your Leg Behind (Arabesque)

The position with one leg lifted behind you is known as *arabesque*. This ballet term is rivaled only by the *pirouette* in its conversational use among non-dancers. And it's one of the most common steps among ballet dancers as well.

The *arabesque* is an extremely versatile little step, which you can do in combination with many other steps. You can do a *battement* into it, or a *développé.* You can do it on a bent leg, a straight leg, in *relevé, en pointe,* while turning — or even in the air!

As usual, we describe all the *arabesque* positions with your right leg lifted. But we strongly advise you to try each one on *both* sides before moving on. Otherwise, you're likely to get a big honking muscle cramp in the right side of your back.

First arabesque

The first position *arabesque* is the most common of all *arabesques*. It's also the easiest: The right arm and leg are both extended back, the left leg is vertical, and the left arm is extended forward. It's all very giraffelike, if you ask us.

1. **Stand facing D-7, in fifth position with your right foot in back, with your arms in low fifth position. With your right foot, do a *battement tendu* to the back as you bring your arms into middle fifth position.**

2. **Lift your right leg into *arabesque*, maintaining the turnout of your right hip, with a straight knee and pointed foot, making sure your heel can't be seen from the front.**

3. **As you lift your leg, open your right arm to second position, palm down, your elbow slightly behind your shoulder. Meanwhile, straighten your left arm in front of your left shoulder, hand at eye level, and focus your eyes on your hand with your chin slightly lifted (Figure 9-4a).**

For professional dancers, this is the *arabesque* of choice. First of all, in this position, dancers have an easier time creating a graceful, flowing line. (For more on the concept of *line*, see Chapter 4.) Second, it comes up a lot in giraffe ballets. Or it would, if there *were* any.

Figure 9-4:
First *arabesque* (a); second *arabesque* (b); third *arabesque* (c); fourth *arabesque* (d); fifth *arabesque* (e).

Second arabesque

The second-position *arabesque* is all about opposition. If your right leg is back, then your right arm is forward, and vice versa. As you might guess, this *arabesque* is more challenging than the first: It requires not only flexibility in the back, but also the ability to rotate your spine simultaneously.

Of course, any flexing and twisting must be done in moderation. If your back or neck yells, listen.

Repeat Steps 1 and 2 from the preceding section. As you lift your leg, straighten your right arm in front of and slightly higher than your right shoulder. Meanwhile, open your left arm to second position, palm down, your elbow slightly behind your shoulder. Turn your head to look over your right arm — as much as you can without getting a neck cramp — while lifting your chin *slightly*, as shown in Figure 9-4b.

Third arabesque

The third-position *arabesque* is considered to have a "Romantic" look; it comes up almost exclusively in good old-fashioned Romantic ballets like *Giselle* and *La Sylphide*. (See Chapter 1 for more on the Romantic style.)

Repeat Steps 1 and 2 from the section "First *arabesque*." As you lift your leg, straighten your right arm in front of and slightly below your right shoulder. Meanwhile, straighten your left arm in front of your left shoulder, bring your left hand level with the top of your head, and focus your eyes between your hands with your chin slightly lifted (refer to Figure 9-4c).

Fourth arabesque

This position of *arabesque* uses a lot of opposition, but not as much as the second *arabesque*. Because you do it on the diagonal, facing the corner, you don't need to rotate your spine quite as much in order to accomplish the same look.

Repeat Steps 1 and 2 from the section "First *arabesque*," but facing corner D-2. As you lift your leg, straighten your right arm in front of your right shoulder at eye level. Meanwhile, straighten your left arm slightly in back of, and lower than, your left shoulder, palm down. Your eyes focus on your right hand, with your chin slightly lifted, as shown in Figure 9-4d.

Fifth arabesque

This *arabesque* is a prehistoric dinosaur. You don't see it often today in choreography, and you may have to really pay attention to catch it in performance. But if you'd like to see it, take a look at Figure 9-4e.

Lifting Your Leg Behind with a Bent Knee (Attitude)

If you practiced the moves in Chapter 8, surely you remember the *attitude*, the graceful bent-knee alternative to the *arabesque*.

The *attitude* is man's best friend — and not just because it looks like a dog at a fire hydrant. It's much easier to perform than the *arabesque* while turned out; it makes you feel looser on those stiff days (especially as you get older);

it makes you appear more limber than you are; and it even looks good when performed low (at 45 degrees off the floor). The weight of your lifted leg in *attitude* is less than in *arabesque*, and the strain on your back is also less. We love the *attitude*.

Herewith, the basic *attitude* positions in center floor.

Crossed and in front (attitude croisée devant)

Stand facing D-8, in fifth position with your right foot in front, arms in low fifth position. Lift your right leg into *retiré* in front of your knee, and lift your arms into middle fifth position. (See Chapter 6 for more on the *retiré*.)

Now, leading with your right foot, extend your right leg out in front until your knee reaches an angle a little bigger than 90-degrees. Remember to keep lifting your right heel, maintaining the turnout of your right leg. Meanwhile, open your right arm to second position, and lift your left arm overhead. Your head faces D-2, as shown in Figure 9-5a.

Figure 9-5:
Attitude croisée devant (a); *attitude croisée derrière* (b); *attitude effacée derrière* (c).

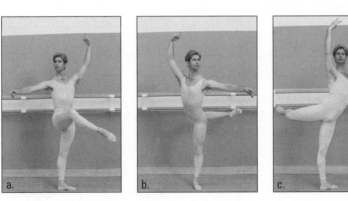

Crossed and behind you (attitude croisée derrière)

Stand facing D-2, in fifth position with your right foot in back, arms in low fifth position. Lift your right leg into *retiré* in back of your left knee, and lift your arms into middle fifth position.

Now extend your right leg out to the back, about halfway. Lead with your knee reaching back, and maintain the turnout of your right leg, which ideally should remain parallel to the floor. Meanwhile, open your left arm to second position, and lift your right arm overhead. Your head faces D-8, as shown in Figure 9-5b.

The attitude is the halfway mark into the full *développé.* At the completion of the motion, the angle of your right leg should be just a little wider than 90 degrees.

Open and to the corner in back (attitude effacée)

Stand facing D-8, in fifth position with your right foot in back, arms in low fifth position. Lift your right leg into *retiré* in back of your left knee, as you lift your arms into middle fifth position.

Now extend your right leg out to the back, leading by reaching back with your right knee, and maintaining the turnout of your right leg. Meanwhile, lift your right arm overhead, and open your left arm second position. Your head is facing D-2, as shown in Figure 9-5c.

An Adagio Combination

Here's a handy combination that allows you to practice many of the moves in this chapter. For music, try Tchaikovsky's *Suite no. 3.,* movement 4, but go forward to Variation X. George Balanchine choreographed a lovely *pas de deux* to this music — and one of your authors has danced it over 80 times.

Count this music *very* slowly. It's a waltz — "OOM-pah-pah" — but the slowest waltz you've ever heard. Each "OOM-pah-pah" gets a single count.

1. **Stand facing D-8, in fifth position with your right foot in front, arms in low fifth position.**

2. **Over counts 1 through 6, do a *développé croisé devant,* with your right leg.**

   Refer to Figure 9-3 again if you'd like a reminder.

3. **On count 7, lower your right leg to *battement tendu croisé devant,* as your arms open to second position.**

4. On count 8, close to fifth position with your right foot in front.

   Keep your arms in second position.

5. Over counts 1 through 6, do a *développé* with your left leg to the side (*écarté derrière*).

6. On count 7, lower your leg to *battement tendu* to the side (*écarté derrière*), opening your arms to second position.

7. On count 8, close to fifth position with your right foot in back, lowering your arms to low fifth position.

8. Over counts 1 through 6, do a *développé* with your left leg back, and left arm forward, in fourth position *arabesque* (*arabesque croisée*).

9. On count 7, lower your left leg to a *battement tendu croisé derrière*. On count 8, close the left leg behind the right in fifth position, as you open your arms to second position.

10. On count 1, lower your arms to low fifth position. On count 2, bring your arms through middle fifth and out to second position as you do a *battement tendu* with your right leg to the side, facing D-1. On count 3, close your right foot behind the left in fifth position as you turn your body to face D-2.

11. On count 4, do a *demi-plié* and lower your arms into low fifth position. On count 5, straighten your knees and bring your arms to middle fifth position. On count 6, open your arms to second position. On counts 7 and 8, lower your arms to low fifth position — preparing to do this combination to the other side.

Now do the mirror image of the entire combination.

Why we do it

We know, we know — if you're new to ballet, this *adagio* stuff is probably frying your brain. You must be asking yourself, "Why would anyone do these exercises day after day, week after week?"

It's true that these slow and deliberate exercises are a challenge. But trust us on this one — the rewards are amazing! The feeling that surges through you after you finish a combination without falling over is not to be believed. It's profoundly satisfying to know that after hours and hours of practice, you have finally found your balance.

And after you find it, how about whirling around on it? We tell you all about that in Chapter 10.

Chapter 10

Ballet's Tasmanian Devil: The Pirouette

*I*f there's one movement that shouts "ballet" to the general public, it's the *pirouette*. That's the incredibly graceful controlled turn that makes a dancer seem to spin like a gyroscope.

If you've ever seen a movement like that during an Olympic figure skating event, you've probably wondered how anyone on earth could do it. Well, you're about to find out. And you're even going to try it yourself.

But wait, you're no doubt thinking, with so much emphasis that you require italics. *These people think that they're going to show ballet newcomers how to do a pirouette in one chapter? Without a teacher? Are they NUTS?!?*

Yes. But you knew that already.

It's All in the Spot

The secret of any controlled turn is called *the spot.* This handy little technique allows ballet dancers to make any number of turns without getting dizzy.

Start by finding a special little spot that you can call your own. In your dance studio or living room, look for something at about eye level to concentrate on. It can be a smudge on a wall, a picture in a frame, your Uncle Ashley's precious Ming vase, or even your own reflection in a mirror. That's your spot.

Caution: Better move the vase.

Face your spot, with your feet in sixth position. Next, keeping your eyes on the spot, slowly turn your body around to the right, in a circle. But wait — although your body turns, your head keeps stationary — forcing you to look farther and farther over your left shoulder, *Exorcist* style.

At some point in your turn, something has to give. You can no longer keep your eyes on the spot — without doing some major damage, that is. At this moment, quickly turn your head around to the right, and find the spot again over your *right* shoulder. Now keep moving your body around to its starting point.

You have completed one spot. Try this a few more times, gradually increasing the pace. When you can spot fluently, you're on your way to mastering the pirouette.

The Pre-Pirouette: Turning on Two Legs

We'll be honest here: There's no such thing as an easy pirouette. The moves in this chapter are among the most complicated in the book. And if you're not careful, you can hurt yourself doing them.

Before you do any kind of turn, always check the surface you're working on to make sure that it has a medium amount of "slide potential." A too-slippery floor can obviously cause you to lose your footing and fall. But even more important, a floor that's not slippery enough can make your foot stick — causing you to twist your knee or ankle.

For an introductory exercise, we hereby introduce the somewhat simpler Turn on Two Legs. Though this is easier than a one-legged pirouette, it presents one considerable challenge: using your stomach muscles to keep the upper and lower halves of your body moving as one.

The turn on two legs is known in French as *soutenu en tournant en dedans* ("soo-tuh-NUE ahn toor-NAHN ahn duh-DAHN"). Say *that* to any ballet dancer, and he'll get that gleam in his eye that only ballet dancers get. Then he'll dare you to do one.

Begin facing D-1 (see Chapter 9 if you need help deciphering that *Battleship*-type reference), in fifth position with your right foot in front, your arms in low fifth position. Your knees are straight, with both heels on the ground (Figure 10-1a). Got it?

1. **Move your arms forward, with your right arm in front, to low fourth position. At the same time, brush your right leg toward the side, as you do a *demi-plié* on your left leg (Figure 10-1b).**

   Chapter 6 tells you all about the *demi-plié*.

2. **Push off your left leg and put all your weight on your right. Step onto the balls of your feet and cross your left leg in front to fifth position, as you open the arms into second position (Figure 10-1c).**

3. **Because your left foot is crossed in front of your right, there's only one way you can turn — to the right. Make one full revolution on the balls of your feet, remembering to spot. At the same time, bring your arms together in middle fifth position. When you finish, your right foot should be in front (Figure 10-1d).**

   See the preceding section for more on spotting.

4. **Now do a *demi-plié* in fifth position. To finish, take your arms to second position. Then straighten your knees to return to the starting position (Figure 10-1a).**

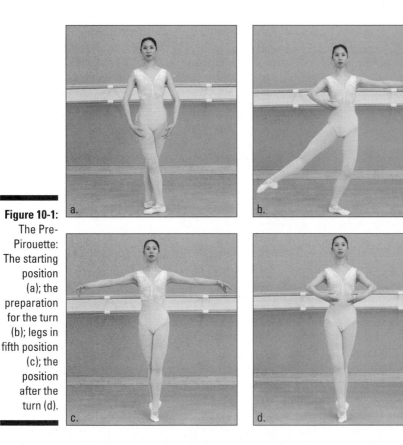

Figure 10-1:
The Pre-Pirouette:
The starting position (a); the preparation for the turn (b); legs in fifth position (c); the position after the turn (d).

When closing your left arm, use plenty of strength, engaging your upper back muscles. The force you gather helps you complete the turn.

Congratulations! Feel free to pause a moment to offer thanks for your first successful turn.

But resting on your laurels is not for you, O Future Principal Dancer. Try putting this turn to music. We suggest the world-renowned Christmas favorite, Waltz of the Flowers (from Tchaikovsky's *Nutcracker*), which works perfectly for this combination. If you can't find that piece, use any moderately quick waltz with a steady beat.

Start the music at the beginning, and wait until the harp finishes playing a long, showy, somewhat self-indulgent flourish (about one minute into the piece). Then listen as the orchestra starts anew with a quick "OOM-pah-pah" rhythm. Count this music in groups of four, where each entire "OOM-pah-pah" gets one count. (Chapter 5 tells you more about counting music for ballet.)

While listening to the first four OOM-pah-pahs, stay in position, but feel free to move your arms outward and back, to feel the beat. Then: Over the next counts 1 through 4, do steps 1 to 4 above, dancing one step on each count.

Don't forget to spot!

Repeat this step till you're tired, dizzy, or facedown on the floor. Then, *switch sides.* Go back to the beginning position, but with the *left* foot in front — and do the whole thing to the left.

When done correctly, this exercise builds killer abs — and transforms your *gluteus maximus* into an impressive *gluteus minimus*.

Turning on One Leg

The actual pirouette, or turn on one leg, is the subject of more testosterone-induced feats of post-ballet-class machismo than any other step. He (or she) who can do the most revolutions in a row acquires a special prestige within a ballet company.

We thought you'd like to know.

Outward from fifth to fifth position

The first pirouettes in this chapter are known as pirouettes outward, or *pirouette en dehors* ("ahn duh-OR"). All English-speaking ballet dancers know this rhyme: *"En dehors,* open the door." There's a reason for that: One leg moves outward — opening a door, so to speak — at the beginning of the turn.

If that's not enough, you may want to remember this: All *en dehors* turns go in the direction of the raised foot. If your right foot is in the air, turn to the right. If your left foot is in the air, turn to the left. It's as simple as that.

Getting the "look"

When mastering any pirouette, all ballet students start by mastering the *look* of the turn. This means mastering all the leg and arm movements — without actually turning. They then graduate to a single turn, and, finally, to multiple turns.

Try following that sequence now: Begin facing D-1, in fifth position with your right foot in front. Hold your arms low and rounded.

1. **Lift your arms through middle fifth position and open them to low fourth with your right arm forward, legs in *demi-plié*.**

2. **Go up on the ball of your left foot. Straighten your left knee as you lift your right leg into *retiré*. At the same time, bring your arms, rounded together, in front of you in middle fifth position.**

   See Chapter 6 for more information on *retiré*.

3. **Close your right leg in fifth position in back, knees bent in *demi-plié*, and open your arms to the side in second position.**

4. **Straighten your legs and bring your arms down to the original low rounded position.**

Now you are in the position you started in, with one exception — your *left* leg is in front. Perfect, in other words, for practicing this move to the other side.

Once around

After you master the "look" of the turn, you can try the turn itself. Don't be intimidated — you're simply doing exactly what you did before, with one added movement. OK — one *really, REEEEEALLY* **BIG** added movement.

When practicing any turn, make sure to hold your supporting knee and ankle steady, so they don't twist.

If you'd like a little help in the support department, go back to the barre. Practice rising onto the ball of one foot *(relevé)* while turning yourself around at the barre with your arms. Try for a feeling of strength and solidity in the supporting leg.

Begin by facing D-1, in fifth position with your right foot in front. Your arms are in low fifth position.

1. **Bring your arms to low fourth position with your right arm forward, legs in *demi-plié* (Figure 10-2a).**

   This is the wind-up!

2. **Push off (you're heading to the right) and *relevé* on your left foot. When the left knee is straight, lift your right leg into *retiré*. As you close your left arm into middle fifth position, rotate to the right (Figure 10-2b), until you face front once again.**

3. **Close to fifth position with your right leg in back, in *demi-plié*, and open your arms to second position (Figure 10-2c).**

4. **Straighten your legs to finish.**

Your next step is to do this turn repeatedly to music. First, make sure that you can do the single turn outward at a moderately quick pace.

Figure 10-2:
The single pirouette: The preparation (a); the turning position (b); the finishing position (c).

The music to Tchaikovsky's *Suite no. 3,* fourth movement ("Tema con variazioni"), is perfect for this exercise. But if you can't find it, you can use any music in a steady, moderate tempo and a very steady beat — say, a little slower than one beat per second.

By the way, the first note of Tchaikovsky's music, played by violins, is the pickup to the beat. The *next* note is beat 1. You count this music in groups of four beats, with each beat lasting a little longer than one full second. ("And-ONE -and-TWO-and-THREE-and-FOUR," and so on.)

Over the next counts 1 through 4, do steps 1 to 4 above, dancing one step on each count. As always, don't forget to spot!

After you have mastered this exercise, try doing it four times in a row. (On step 3, the first three times, close your right leg in front. The fourth time, close the right leg in back in *demi-plié.*)

Now repeat the whole exercise to the left!

Outward from fourth to fifth position

The pirouette described in the preceding section may be the *simplest* of all pirouettes, but the next one is the most *common*. What's the difference? Well, in this one you take off from a different position — fourth instead of fifth.

When you take off in fourth position, you suddenly have much more force available to generate the turn. That makes the turn more spectacular. Anytime you see a dancer showing off, spinning around and around, chances are he or she started in fourth position.

That extra force also makes this turn more dangerous! Be careful, as always, that the floor doesn't cause you to slip or stick.

As in the previous turn, we recommend trying the "look" of the pirouette before attempting the whole thing. So, first, follow these steps, *leaving out the turn itself*. Then, after you master the position, go for the turn.

Begin in fifth position, with your right foot in front, arms in low fifth position (Figure 10-3a).

1. **Point your right foot to the right side (*battement tendu*) with a straight knee. Meanwhile, bring your arms through middle fifth position and open them out to second (Figure 10-3b).**

2. **Now for the windup: Bring your right leg back, foot pointed (*demi rond de jambe*), and do a *demi-plié* in fourth position. Meanwhile, your left arm stays to the side, and your right arm is rounded in front of you, in fourth position (Figure 10-3c).**

3. **Push off the right leg and bring it up into *retiré*. Meanwhile, do a *relevé* on the left foot, left knee straight, and rotate to the right. As you turn, bring your arms together in middle fifth position, to help you get all the way around (Figure 10-3d).**

Don't forget to spot!

4. **Close to fifth position with your right foot in back, in *demi-plié*, and open your arms to second position (Figure 10-3e).**

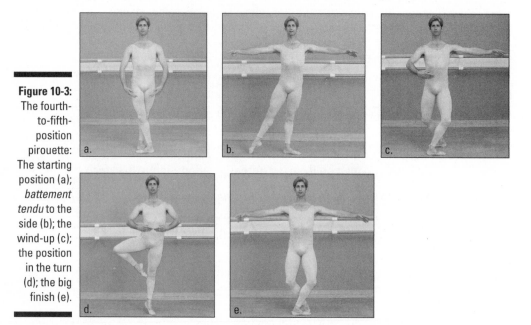

Figure 10-3:
The fourth-to-fifth-position pirouette: The starting position (a); *battement tendu* to the side (b); the wind-up (c); the position in the turn (d); the big finish (e).

Now for a musical workout. A good piece of music to use for this turn is the Ballroom Scene from Prokofiev's great ballet, *Romeo and Juliet*. This music is absolutely spectacular — it usually provokes sighs of ecstasy, not only from the audience, but from the dancers, orchestra members, stage managers, and half of the costume department as well.

The music begins with four heavy beats. Then the main theme begins — and this is where you begin to count and dance. For this music, count to 4, where each beat lasts about one second.

On each count, do one step above. (The entire preparation and turn takes four counts.) Now repeat the turn to the other side.

INJURY ALERT

Multiple pirouettes

In principle, multiple pirouettes are just as easy to grasp as single pirouettes. After a professional dancer completes a full revolution, he doesn't stop — he just keeps spinning as long as he can.

But we don't recommend that you attempt multiple pirouettes at this stage of your development.

They're very, *very* difficult to do. Even professionals differ in their spinning aptitude. Some can do triples or more; others are content to do a good double turn. So don't try the multiple pirouette yet. We like you too much.

Inward from fourth to fifth position

If you like the pirouette outward, you are going to love the pirouette inward (*pirouette en dedans* — "ahn duh-DAHN").

If you've read the preceding section, you may remember that for outward turns, you always turn in the direction of the raised foot: *"En dehors, open the door."* Well, for inward turns, you turn as if you are *closing* the same door — toward the standing leg.

But be warned: This move is a little trickier. When turning inward, it's a little harder to maintain that all-important "turned-out" leg position that is the basis of all ballet.

Here's the most important thing to remember: Keep your standing leg strong.

As in other turns, you should start with the "look" of the turn. After you feel comfortable, add the turn itself.

Begin facing D-8, in fifth position with your right foot in front, arms in low fifth position (Figure 10-4a).

1. **Point your right foot forward to D-8 (*tendu croisé*) with a straight knee. Meanwhile, bring your arms through the middle and open them to second position (Figure 10-4b).**

2. **Lower your right heel and bend your right knee, in fourth position (*demi-plié*). Meanwhile, bring your right arm to the front. Your left arm remains to the side in fourth position (Figure 10-4c).**

3. **Quickly rise to the ball of your right foot, with your right knee straight. As you do, bring up your left leg in *retiré*. Meanwhile, bring your left arm in to meet the right in a rounded middle fifth position (Figure 10-4d), as you turn.**

Because you're turning to the right, look at your right foot in the preparation position and turn in the direction it is pointing.

Don't forget to spot!

4. **After one turn, close your left leg in front in fifth position, facing D-2 (*croisé*). Do a *demi-plié* to absorb any extra force, and bring your arms to second position to help you to stop (Figure 10-4e).**

5. **Straighten your knees to finish.**

"That was a *pirouette en dedans*," you can triumphantly proclaim to your party guests.

Did you notice — your feet are now in exactly the opposite position from the start. You know what that means — you are ready to repeat the turn to the left. Go for it!

During this turn, keep the inner thigh muscles of your supporting leg reaching forward. Your pirouette is much more likely to succeed this way.

Figure 10-4: *Pirouette en dedans:* The starting position (a); pointing the right foot forward (b); the fourth position preparation (c); the turning position (d); the finish (e).

a.

b.

c.

d.

e.

To try this turn to music, we suggest the *pizzicato* movement from Glazunov's ballet *Raymonda*. Count this music in groups of four.

Over counts 1 through 4, do Steps 1 to 4 — one step on each count of the music. Over the next counts 1 through 4, repeat this exercise to the other side.

As you see, you can constantly alternate sides as you repeat this move: right, left, right, left.

Traveling Turns

Almost anyone can do traveling turns. What makes them different from all the other turns we mention in this chapter is that they involve traveling across the floor — on purpose, that is.

On one leg

With the traveling turn on one leg, you can cover a lot of space in a short period of time — impressing your friends, neighbors, and anyone who may be looking in the window. The traveling turn on one leg is known in French as the *tour en dedans piqué* ("TOOR ahn duh-DAHN pee-KAY"), or simply *piqué* turn for short.

By the way, the word *piqué* literally means "stung," or poked. (Imagine your pointed foot briefly "poking" the ground just before the turn.) May you win your next game of Trivial Pursuit.

In performance, the ballet dancer frequently executes many of these turns, one after another. If you were to watch from above — from the balcony, for example — you could see the ballerina creating a large circle on the floor with a series of these turns, called a *manège*. Or sometimes, instead of a large circle, she creates a *diagonal*, in which the series of turns forms a long diagonal line from a far corner of the stage toward the audience.

Often these turns are combined with other kinds of turns, and performed at a dazzling pace, driving the audience wild. Afterwards, the dancer often freezes for a moment in a graceful pose. After the *bravos* have started, she takes center stage to bow, with great humility. (She's lovin' every minute.)

In ballet, not every move gets performed by both men and women. Some were invented strictly for one gender or the other. Though our male readers are welcome to try our *piqué* turns, we should point out that you almost never see men *piqué*-ing away in performance.

Again, make sure to start with the "look" of the turn before you attempt the turn itself.

Start facing D-1, in fifth position facing front (*en face),* arms in low fifth position.

1. **Extend your right leg forward, pointing your right foot (tendu); lift your arms through the middle to low fourth position — your left arm opens to the side, while your right arm rounds in front of your stomach (Figure 10-5a).**

2. **With your right leg, draw a quarter circle on the floor from the front to the side (*demi rond de jambe*), and bend your left knee (*demi-plié*). Your arms stay in low fourth position (Figure 10-5b).**

3. **Push off your left leg and step onto the ball of your right foot (*demi pointe*), with your right knee straight. Meanwhile, bring your left leg into *retiré* back. Keep your arms rounded in front of you (Figure 10-5c).**

   This, by the way, is your "*piqué* turn" position. Later you actually make the turn at this point. But for now, try to balance there for at least a second, to get the feeling of a sustained pose. Imagine turning in this position. Thrilling, isn't it?

4. **When you are ready to come down — or if gravity is ready for you — bring your left leg down behind your right into a fifth position *demi-plié*. (Figure 10-5d).**

5. **Now, to prepare to repeat the move, brush your right leg to the side (*dégagé*), simultaneously returning your arms to low fourth position (Figure 10-5e).**

You are now ready for the next *piqué*. Note that this move (beginning with step 3) is repeated the exact same way until you reach the opposite corner.

We suggest that you try this move several times across the floor to the right — and then repeat it to the left — before trying to add the turn.

Ready to try? Courage, young balletomane. All you have to do is use a little more force in the push-off and the closing of the arms, and you'll find yourself completing one turn to the right.

Figure 10-5:
Tour en dedans piqué: right leg *battement tendu* to the front (a); right leg *battement tendu* to the side, ready for push-off (b); the turning position (c); the finish of the turn (d); preparing to repeat the turn (e).

When turning, don't let yourself get tempted by bad technique. It would be very easy to turn your knee inward to get around faster. But good technique calls for your lifted knee to stay rotated outward. It's also common to lift your shoulders. — another ballet *non-non*. Keeping your arms lower while you turn can help to hold your shoulders down and free up your neck for its spotting duties.

Which reminds us — remember to spot your head so that you don't get dizzy! When you turn and travel across the floor at the same time, keep your eyes on the direction you want to go. So when you turn to the right, spot the wall to your right — and when you turn to the left, spot the wall to your left.

When doing traveling turns, be aware of exactly where you place the *piqué* leg (the leg you're turning on). This dictates the direction in which you're going to be traveling!

To practice this kind of traveling turn, pick some music with a beat you can hear clearly — almost any *pas de deux* would work beautifully. (For instance, you could use the "Wedding" *pas de deux* from the ballet *Don Quixote*.) Now repeat this step from one side of the room to the other.

On two legs

If you've watched any ballet at all, chances are you have seen repeated turns on two legs (*tours chaînés déboulés* — "TOOR sheh-NAY day-boo-LAY"). They make quite an impression — especially fast! But when broken down, they are really only a succession of simple half-turns. Each one is lovely, but when connected together, they resemble a string of pearls.

For once, the English description is just as beautiful as the French is. The word *chaîné* literally means "in a chain."

1. **Begin with your heels together, feet pointed outward in first position. Your arms are low and rounded just in front of your thighs, in low fifth position.**

2. **Rise to the balls of your feet, keeping your knees straight and ankles strong, with your weight in the middle of your feet (first position *relevé*). Lift your arms through middle fifth position into second position (Figure 10-6a).**

3. **Close your arms into the rounded middle-fifth position in front of your body. This gives you the force to lift your left leg slightly off the floor and rotate to the right, halfway around. Keep your feet in first position, with your knees straight (Figure 10-6b).**

   Now you're facing the back wall.

4. **Open your arms to the side, into second position, while lifting your right leg off the ground ever so slightly. Rotate to your right, coming around to the front again in first position, as in Figure 10-6a.**

Figure 10-6:
Chaîné déboulé: The position facing front (a); halfway around the turn (b).

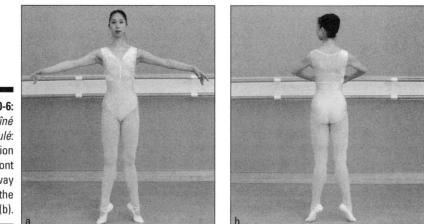

TRY IT!

In the Just for Fun Department

Okay, you've discovered how to do multiple turns on one leg — and multiple turns on two legs. Now, why not combine 'em? Ballet dancers and choreographers do this all the time, and so can you.

Try doing four *piqué* turns, followed by four *chaîné* turns. (Poked and chained. And they say ballet is non-violent.)

Now try the opposite: Four *chaîné* turns, followed by four *piqué* turns.

With a little imagination, you can create your own combinations. Mix and match — keeping the flow of movement going. You're on your way to great choreography.

Repeat this as many times as you can, until you run out of room or fall over in a pearllike heap. Then try it to the left.

TIP

When doing the *chaîné* turn, keep in mind where you point your "first" foot — because that's the direction you are going to travel. For example, when turning to the right, point your *right* foot where you want to go.

TIP

Once you feel very comfortable with the *chaîné* turn, try to keep your arms in middle fifth position throughout the whole movement. That is the proper way to look when *chaîné*-ing

A two-legged traveling turn combination

Here's an exercise for practicing your traveling turns on two legs (*tours chaînés déboulés*). For music, we suggest the "Four Little Swans" from Tchaikovsky's *Swan Lake*. Count this music in groups of four. (This music has an "OOM-pah, OOM-pah" sound, and each "OOM" gets a new count.)

1. **Start in the D-6 corner with your right foot front, in fifth position, with your body facing D-8 (*croisé*). Your arms are in low fifth position.**

2. **On the first four counts, prepare to turn. Point your right foot, knee straight, toward D-8 (*tendú croisé*). Bring your arms through middle fifth position into low fourth position, with your right arm rounded in front.**

3. **On the fourth count of this preparation, do a *demi-plié* on your left leg.**

4. **Over counts 1 and 2, push off your left leg and transfer your weight to the right on demi pointe. As you do, bring your left foot in to meet your right in first position, while making a half turn and bringing your arms to middle fifth position.**

   You should now be facing D-5.

5. **On count 3, continue to turn half a revolution to your right, until you are facing D-1. As you turn, open your arms to second position.**

6. **On count 4, continue turning to the right until you are facing D-5, with your arms in middle fifth position and your legs in first position.**

   Now keep repeating Steps 4, 5, and 6. Depending on your level of ability or your mood, you can alternate between steps as quickly or as slowly as you like. For example, you can start by taking one turn for every four counts. As you get more confident, try one turn for every two counts. And finally, when you've really mastered the motion, do one turn on *each* count.

7. **Now for the big finish. Slide your right leg through a fourth position *demi-plié,* facing D-2. Your left leg is back in *battement tendú arrière* as you straighten your right knee and transfer your weight to your right foot. Meanwhile, bring your arms from middle fifth position to high fourth position with your left arm up, and try to combat your dizziness.**

Whipping It Up: The Famous Fouetté

The incomparable, jaw-dropping, eye-popping, heart-stopping, floor-mopping turn, the *fouetté en tournant,* is known to the entire ballet world simply as *fouetté* ("foo-et-TAY").

Literally, *fouetté* means "whipped." As the ballerina executes multiple turns on one leg, she raises and lowers herself on that leg (the very same *relevé* you can read about in Chapter 6), while simultaneously whipping the other leg around and around (see Figure 10-7). Whip! Whip! If you stand anywhere in the general vicinity of a *fouetté*-ing ballerina, you can feel the change in air pressure every time that lethal gam whooshes by.

When a ballerina starts to do *fouettés,* you can bet that all dancers, students, critics, and balletomanes in the audience will start counting. In the final "coda" section of many a *pas de deux,* where the flashiest steps are danced, the ballerina is expected to execute no fewer than 32 *fouettés* without pause! The famous "Black Swan Pas de Deux" from *Swan Lake* is a classic example. Talk about pressure: Many dance aficionados feel that the success of an entire performance depends on the outcome of these turns.

Figure 10-7:
The Famous
Fouetté (a
and b), and
the big
finish (c).

In fact, this move is such a staple of the classical ballet repertoire that today, most ballerinas must be able to complete 32 good *fouettés* — or else have something equally amazing to offer — before being considered for a role with a major dance company.

To make matters just a little more interesting, this most challenging of steps is usually performed toward the very end of a ballet — say, in Act III — when the ballerina is already tired out from a long evening of dancing. Therefore, the showiest ballerinas never fail to demonstrate their superhuman stamina by throwing in a few double or triple turns — just because they can.

By the way, the *fouetté* is primarily the province of females. But men sometimes integrate one or two into their *grand pirouette* turns in second position, during the coda — just because *they* can.

The practice of pirouettes is a years-long endeavor — but one that offers some of the most gratifying rewards in ballet. May your revolutions never end.

Chapter 11

Linking It Together: The Steps Between the Steps

*Y*ou may have tried — and maybe even mastered — several different ballet steps while reading this book. But after you master the steps, how do you put them together into something that looks like a dance? That's the problem that dancers and choreographers have faced ever since ballet was young.

Enter the *linking steps*. These steps help you to get from one tricky move to the next. Linking steps also play an important role in giving every exercise a clean and polished look.

Galloping in the Air (Chassé)

Ballet dancers and choreographers have long found inspiration in horses — those smelly, yet graceful, beasts. The equestrian *pas de cheval* from Chapter 7 is one example. Here's another step that imitates a horse.

If you've ever watched a horse in full gallop, you've probably noticed the particular pattern that his legs make. He brings his front and back legs together while in the air. Then he lands on the back legs as the front legs extend forward. And once again, he brings all his legs together in the air.

Bringing all your legs together in the air in ballet is called *chassé* ("shah-SAY"). The French word literally means "chased" — describing how one foot chases the next in this step. (We don't even want to *ponder* what ballet would be like if we had four legs.) Care to give it a try yourself?

The basic chassé

As we describe this step, we use the handy system introduced in Chapter 9 to number the corners of the room. Stand facing D-8, in fifth position with your right foot in front, and your arms in low fifth position.

1. **Do a *demi-plié* and slide your right foot to the front into fourth position. Meanwhile, lift your arms into low fourth position, right arm in front (Figure 11-1a).**

2. **As you bring your left leg in to meet the right, push off the ground just enough to lift your body into the air. Join your feet together and point them in the air, as shown in Figure 11-1b.**

3. **Land in fifth position with your right foot in front and do a *demi-plié* (Figure 11-1c).**

   That's the *chassé.*

Figure 11-1: The *chassé* — the *demi-plié* in fourth position (a), the jump in fifth position (b), and the landing in a fifth position *demi-plié* (c).

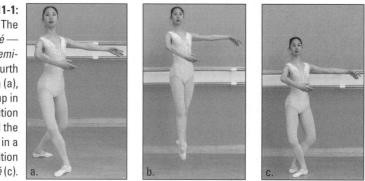

You can do these steps many times in quick succession. Try a few in a row — it feels good, it builds confidence very quickly, and it keeps them thar horse wranglers away.

How about the other direction? To do the mirror image of the exercise, start by facing D-2 with your left foot in front.

Did we mention that this exercise can be done in every direction — and also while turning in the air? But that's the subject of another book.

A chassé combination

For music, we suggest a selection from Adolph Adam's *Giselle:* the *pas de deux* for Giselle and Albrecht from Act I. This music sounds a little bit like a horse's canter. Count the music in groups of eight, where each count lasts about one second.

1. **Stand facing D-8, in fifth position with your right foot in front, arms in low fifth position. Over counts 1 through 4, do nothing.**

2. **Over counts 5 through 8, bring your arms through middle fifth position to low fourth position with your left arm in front.**

3. **Over counts 1 through 6, do consecutive *chassés* on each count.**

4. **On count 7, do a fifth position *demi-plié,* with your right foot in front. Immediately do a *battement tendu* with your right leg to the side, turning your body to face D-1.**

5. **On count 8, close your right foot in fifth position in back, and face D-2.**

Now you're ready to rock with the other leg. Repeat this exercise to the left. When you feel comfortable doing this exercise to both sides forward, try doing it to both sides in reverse.

The *sequence* of movements is the same — only the *direction* changes.

Gliding between Steps (Glissade)

The *glissade* ("glee-SAHD") is the most common of all the connector steps in the classical ballet vocabulary. This step was initially created to portray the illusion of gliding along the floor, but today it has developed into a more aerial motion.

The most popular direction of a *glissade* is to the side. In fact, you have a healthy imagination, the *glissade* may remind you of a crab walking. Except, of course, that in a *glissade* you join your feet in fifth position — something crabs almost never do.

The basic glissade

Stand facing D-1, in fifth position with your left foot in front, arms in second position.

1. Do a *demi-plié* on both feet in fifth position.

2. Brush your right foot sideways into a *dégagé* in second position, as you maintain *demi-plié* on your left leg (Figure 11-2a).

3. Push off your left leg, straightening your left knee.

   Both knees should straighten in the air simultaneously, as shown in Figure 11-2b.

4. Land on your right leg, and lower into *demi-plié* on your right leg with your left foot out to the side in *dégagé* (Figure 11-2c).

5. Finally, close your left leg in front into a fifth position *demi-plié* (Figure 11-2d).

As you do this step, try to visualize the ideal position while both your feet are in the air: You want both your knees straight and your feet pointed. The more you can see this position in your mind's eye, the better you'll be able to do it.

The *glissade* can (and should) be danced in other directions as well — front and back, for example. But wait until you've done the *glissade* to the side about a thousand times. For starters, try the combination in the following section.

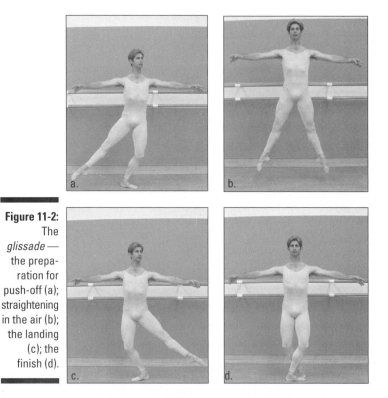

Figure 11-2: The *glissade* — the preparation for push-off (a); straightening in the air (b); the landing (c); the finish (d).

A glissade combination

This combination allows you to practice the glissade to both sides. For music, we suggest the waltz from Tchaikovsky's *Serenade for Strings.* Count this music in groups of four, where each "OOM-pah-pah" of the orchestra gets one count.

1. **Stand facing D-1, in fifth position with your left foot in front, arms in low fifth position.**

2. **Over counts 1 through 3, lift your arms through middle fifth into second position. On count 4, do a** *demi-plié.*

3. **Over counts 1 through 3, do a** *glissade* **to the right on each count. After the third glissade, immediately do a** *battement tendu* **with your left leg to the side.**

   See Chapter 6 for more information on the *battement tendu.*

4. **On count 4, close your left leg behind your right in fifth position and do a** *demi-plié.*

   You are now in position to repeat this combination to the left. Continue doing *glissades* in both directions until you get tired or the cows come home — whichever comes first.

Doing the Three-Step

Ballet technique includes several steps called "three-steps" — steps that have three different components. The most popular of these are the Grapevine (used often to connect big jumps) and the Classic Waltz Step (used to connect jumps, turns, and people). Sure, we could name other "three-steps" — but practice these two, and you'll be set for most ballet situations.

The Grapevine (pas de bourrée)

The famous Grapevine is best known from all kinds of ethnic dances. If you are Greek or Jewish, you have been dancing the Grapevine for centuries. The popular Jewish dance "Havah Nagilah" is nothing more than a Grapevine.

But the Grapevine isn't just for weddings anymore. Its ballet equivalent, the *pas de bourrée* ("PAH duh boo-RAY"), crops up everywhere — from the classical *Swan Lake* and *Sleeping Beauty* to the romantic *Giselle* and *La Sylphide,* to the more contemporary ballets choreographed by George Balanchine, John Cranko, Jiri Kylian, and Mark Morris. In fact, we'd be hard pressed to think of a ballet in which a *pas de bourrée* doesn't appear at one time or another.

The back-side-front pas de bourrée

To remember the order of movements in this exercise, say to yourself, "Back, Side, Front" — describing the placement of your feet in *pas de bourrée.* (Centuries ago people used to be hanged as witches for talking to themselves, but in ballet studios, that hardly ever happens.)

Stand facing D-1, in fifth position with your right foot in front, arms in low fifth position. In preparation for the *pas de bourrée,* lift your left foot into the *cou-de-pied* position in back and do a *demi-plié* on your right leg, lifting your arms into low fourth position with the right arm in front (Figure 11-3a). Then follow these steps:

1. **Rise up to the ball of your right foot as you close your left foot in back in fifth position.**

   Your arms are still in low fourth position (Figure 11-3b).

2. **Step your right foot to the right into second position (still in *relevé* on both feet) and open your right arm to second position (Figure 11-3c).**

3. **Close your left foot in front of the right and do a *demi-plié* on the left leg, as you bring your right foot into *cou-de-pied* in back, closing your left arm in front in low fourth position. Complete all these positions simultaneously (Figure 11-3d).**

Now repeat the *pas de bourrée* to the other side.

The front-side-back pas de bourrée

The "Back, Side, Front" combination is just one possibility. Try doing the Grapevine in reverse order: Front, Side, Back. Start facing D-1, in fifth position with your right foot in front, arms in low fifth position. In preparation for the *pas de bourrée,* lift your right foot into *cou-de-pied* in front and do a *demi-plié* on your left leg. Meanwhile, lift your arms through middle fifth into low fourth position, with your left arm in front.

1. **Rise up to *relevé* on your left foot as you close your right foot in front in fifth position, your arms still in low fourth position.**

2. **Step your left foot to the left into second position (still in *relevé* on both feet). Open your left arm to second position.**

3. **Close your right foot in back of the left and do a *demi-plié*. Bring your left foot to *cou-de-pied* in front, and bring your arms to low fourth position, right arm in front.**

Now repeat the whole exercise to the other side.

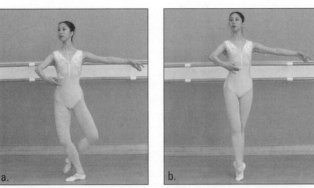
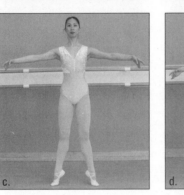

Figure 11-3:
Pas de bourrée — the preparation (a); step to the balls of your feet (b); step to second position (c); step to *cou-de-pied* (d).

A pas de bourrée combination

For music, we suggest the coda of the "Bluebird *pas de deux*" from Tchaikovsky's *Sleeping Beauty*.

1. **Start facing D-1, in fifth position with your right foot in front. Over counts 1 through 4, do nothing.**

2. **Over counts 5 through 8, bring your arms up through middle fifth and open them to second position.**

   Leave your arms in second position for the remainder of the combination.

3. **Over counts 1 through 4, do the preparation and Steps 1, 2, and 3 of the back-side-front *pas de bourrée*, replacing the *cou-de-pied* in back with a *degagé* of your right leg to the side and keeping your arms in second position throughout.**

4. **Over counts 5 thought 8, do the preparation and Steps 1, 2, and 3 of the front-side-back *pas de bourrée*, again replacing the *cou-de-pied* in front with a *degagé* of the left leg to the side and keeping your arms in second position throughout.**

Now *repeat all the steps again* in this order until you feel comfortable or tip over. Then try the combination to the other side.

The Classic Waltz Step (balancé)

The waltz is one of the most elegant and beautiful things that two people can do together. The dancers hold each other in their arms. Eyes meet, and starry-eyed sentiment ignites. They move in harmony, breathing as one, intimately intertwined in a passionate embrace, spinning in circles, around and around, quicker and quicker, whipping up a whirling vortex of ever-increasing velocity!

> (Publisher's note: We apologize for the preceding excess. The authors have been hosed down.)

You can even do a waltz by yourself, although that's much less fun. You can do it from side to side with one leg in back, with one leg in front, traveling across the floor on the diagonal, traveling in circles, and even backwards. What a versatile step! For now, we concentrate on the waltz step from side to side — known as a *balancé* ("bah-lahn-SAY").

We suggest Johann Strauss's greatest waltz, *On the Beautiful Blue Danube,* for trying out your waltzing legs — but nearly any waltz will do. Strauss's waltzes nearly always begin with a slow introduction, so wait until the music starts moving at a good "OOM-pah-pah" clip.

As you begin to practice this step, give one count to each "OOM-pah-pah" of the orchestra. But later, as you feel more comfortable, you can give THREE counts to each "OOM-pah-pah" — put count 1 on OOM, count 2 on "pah," and count 3 on the other "pah."

Start facing D-1, in fifth position with your right foot in front, arms in low fifth position. Over counts 1 though 5, do nothing. On count 6, brush your right leg to the side in *dégagé*, and lift your arms through middle fifth position into second position (Figure 11-4a). Then follow these steps:

1. **On count 1, step onto your right leg, bringing your left arm into low fourth position in front, and bringing your left leg to *cou-de-pied* in back (Figure 11-4b).**

2. **On count 2, close your left leg in back of the right, putting your weight onto the ball of your left foot. Lift your right foot off the ground slightly as you close your arms to low fourth position with the left arm in front (Figure 11-4c).**

3. **On count 3, lower your right foot back to the floor, and allow it to take the weight of your body, as your arms stay in low fourth position and your left leg arrives in *cou-de-pied* back. (See Figure 11-4d.)**

Figure 11-4:
Balancé —
the prepa-
ration (a);
step to the
right foot,
left foot in
cou-de-pied
back (b);
step to
the ball of
the left foot
(c); step
forward on
the right
foot, left foot
returning to
cou-de-pied
in back (d).

4. **Now do a *degagé* with your left leg to the side in preparation for the
next *balancé*.**

Repeat Steps 1, 2, and 3 to the other side to get a balanced impression of
the waltz.

We're not just showing you ballet — we're actually preparing you for your
next ballroom competition.

Getting from One Place to Another

Though ballet offers a multitude of choices for moving from one place to
another, sometimes you just gotta walk or run. But of course, even walking
has a specific formula in ballet.

Walking and running

Remember these pointers as you walk ballet-style:

✔ First of all, when walking, you must maintain turnout at all times. So you can't just walk straight ahead; you have to keep your hips rotated out to the sides and walk like a barnyard fowl. This is considered beautiful. (See Chapter 4 for more information on turnout.)

✔ Second, don't forget that in ballet, you must point each foot every single time that it leaves the floor. Then, as you return each foot to the ground, place your toe down first, and transfer your weight to the ball of your foot, and finally to the heel. *Toe-ball-heel* — that's what ballet dancers are always mumbling to themselves in their sleep.

Finally, don't forget to walk the walk of your character. For example, say you're portraying the Swan Queen, Odette, in *Swan Lake.* You would never walk with quick, small steps. For one thing, you're a swan, with long bird-legs. And for another, you're a queen, who must appear regal at all times. Walk slowly and deliberately, even when entering and exiting the stage. And even when running, make sure that your steps are large, and keep your feet in front of your hips to maintain a regal and graceful look (for a bird).

As you walk, try to keep your head at a steady height without bobbing it up and down. That barnyard fowl analogy does have its limits.

This same formula works for the ballet run — it all just happens a little faster. Make sure to reach forward with each running foot, and keep your foot pointed, directly in front of your hips.

The traveling step (bourré)

The *bourré* ("boo-RAY") is the most labor intensive, slowest, and most painful way for a dancer to get from one place to another.

The *bourré* (not to be confused with the *pas de bourrée* from earlier in this chapter) consists of about a million teeny, tiny baby steps danced in sequence, usually *en pointe,* to create a deceptively seamless traveling line. The sheer speed of these steps — tip tip tip tip tip tip tip tip — makes the dancer seem to hover across the floor.

A beautifully executed *bourré* can elicit multiple ooooohs from the audience. One of the most ooooooh-inducing *bourrés* occurs in Act II of the ballet *Giselle.* As the curtain rises on a haunted forest, the veiled Myrta, (Queen of the Dead

Jilted Virgins) dances a beautiful *bourré* all the way across the stage, from one side to the other. At that moment, we know that she's a ghost — she seems never to touch the ground. A spiritual and chilling moment — it gives us the willies every time.

Wanna *bourré?* Follow these steps. (This is going to take some practice).

Stand facing D-1, in fifth position with your right foot in front, arms in low fifth position.

1. **Rise up onto the balls of your feet and close your left foot so that the left toes are directly behind the right, as shown in Figure 11-5a.**

2. **With the weight of your body on your right foot, move your left foot an inch or two to the right, still keeping it behind the right foot (Figure 11-5b).**

3. **Now slide your *right* foot to the right a couple of inches.**

4. **Keep repeating these two steps endlessly, or until your feet beg for mercy.**

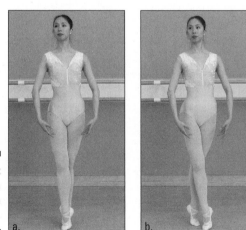

Figure 11-5:
Hovering in space with the *bourré.*

Don't be dismayed if you need to bend your knees slightly as you *bourré.* A slight knee bend is natural, and even encouraged. (The operative word is *slight.*) Keep going till you run into the wall, then try the other direction.

Lift your feet ever so slightly off the floor, by bending your knees, when doing a *bourré,* in order to avoid tripping.

Swan luck

Long ago, a ballerina we know was dancing the role of the Swan Queen in *Swan Lake* at a gala opening night performance in a major city, in front of thousands of people and the international press. In the *Grand pas de deux* of Act II, she entered the stage doing a beautiful *bourré,* floating gracefully and seemingly effortlessly across the stage — and tripped, landing on her rear end with a thud. This is not the kind of thing you want to have happen to you in a tutu.

But she got up, brushed herself off, and danced the pants off of *Swan Lake* — her best performance to date.

Even swans can make a big splash.

Running fast, feet to the front (pas de couru)

Earlier in this section you experienced the wonderful exhilaration of the wind in your hair as you ran wildly across the stage. Now it's time to step it up a notch. Meet the *pas de couru* ("pah duh koo-RUE" — literally, "step of run") — taking the basic ballet run into extreme territory.

In this step, you follow the same pattern as in the basic run. (See "Walking and running" earlier in this chapter.) The difference is that as you begin the motion, you throw your first leg up into the air in front of you at a 45 degree angle, with great force, lifting your body into the air — so much so that you can touch the floor with three legs in succession before your weight comes tumbling down. The overall effect is overwhelmingly joyous and bubbly — the ballet version of Happy Feet.

When you dance a *pas de couru,* be careful not bang your heels together as you toss the legs in the air. For that matter, be careful not to fall as your heels do a tango in front of you.

Faking It Gracefully (Coupé)

Even with decades of practice and strict technique, any dancer can have a bad night. Sometimes technique is not enough — sometimes you need to fake it.

When the balance of a pirouette is off a hair, when an *arabesque* starts to lean too early, when the music seems too slow and you can no longer hold a position, what do you do? Run offstage? Never. You "*coupé* out."

The *coupé* ("koo-PAY") is a dancer's "Break Glass in Case of Emergency." It's a step to fall back on — literally.

If gravity pulls you in an unchosen and unintended direction, step that way with one foot — as if you meant to all along. Then do a *demi-plié*, and bring the other leg into the *cou-de-pied* position in back (as in Figure 11-6) — or in front. This is *the coupé* — a friend in time of need.

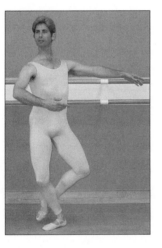

Figure 11-6:
The *coupé*
with the left
foot in back.

This graceful fake step allows you to look really good as you regroup and carry on. So good, in fact, that there isn't a ballet dancer alive who doesn't know this Golden Rule:

𝔚𝔥𝔢𝔫 𝔦𝔫 𝔇𝔬𝔲𝔟𝔱,

ℭ𝔬𝔲𝔭é ℭ𝔲𝔱.

Chapter 12

Ground Control to Ballet Dancer

In This Chapter

▶ Jumping in place and across the floor

▶ *Sautés* aren't just for mushrooms

▶ Doing the Can-Can

▶ Desperately seeking *sissonne*

In this chapter you are going to explore your abilities to defy gravity, and feel airborne, even if it's just for a second or two. Jumping is one of the greatest thrills in ballet.

Before attempting to jump, however, we strongly suggest that you cover some of the earlier chapters in this book. Chapters 6 through 11 help you build the strength and coordination that you need for jumps.

Of course, like everything else in ballet, jumping takes practice. But when you're flying gracefully through the air, you'll be glad you know how to land.

Small Jumps on Two Legs (Petit Allegro)

First things first. *Petit allegro* ("puh-TEET a-LEG-row") refers to the category of small jumps that dancers master before they attempt those breathtaking leaps.

In the simplest jump, called a *sauté* ("soh-TAY"), you stand on both legs, jump — but not too high — and return to both legs. We're pretty sure you can handle this challenge.

In first position

This is the easiest position in which to experience the thrill of momentary weightlessness. You can concentrate on the coordination of bending and straightening your knees, pointing your feet while jumping, and the inevitable landing. Through all this, your arms and legs stay in one position, freeing your mind to focus on the jump.

Start in first position, arms held in low fifth position.

1. **Do a *demi-plié* (as shown in Figure 12-1a).**

2. **Do a *relevé* and return to the *demi-plié*.**

   See Chapter 6 for more information on the *relevé*.

   Repeat this as many times as you want — up, down, up, down. Shake out your legs to rest.

   Now you're ready to jump.

3. **From the *demi-plié*, push as if you are going to do a *relevé* — but this time, let your feet leave the ground. As you do, straighten your knees and point your feet (Figure 12-1b).**

4. **When you land, immediately bend your knees into a *demi-plié* — that's your shock absorber. Now straighten your knees again to finish.**

Congratulations: your first *sauté*.

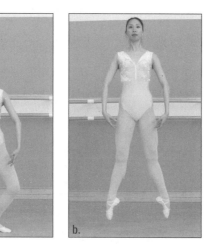

Figure 12-1:
Sauté in first position: First-position *demi-plié* (a); the jump with pointed feet (b).

a.

b.

Try to do this step in a steady rhythm, with one move on each count: (1) *Demi-plié.* (2) Jump. (3) Land/*demi-plié.* (4) Straighten. Then rest for four counts — and do the step again. Try this over and over, always resting for four counts between repetitions.

Ready to increase your endurance? Try this same sequence, but *without* the four-count rest between repetitions.

What's that you say? You want *more?* Try doing three jumps in a row. After you land the third time, straighten your knees and do a *demi-plié,* ready to jump three more times. Then shake out your legs and stretch out those calf muscles.

In fifth position

The *petit allegro* jump in fifth position is known as a *soubresaut* ("soo-bruh-SOH"). The difficulty of this jump lies in trying to keep your legs together in the air.

Stand in fifth position with your right foot in front, your arms down in low fifth position (where they will stay throughout the *soubresaut*).

1. **Do a *demi-plié* in fifth position, right foot in front (Figure 12-2a).**

2. **Jump and cross your feet just a little bit more, so that the toes of one foot are directly in front of the toes of the other (Figure 12-2b).**

   This masochistic little move is known as "fifth position in the air."

   As you jump, make sure to use your abdominal muscles to keep your feet from moving behind you in the air. If your feet get behind you, you could strain your lower back muscles on the landing.

3. **As you prepare to land, open your feet just slightly to land in a fifth position *demi-plié*; then straighten your knees.**

Repeat this jump six more times — then do a *battement tendu* with your right leg to the side, and close it behind your left leg in fifth position. Now you're in position to repeat the entire sequence with your left foot in front.

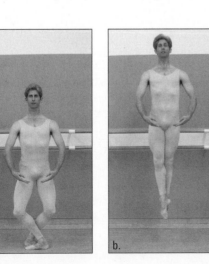

Figure 12-2: *Soubresaut:* Fifth-position *demi-plié* (a); the jump, with feet crossed (b).

a.

b.

After you practice this step a few times, try a little variation on it. Starting with your feet in fifth position with the left foot in front, move diagonally forward ever so slightly with each jump — from D-6 to D-2 — and keep your arms in third *arabesque* arm position. (For more on the *arabesque* arm positions, see Chapter 9. But note: only the *arms* are in *arabesque* here — not the legs.) This is a move from the ballet *Giselle,* and if you feel inspired, we suggest that you try dancing it to the music from the *pas de deux* in Act I of that ballet.

Changing your feet during the jump

Your challenge, if you choose to accept it, is to change the position of your feet as you jump. This move, known in French as a *changement de pieds* ("shahnj-MAHN duh pee-AY"), is the starting point for the beating of your legs — that virtuosic flapping motion that the pros do. There are several ways to change feet while jumping, and this is your chance to practice the first stages of several different jumps.

Fifth to fifth

Start in fifth position with your right foot in front, arms in low fifth position.

1. Do a *demi-plié* (Figure 12-3a).

2. Now jump, opening your legs into first position in the air (Figure 12-3b).

   Remember to straighten your knees and point your feet fully in the air.

3. Land in fifth position with your *left* foot in front, and go into a *demi-plié* (Figure 12-3c).

There you have it — a *changement de pieds.*

George Balanchine, one of the greatest choreographers of the twentieth century, influenced the evolution of this step. He added an additional change of the feet in the air. Today, after opening the legs to first position in the air, you would immediately bring them into "fifth position in the air" before landing. This change caught on in the dance world. We know that's a lot to do in the air — but hey, blame George.

If you want to put a fine point on your *changement de pieds,* you can add a little move of your head. In pure classical jumping technique, your head should always turn *slightly* in the direction of your forward foot. That is, if your right foot is in front, you turn your head *slightly* to the right. When you change feet in the air, your head should follow — subtly, of course, to avoid becoming airsick, which would be decidedly unballetic.

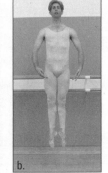

Figure 12-3:
Changement de pieds:
Fifth-
position
demi-plié (a);
the jump (b);
the land-
ing (c).

Fifth to second and back (petit échappé)

In Chapter 8, we tell you about a little move called the *échappé*. The *petit échappé* is nothing more than an *échappé* with two jumps attached.

Start in fifth position with your right foot in front, arms in low fifth position.

1. **Do a *demi-plié* (Figure 12-4a).**

2. **As you jump, immediately open your legs into second position, and bring your arms up through middle fifth to second position (Figure 12-4b).**

3. **Land in a second position and do a *demi-plié* (Figure 12-4c).**

4. **Now push off into another jump, and change your legs into fifth position with your left foot in front, bringing your arms back to low fifth position (Figure 12-4d).**

That was one handsome looking *petit échappé*.

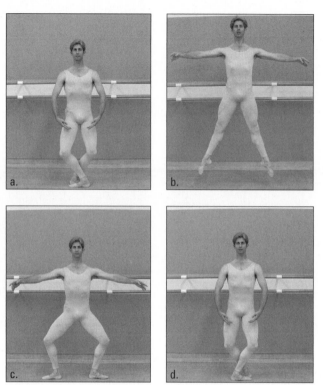

Figure 12-4:
Petit échappé: Fifth-position *demi-plié* (a); opening the legs in the jump (b); the landing (c); the second landing, feet in fifth position (d).

Repeat this move several more times, with a rest in between. When that seems easy, try doing several of them in a row without a rest.

Want more? Try alternating the *petit échappé* with the *changement de pieds:* one *échappé,* one *changement de pieds,* one *échappé,* one *changement de pieds,* and so on. Finally, finish with two *changements de pieds,* then repeat all this to the other side. If you feel like using music for this combination, we suggest the Polonaise from Tchaikovsky's *Swan Lake.*

The grand échappé

In this section on small jumps, we'd like to introduce you to one larger one. The *grand échappé* is just like the *petit échappé* — but bigger.

In performance, this step is usually danced by men, because it has a heavy, macho look. You may need almost twice the force for this jump that you use in the smaller jump. But imagine how much more you can do in the air with that added height.

Don't attempt this jump until you have completely warmed up and have successfully done several small jumps.

Start in fifth position with your right foot in front, arms in low fifth position.

1. **Do a *demi-plié*.**

   Refer to Figure 12-4a.

2. **Now jump — high! Bring your legs into fifth position in the air, and bring your arms to middle fifth position.**

3. **Now open your legs and arms into second position in the air (see Figure 12-5).**

4. **Land and do a *demi-plié* (as in Figure 12-4c). Now push off again with enough force to sustain second position in the air for a moment.**

5. **Close your left foot in front in fifth position in the air; then land and do a *demi-plié*.**

   Refer to Figure 12-4d.

Figure 12-5:
The *grand échappé:* second position in the air.

Small Jumps on One Leg (More Petit Allegro)

After you experience the excitement of jumping from two feet (see the previous section), you may want to attempt to jump from *one* foot. In these jumps there are many ways to land — on the same foot, on the other foot, or on both feet.

Pushing off and landing on one leg (temps levé)

Jumping repeatedly on the same foot (*temps levé* — "tahn luh-VAY") is extremely easy to describe — and extremely challenging to do. The difficulty is not in the technique, but in the strength and endurance that you need to be a human pogo stick.

To start, stand in first position, arms in low fifth position.

1. Do a *demi-plié,* and then jump.

2. Land on your right leg, with your left leg in *cou-de-pied* back position (Figure 12-6a).

3. Keeping your left foot where it is, jump straight up with your right leg, straightening your right knee and pointing your right foot fully (Figure 12-6b).

4. Land on your right leg, and do a *demi-plié* on your right leg.

5. Push off your right leg again, and land back on both feet in first position.

6. Do a *demi-plié* and straighten your knees.

Repeat this step to the other side, with your right leg in the *cou-de-pied* back position — and then repeat both sides again.

Figure 12-6: *Temps levé:* The first landing on the right leg, left leg in back *cou-de-pied* position (a); the second jump (b).

Whenever you jump from one leg and land on one leg, make extra sure that your knee is over the middle of your supporting foot, to protect your knee from twisting.

After you get the feel for this jump, why not try it to music? We suggest using the Scherzo movement from Mendelssohn's *Midsummer Night's Dream.*

In attitude (emboîté)

In this step, the *emboîté* ("ahm-bwah-TAY"), you jump from one leg and land on the other, while keeping your raised leg in *attitude* (for much more on *attitude,* refer to Chapter 8).

The *emboîté* resembles that old French cabaret step, the Can-Can — with the exception that your legs are turned out, and your feet pointed.

Start in fifth position with your right foot in front.

1. **Brush your right foot out to *attitude* front. Bring your arms halfway between low fifth and second position and do a *demi-plié* (Figure 12-7a).**

2. **Push up off your left leg. In the air, switch legs — so that your left leg is now in *attitude,* and your right leg is straight with a pointed foot (Figure 12-7b).**

3. **Keeping the left leg in *attitude,* land on your right leg and do a *demi-plié* (Figure 12-7c).**

Now do another *emboîté* to the other side.

Want to put this step to music? Nothing's more appropriate than the Can-Can from Offenbach's *La vie Parisienne.* Start by taking two counts for each *emboîté,* and when the movement becomes really fluent, do one per count.

Brushing Your Feet into a Jump

When you practice at the barre, one of the first exercises you do is the *battement tendu* — brushing one foot along the floor (see Chapter 6 for more information on the *battement tendu*). You can create an immense amount of force with this brushing motion. Doing a *battement tendu* is like loading a slingshot. If you then release your leg into the air, your body has little choice but to follow. Trust the force, and you too can be a skywalker.

Brushing and joining your feet in the air (pas assemblé)

The *pas assemblé* ("PAH ah-sahm-BLAY") is similar to the *soubresaut* (see "In fifth position," earlier in this chapter) — except that your feet are at a slight angle.

Figure 12-7:
Emboîté:
The
prepara-
tion in
attitude (a);
changing
the legs in
the air (b);
the landing
on the right
leg (c).

Stand in fifth position with your left foot in front, arms in low fourth position with your right arm in front.

1. **Do a *demi-plié*. Now brush your right leg in *dégagé* to the side (Figure 12-8a).**

2. **Jump off your left leg and lift your left leg up to meet your right leg — *assembling* your legs in the air. Your left leg should be crossed in fifth position in back (Figure 12-8b).**

3. **Land in fifth position with your right foot in front, and do a *demi-plié* (Figure 12-8c).**

   This jump should not travel, but simply go straight up and down.

Now try repeating the step to the left.

How about doing this step to music? For a change of pace, try Scott Joplin's *Maple Leaf Rag*.

Figure 12-8:
Pas assemblé: The preparation (a); the jump — some assembly required (b); the landing (c).

Brushing, drawing a 4, and landing on one leg (pas jeté)

In the *pas jeté* ("PAH juh-TAY") you brush one foot, then jump, keeping one leg straight while the other leg bends and touches the straight leg behind the calf. This unique step creates the shape of a "4" in the air — try *that* the next time you have to deliver a financial report.

Start in fifth position with your left foot in front.

1. **Do a *dégagé* with your right leg to the side while you *demi-plié* on your left leg, and bring your arms into low fourth position with your right arm in front (Figure 12-9a).**

2. **Push off your left leg into the jump. As you leave the floor, bring your left leg into the *cou-de-pied* position behind your right leg (Figure 12-9b).**

3. **Maintain this position as you land, and do a *demi-plié* on your right leg, keeping your arms in low fourth position (Figure 12-9c).**

Now try this jump to the left, and change your arms to low fourth position with your left arm in front, as you brush your left leg to the side.

Figure 12-9:
Pas jeté:
The take-
off (a);
the jump,
creating
a number 4
in the air (b);
the land-
ing (c).

Traveling Jumps

All the jumps described so far in this chapter, on one or two legs, have something in common: They go straight up and down. After you feel completely
comfortable with these jumps, you can start to jump in different directions
as well — *traveling,* as they say in the ballet biz.

But be careful. Nearly every professional ballet dancer has sprained an ankle
at least once — usually from landing wrong from a traveling jump. We'll say it
again: Practice only those moves that you're comfortable with.

The cat step (pas de chat)

In Chapter 7 we show you the *pas de cheval*, or horse step. That's not the
only step that takes its inspiration from the animal kingdom.

Cats are admired for two abilities, which far exceed our own: licking themselves and jumping. Though the first of these abilities doesn't come up often
in ballet, the second certainly does. These flexible little animals have inspired

two jumping steps: the cat step (*pas de chat* — "PAH duh SHAH") and the Big Honking Cat Leap (*grand saut de chat* — "GRAHN SOH duh SHAH") — okay, that's not a direct translation. For now, we want to stick to the *pas de chat,* and save the larger leap for Chapter 13.

For this jump, we suggest that you stand way over to the left side of your room, because you're gonna be traveling sideways, to the right.

1. **Stand facing D-1, in fifth position with your left foot in front, arms in low fourth position with your right arm in front.**

2. **Lift your right leg into** *retiré* **as you do a** *demi-plié* **on your left leg (Figure 12-10a).**

3. **Push off your left leg into the air, and bring your left leg into a** *retiré* **position (Figure 12-10b).**

   Notice that you're making a diamond shape with your legs.

4. **Land on your right leg, maintaining your left leg in** *retiré* **(Figure 12-10c), and finish by closing your left leg in front of the right in fifth position (Figure 12-10d) — ready to repeat the whole step.**

You can dance this step over and over in succession, all the way across the dance floor. Try it! For music, we recommend the ballet music from Verdi's opera *I vespri siciliani.*

Traveling to the side and forward (pas de basque)

Like the waltz step that we show you in Chapter 11, this step has three components. What's unique about the *pas de basque* ("PAH duh BAHSK"), though, is that it travels *both* sideways and forward — like a knight in the game of chess. Or like your Uncle Harry last St. Patrick's Day.

Stand facing D-8, in fifth position with your right foot in front, arms in low fifth position.

1. **Do a** *battement tendu* **with your right leg to the front, bringing your arms to middle fifth position (Figure 12-11a).**

2. **Do a** *demi rond de jambe* **(see Chapter 6) with your right leg to the side, and push off your left leg into the air, sideways to the right, with both legs extending into second position in the air. Meanwhile, open your arms to second position (Figure 12-11b).**

   Because you're traveling to the right, you will land on your right leg first.

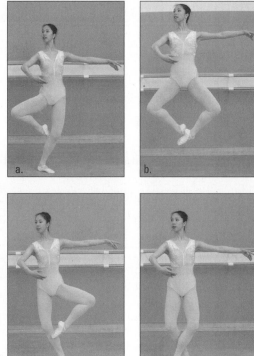

Figure 12-10:
Pas de chat: The take-off (a); the position in the air (b); the landing on the right leg (c); the finish in fifth position (d).

3. **Close your left leg into a first-position *demi-plié* (Figure 12-11c).**

4. **Staying in the *demi-plié*, slide your left leg forward through fourth position, transferring your weight to the left leg and straighten it. Meanwhile, do a *battement tendu* with your right leg to the back, bringing your arms through middle fifth position, and open them into second position (Figure 12-11d).**

5. **To finish, close your right leg behind the left in fifth position, arms lowering to low fifth position (Figure 12-11e).**

   Now you're ready to repeat the *pas de basque* starting with your left leg, traveling to the left and forward.

We're pretty sure Basques never walked this way. But if you'd like to give this step a try to music, try the *Braul* movement from Bela Bartók's *Romanian Dances.*

Figure 12-11:
Pas de basque: the *battement tendu* to the front (a); second position in the air (b); first position following the landing (c); after the slide forward, in *battement tendu* to the back (d); the finishing position (e).

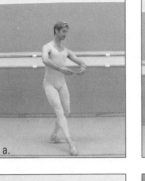

Landing "closed" (sissonne fermée)

The *sissonne* ("see-SONE") is a jump from two legs onto on one leg. In the *sissonne fermée* ("fair-MAY"), or "closed," you land on one leg and then "close" the other into fifth position.

Start facing D-1.

1. **In fifth position with your right foot front, arms in low fourth position with your right arm in front, and do a *demi-plié* (Figure 12-12a).**

2. **Jump from both legs and travel to the right, opening your arms into second position (Figure 12-12b).**

3. **Land on your right leg, with your left leg still extended to the left side, arms in second position (Figure 12-12c).**

4. **Close your left foot in front of the right in fifth position, and bring your left arm in front to low fourth position (Figure 12-12d).**

That's all there is to it!

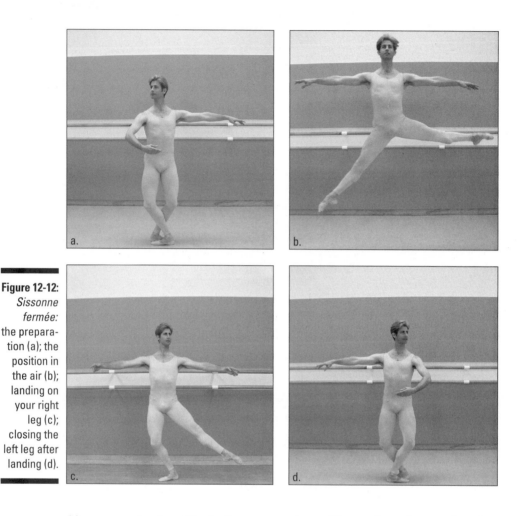

Figure 12-12:
Sissonne fermée: the preparation (a); the position in the air (b); landing on your right leg (c); closing the left leg after landing (d).

After you understand the feeling, you are in position to do a *sissonne fermée* to the left.

Here's an easy way to remember which way to jump in the *sissonne fermée:* Let the *front* foot point the way. For example, if your right foot is in front, jump to the right.

If the spirit moves you, try doing a bunch of *sissonnes* set to music. We suggest the opening of the final movement of Tchaikovsky's Suite for Orchestra no. 3 in G major. This is the music that the choreographer George Balanchine chose for his masterpiece *Theme and Variations.*

Landing "open" on one leg (sissonne ouverte)

The *sissonne ouverte* ("oo-VAYRT"), or "open," is very similar to the *sissonne fermée* — with the exception that after landing, you hold your raised leg "open" for a second before closing it.

Stand facing D-2.

1. **In fifth position with your right foot in front, arms in low fifth position, and do a *demi-plié* (Figure 12-13a).**

2. **Push off both legs, shooting your right leg forward as you lift your left leg back and bring both arms into a first position *arabesque* (Figure 12-13b).**

   You should travel forward on this jump.

3. **Land on your right leg, keeping your left leg behind you, in *arabesque;* keeping your arms in first position *arabesque* (Figure 12-13c).**

The open-legged landing of the *sissonne ouverte* gives you a wealth of options. As you stand there with your legs open, you can say to yourself, "Hmmmmm. What would I like to do now? Close my raised leg into fifth position? Go on to another step? Or hold this open position indefinitely?" This last option is useful if you're onstage and your partner is taking too long in the dressing room.

Say that you decide to close your left leg behind your right in fifth position, with straight knees. (A good choice.) You can now do a *demi-plié* and repeat the *sissonne ouverte* to the right. After several repetitions to the right, do a few to the left.

Make sure to plan which direction you are going to dance the *sissonne* before dancing it. That way, you won't accidentally twist something because of a last-minute decision.

Try the following combination, using the same music that we suggest for the *sissonne fermée*.

1. **Begin facing D-2. Dance four *sissonnes ouvertes* and a *pas de bourré* to the right, ending with your left foot in front.**

2. **Now turn your hips and torso to face D-8, and repeat the sequence to the left.**

As ballet dancers have been saying for centuries: *Vous cuisinez au gaz.* (You're cooking with gas.)

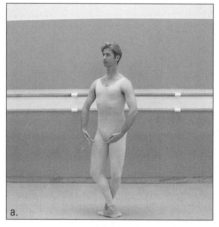

Figure 12-13:
Sissonne ouverte: The starting position (a); the position in the air, in first position *arabesque* (b); the landing (c).

Chapter 13

Getting More Air Time

*I*n this chapter we help you reach your personal best — vertically speaking.

But no need for acrophobia. All the moves in this chapter are built on techniques from earlier in this book. For example, Chapter 12 shows you the two-legged push off, that fluid coordination of bending and strengthening your knees. Now you are going to push off with more strength, attain more height, and beat your legs twice, three times, or even four times in the air. You can also use your old friend, the *grand battement* (Chapter 8) to propel you into the air in a *grand jeté*. And just for fun, you can discover how to do the one-legged jump and landing known as a *cabriole*.

If all this ballet terminology makes your stomach seize up, don't panic. A lot of ballet words sound confusing at first. But we're going to make you a guarantee: If you read on, you'll be able to understand every single term in the previous paragraph — *or you give us $1,000,000!*

Doing the Impossible: Stationary Jumps

Sounds like an oxymoron, doesn't it — a stationary jump? But with these words, we mean that if you were tracked from above by a Global Positioning Satellite, you would not appear to move. You'd jump straight up and down, landing in the same place you started. This seemingly easy jump is very exciting when danced well — especially in repetition.

The simple beat and change (royale)

In the so-called *royale*, you jump straight up in the air and beat your legs together before landing.

In Chapter 12, we introduce you to the *changement de pieds*. In that jump, you start in fifth position, jump straight up, open your feet into first position in the air, and then land in fifth position with the other foot in front, going into a *demi-plié*.

Simple, no? The *royale* simply takes this jump one step further.

1. **Start in fifth position with your right foot in front, and your arms in low fifth position (Figure 13-1a).**

2. **Jump into the air and open your legs into first position (Figure 13-1b).**

3. **Now here's the tricky part.** *While still in the air,* **bring your right foot in front in fifth position (Figure 13-1c) — and then open your legs into first position once again.**

4. **Land with your left foot in front in fifth position, and go into a *demi-plié* (Figure 13-1d).**

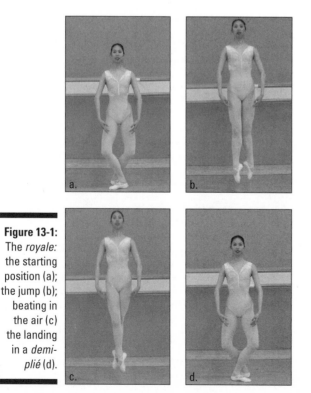

Figure 13-1:
The *royale:*
the starting
position (a);
the jump (b);
beating in
the air (c)
the landing
in a *demi-plié* (d).

With so many moves to do in the air, be careful how you land — in order to avoid giving yourself a *royale* pain.

Beating and landing on one leg, with the other leg back (entrechat trois)

The word *trois* may have tipped off you Francophiles that in this next jump, you beat your legs together *three* times before landing. The *entrechat trois* ("ahn-truh-SHAH TWAH") jump is surprisingly similar to the *royale*. Only the landing is different.

1. **Begin in fifth position with your right foot in front, and your arms in low fifth position (see Figure 13-1a).**

2. **Jump and open your legs into first position in the air (the first beat — Figure 13-1b).**

3. **While in the air, close your right leg in front of your left in fifth position (the second beat — Figure 13-1c).**

4. **Bring your legs into first position in the air (the third beat).**

5. **Now here's the difference: Bring your right leg into *cou-de-pied* in back, land on your left leg, and go into a *demi-plié*. As you land, bring your arms into fourth position with your right arm in front (Figure 13-2).**

Figure 13-2:
The *entrechat trois* landing.

When practicing this jump, as in all other ballet moves, don't forget to try it to the other side, to keep yourself from getting lopsided.

The entrechat quatre

After witnessing the runaway success of the three-beat *entrechat trois* (see the previous section), choreographers wasted no time inventing such still-more-complicated sequels as the *entrechat quatre* (4 beats), *entrechat cinq* (5), *entrechat six* (6), *entrechat sept* (7), *entrechat huit* (8) — the list goes on and on, as do the injuries.

For safety reasons, we recommend that you stay away from most of these steps, unless you happen to live in a zero gravity environment. But if you feel *extraordinarily* comfortable with the *entrechat trois,* then you may want to try the *entrechat quatre.*

This jump begins and ends with your feet in the same position. What goes on in between is a whole different story — and if you blink, you miss it.

Once again, begin in fifth position with your right foot in front, arms in low fifth position. As you jump, open your legs into first position. While in the air, close your right leg in back of your left in fifth position. Now open your legs again into first position; then close your right leg in fifth position in front. (All this transpires in the air.) Finally, land in a *demi-plié.*

There you have it: a four-beat wonder. But you should definitely stop there. Don't try a greater number of beats— leave *that* to the pros.

A jump you shouldn't try — the double tour en l'air

In the *double tour en l'air,* the dancer leaps into the air, spins around twice, and lands gracefully. Don't even think about it. This step may look easy enough — but that's only because world-class ballet dancers are paid to create that illusion.

In reality, a couple of factors make the *double tour* extremely dangerous to do.

✔ It's a jumping turn. As such, it combines two elements, jumping and turning — each of which requires strength, practice, and coordination.

✔ The turn factor itself puts your knees and ankles at risk of twisting.

✔ The jump element requires enormous strength to control the landing. Ballet's worst sprains have resulted from jumping turns gone bad.

So instead of attempting the *double tour,* just sit back and marvel at the sheer beauty of its execution. In classical ballet, you can find it in almost every male solo.

By the way, although all professional ballet dancers practice this step, it is primarily the province of male dancers. For men, the *double tour en l'air* is pretty much a prerequisite for any company contract.

In the coda of the *grand pas de deux* from *The Nutcracker,* the Cavalier often dances up to 20 "stationary" jumps in a row, beating his legs up to 6 times with each jump. But the real test of a male dancer's technique comes in the Bluebird solo from *Sleeping Beauty.* This variation consists of nothing but jumps. It finishes with a series of six consecutive six-beat jumps, followed by a double turn in the air, landing on one knee as only a Bluebird can. Talk about showing off. Sheesh.

Jumping Across the Floor (Grand Allegro)

If you've tried out some of the exercises earlier in this book, you know first-hand the kind of commitment required to coerce a body into an unnatural position. Now imagine hurling that position through the air — and you have some idea of the big jumps known as *grand allegro* ("GRAHND a-LEG-row").

For this book, we show you the big jumps with the lowest level of risk. Be aware, though, that the risk still exists. You have to admit that somewhat superhuman factors are involved when people throw their bodies into the sky, create bizarre shapes, and plummet back down to earth. To ensure a safe landing, always land with your knees directly over your feet, and immediately go into a *demi-plié,* ballet's own patented shock absorber.

Running and jumping forward in the splits (grand jeté)

The *grand jeté* ("GRAHN juh-TAY") is the fastest way to get from one side of the stage to another. This "big *jeté*" resembles the graceful leap of a gazelle, or of those sheep you've counted on sleepless nights.

This step owes its power to the *grand battement* (or high Rockette-style kick) we tell you about in Chapter 8. You kick one leg into the air and follow it with your body — flying up at an angle, splitting your legs at the top, and returning to earth on a downward diagonal, landing on one leg.

We suggest that you read all the way through these instructions before starting. Otherwise, you may find yourself stuck to the ceiling after Step 3.

1. **Start in corner D-6. Point your left leg in front in *battement tendu croisé devant,* with your body and left foot facing toward D-2.**

   You can find out all about the *battement tendu croisé devant,* as well as the system for numbering the directions of the room, in Chapter 9.

2. **With your arms in second position, take two steps forward — left, right. As you begin to step with your left leg again, do a *demi-plié,* and brush your right leg into a *grand battement* to the front. Meanwhile, lower your arms through low fifth position, and lift them into middle fifth position (Figure 13-3a).**

3. **As your right leg lifts, allow it to pull you up into the air, as you push off the ground with your left leg. Lift your left leg into *arabesque* behind you (splitting your legs as widely as possible without changing your religion), and lift your arms into high fourth position with your left arm high (Figure 13-3b).**

   Now for the descent.

4. **Land on your right leg and do a *demi-plié* as you lift your left leg in *arabesque.* Keep your arms in high fourth position (Figure 13-3c).**

5. **Brush your left leg through first position to begin stepping twice, (on your left leg, then right) with your arms in second position, in preparation for the next *grand jeté.***

   The next *grand jeté* begins with a *battement* of your left leg.

That's it: two steps and a *grand jeté.* If this step feels relatively easy, try it in succession, all the way across the floor in a diagonal, until you run out of room. Then come back: Start from D-4 and travel from the right to the left side of the room, ending in D-8.

This very sequence is danced by Prince Siegfried in *Swan Lake,* in his third act coda entrance. He travels in a circle, from D-6 around to the front D-8. (You can read more about this solo, and find out how to do it yourself, in Chapter 15.)

The split jump through a bent knee (grand jeté saut de chat)

If you've mastered the *grand jété* (see the previous section), you won't have any trouble with the *grand saut de chat* ("GRAHN soh-duh-SHAH"). Because it starts with a *bent* knee, the *grand saut de chat* is actually a bit easier than the *jété.* (Just as an *attitude* is less strenuous than an *arabesque.*) You raise one knee and — when it reaches its highest point — you straighten it, propelling you into the air.

Figure 13-3:
The *grand jeté:* takeoff (a); jump (b); and landing (c).

This *jeté* is the jump of choice for most modern dancers. The preparation of the jump enables dancers to reach the same height with less effort and a greater sense of freedom.

By the way, *grand saut de chat* means Large Step of the Cat. Just imagine a cheetah during a full-out run. That's how you want to look, minus the spots.

1. **Go to corner D-6 and face D-2. Point your left foot to *croisé devant*, and lift your arms into second position.**

   See Chapter 9 for more information on the *croisé devant.*

2. **Take two steps, left and right. On the next step of your left leg, do a *demi-plié* and lift your right leg up through *retiré*. Meanwhile, bring your arms through low fifth position and into middle fifth position (Figure 13-4a).**

3. **Straighten your right leg (so that it points diagonally upward) as you push off your left leg. Then straighten your left leg behind you in** *arabesque*.

   Your arms open into third position *arabesque* as you arrive in the full jump position (Figure 13-4b).

4. **Land on your right foot and do a *demi-plié*, as you bring your left leg through first position into a *demi-plié* in fourth position, (this step is known as *failli*) left foot in front. Arms in low fourth position right arm in front (Figure 13-4c).**

But don't stop there. Take two more steps, bringing your arms to second position, and do another *grand saut de chat*, with the right leg. Keep repeating this move all the way across the room. Then do it all to the other side.

Figure 13-4: The *grand saut de chat:* preparation (a); jump (b); and landing — first the right leg, then the left (c).

Care to do the *grand saut de chat* to music? Try the final waltz (the *Finale*) in Act II of Tchaikovsky's *Nutcracker.* Do one *grand saut de chat* after another across the floor — taking two steps before each jump.

What's that you say? You want an *even* more challenging variation on the *grand saut de chat?* Do the same move as before, but this time omit the two steps between the jumps. The result is a series of quick, pure *grands sauts de chat* across the floor.

Traveling beat at 45 degrees front and back (cabriole)

The steps earlier in the chapter let you jump across the floor with the agility of a feline and the abandon of a maniac. The next jump combines those talents by and adding a beat to a traveling jump. In the resulting move — called a *cabriole* ("kah-bree-OLE") — the legs beat together at a 45-degree angle away from the body.

Cabrioles can be danced both to the front and to the back, and even to the sides. They can also be danced quick and small, or slow and high. We suggest that you start quick and small; as you gain confidence, you can make them bigger.

To the front

Here's how to dance the *cabriole* to the front:

1. **Start in corner D-6, facing D-2. Point your left foot to the D-2 corner, with your arms in second position. Step onto your left leg, do a *demi-plié*, and brush your right leg up to a *dégagé* in front. Meanwhile, bring your left arm in front of you in low fourth position (Figure 13-5a).**

   See Chapter 6 for more information on the *dégagé.*

2. **Push off the floor with your left leg, then bring your left leg up to meet your right leg, touching it in fifth position in the air, with your right foot in front (Figure 13-5b).**

3. **Land on your left leg in *demi-plié* and step out onto your right leg, opening your left arm into second position — ready to step on your left leg once again to repeat the *cabriole*.**

Your ending position should look exactly like the one you started in (see Figure 13-5a).

As you've no doubt guessed, this step can be danced all the way across the floor. But for a bit more fun, add a *pas chassé* (see Chapter 11 for a quick review) and one more quick step between the *cabrioles.* This technique also lets you travel farther. After traveling to your right for a few repetitions, you should repeat the step to the left side, to keep balanced.

Figure 13-5:
Cabriole to
the front:
takeoff (a);
beat in
the air (b).

To the back

Now for the *cabriole* to the back.

1. **Start in corner D-4 and face corner D-8. Point your right foot and do a *battement tendu* to the front. Meanwhile, lift your arms into second position.**

2. **Step out on your right foot as you bring your arms into middle fifth position; then step on your left foot and do a *demi-plié* in preparation, as you lift your right leg and your arms into a first position *arabesque* (Figure 13-6a).**

   Now for the hard part.

3. **Push off your left leg and bring your left leg up to meet the right in fifth position with your right foot in back in the air (Figure 13-6b).**

4. **Quickly return your left leg to the ground, safe and sound, in a *demi-plié.* Momentarily keep your right leg in *arabesque* before bringing it down, through first position *demi-plié,* into fourth position *demi-plié* with your right foot in front.**

Your landing position should be just like the one you started in (see Figure 13-6a).

If you're so inclined, try doing a series of *cabrioles,* both front and back, to the music of the Jean de Brienne's variation from Glazunov's ballet *Raymonda.*

Figure 13-6:
Cabriole to the back: the preparation in *arabesque* (a); beating the legs in the air (b).

Too cool for school?

If you're excited by the exercises in this book, and want even more, then you may be in the market for a neighborhood ballet class. But finding the right school is very important.

Your best bet is a school attached to a professional ballet company. If there's one in your town, then call and inquire if they offer adult ballet classes. Chances are, they provide very good training. You may even find that your instructor is your favorite retired dancer!

If there's no professional ballet company around, then look for a teacher who has a Cecchetti or Royal Academy of Dance certification, or who has professional ballet experience. Or try to find a school that has prepared some former students for professional careers. That's especially important if you're seeking a class for your children. The better training they get from the start, the more likely they are to succeed.

In ballet classes, prices vary widely. But $10 per class is about average. Most ballet schools offer "bulk rates" — charging less for doing more. Each class lasts approximately one hour.

If you do decide to begin ballet classes, make the commitment to stick it out for at least six months. Ballet dancers are not trained overnight. In six months you'll see some return on your investment — and you can decide whether to continue.

There's nothing in ballet that can't be made twice as difficult. Such is the nature of the *double cabriole.* In this masochistic little number, you touch your legs together *twice* before returning them to the floor. But don't try it — just watch. Look for the double *cabriole* danced by the principal male dancer in the coda section of Act III of *Swan Lake*, the second act of *Giselle,* and the third act of *Sleeping Beauty* — to name just a few.

The Reverent Stretch and Bow (Reverance)

For centuries, ballet dancers have been doing things that seem downright weird to the rest of the world. No reason to stop now.

At the very end of a classical ballet class, the dancers traditionally express their gratitude and respect for their teacher and rehearsal pianist with a move known as a *reverance.* Even if you're practicing in your living room, for the entertainment of your dog, you can end your workout this way. It's the very least Sparky deserves.

Stand with your feet together, facing D-1, with your arms in first position and feet in sixth position.

Starting with your right foot, take two steps toward the D-2 corner, bringing your arms up through middle fifth position on the first step, and opening to second position on the second step.

Then men close the right leg into a position halfway between first and sixth, keeping the arms in second. Women (now standing on the left leg with the right leg behind) bend the right knee so that the inner parts of the knees are touching, keeping the right foot fully pointed.

For everyone: Lower your head as you lower your arms to your sides.

Men may take a gracious pose, with one hand on the chest as shown in Figure 13-7. Women do a *demi-plié* on the left leg — either a little, or very deeply, depending on the level of gratitude.

Now you know what to do the next time the British Empire grants you a knighthood.

If you can complete the exercises from Chapter 3 through this chapter, you're amazing. That's the entire set of floor warm-ups, barre exercises and center floor work that professional ballet dancers do every day.

Figure 13-7:
The
reverance.

Even if you only decide to *read* these chapters, you're on your way to developing an understanding of how ballet works. Not only does that help you decipher what people are talking about in conversations about dance (and in ballet program booklets), but it also lets you identify steps as you see them in performance.

And when *that* happens, it's a great feeling. Even unfamiliar choreography has familiar elements, making you much more at home — no matter where your feet take you.

Part IV
Living the Ballet Life

The 5th Wave   By Rich Tennant

THE IMPROVISATIONAL WARDROBE BALLET COMPANY PRESENTS: AFTERNOON OF A SHOWER CURTAIN

In this part . . .

When you see or dance ballet, you may be swept away by the passion . . . overcome by the majesty . . . uplifted by the joy of movement to glorious sound. You may completely forget that you're basically watching a bunch of people balancing on shoes made of newspaper, canvas, and acrylic, and using tree sap to not fall over.

This part is about the whole process of creating and performing ballet — from the vision of the choreographer to the performance onstage. It's about all the little steps that join together to create art. It's about time. It's about space. It's about four chapters long.

Chapter 14

Partners Aren't Just for Square Dancing

Sharing the ballet-performing experience with another person is the greatest feeling in the world. And no shared experience is more intense than the teamwork of *partnering*.

In traditional classical partnering technique, the man always supports or lifts the woman, while she performs a lovely move. Yes indeed — chauvinistic. But that's the history of the art form, and we stick with it in this chapter. That's why, throughout this chapter, we describe techniques in terms of a man-woman team.

After you explore the traditional technique, feel free to switch roles at will: Today's choreography calls for all kinds of combinations. And switching now and then gives you a greater understanding of what your partner is going through.

Because the success of each movement depends on the sympathetic collaboration of the man and woman, partnering has often been compared with marriage. So as you begin to explore the *pas de deux* experience, pick a partner you enjoy spending time with.

And above all, remember: Patience is a virtue. A *big, fat, hairy* virtue.

Partnering 101: Finding Her Balance

The first step in any dancing partnership is finding the woman's *balance* while the man holds her. As long as the woman keeps at least one leg on the floor, there is a certain spot where it seems effortless to stay upright. If the man were to let go of her at this moment, the woman would not tip over. This is sometimes called the *sweet spot*.

Finding the sweet spot may be harder than you might think. Often, in the great ballets, the woman balances her entire weight on the ball of one foot, (or, in the case of professional dancers, on the points of her toes), so even the slightest angle can send her headfirst into the orchestra pit.

With both feet on the floor

To follow the tradition of classical ballet, and for reasons of safety, you should begin to find the woman's balance while all feet remain on the ground.

1. **The man stands directly behind the woman, with his feet in a somewhat open first position. The woman stands in fifth position with her right foot front on *demi pointe* (Figure 14-1a).**

   The woman's feet should be approximately 12 inches in front of the man's feet, so that he can hold her waist with slightly bent elbows. Her arms are in low fifth position.

2. **The man takes hold of the woman's waist.**

   He never squeezes with his fingertips, but instead uses his palms and fingers together as a unit to control the weight of the ballerina (see Figure 14-1b).

3. **The man uses his arms to lean the woman forward slightly, then to each side, and finally, back toward him. Meanwhile, the woman holds her position without compromise.**

   The man tries to find that "sweet spot," where there is no resistance in his hands. By feeling how her weight changes as she goes in each direction, the man also develops the ability to compensate when she is off balance.

On one leg

When the man has found the woman's balance on both feet (see the preceding section), he must find her balance while she stands on one leg.

Begin in the position that we describe in "With both feet on the floor."

 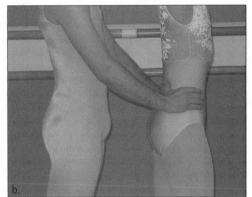

Figure 14-1:
Finding her balance (a); close-up of correct partnering hands (b).

a.   b.

1. **The woman lifts her right leg into *retiré* as she lifts her arms into middle fifth position.**

   To do this, she must transfer the weight of her body slightly to the left, in order to balance over her left foot.

2. **The man finds that "sweet spot" by leaning the woman slightly to the front, sides, and back.**

   The woman should hold the *retiré* position strongly as he does this.

3. **Now the woman closes her right leg into fifth-position *demi pointe* (Chapter 10), and then lowers to *demi-plié*.**

   The man should note all the small transfers of her weight as he assists her into this *demi-plié*.

4. **From here, with the help of her attentive partner, the woman rises directly up to the ball or her left foot, bringing her right foot into *retiré*.**

If you're both still standing, you are well on your way to trying more advanced skills and pirouettes.

Promenading

You may remember this move from junior high school square dancing — America's own ethnic dance. As you may recall (in your traumatized little eighth-grade mind), the *promenade* involved two people walking around each other. Well, in ballet, the woman doesn't have to walk. She simply holds her leg up in a lovely position as the man strolls around her, turning her as he goes. You're about to discover that this is *nowhere near* as easy as it sounds.

While he holds her waist

In this most basic of promenades, the man makes the smallest possible circle around the ballerina while holding on to her waist. The move goes something like this:

1. **The woman stands in a fifth position *relevé* with her right foot in front, arms in low fifth position. The man takes her waist, with his feet together in first position.**

2. **The woman lifts her right leg to *retiré* and lifts her arms into middle fifth position (Figure 14-2a).**

   Now the journey begins.

3. **The man takes a step with his left leg to the left, and then slowly crosses his right leg over his left. He continues, alternating legs, and walks in a circular pattern.**

   As he moves, so does she, rotating ever so slowly on one leg. Throughout the journey, his view of her back never changes.

   For the man: Try to keep your partner balanced over her standing leg; concentrate on keeping her leg perpendicular to the floor. Also, as you complete a circle on the floor, try to maintain the same distance from the woman's standing leg at all times.

4. **After the man completes one full revolution, he allows the weight of the woman's body to shift slightly toward her left heel. This helps her to do a *demi-plié* in fifth position without falling over, closing her right leg in back.**

Now try the mirror image of the entire promenade, going in the other direction, and giving the ballerina the chance to lift her *other* leg.

Promenades can be done to both directions, and the woman can stand on either leg, with the other leg in any number of different positions — *attitude* or *arabesque,* for example. Feel free to mix up your own combinations, drawing creatively from Chapters 9 through 12.

In most classical ballets, the ballerina wears a tutu. This bizarre little dress, which highlights the ballerina's legs to the audience, has one major disadvantage — it completely hides her legs from her partner. The easiest way to find a ballerina's balance is by looking at her legs. But in practice, every male dancer has to partner the ballerina *without* looking at her legs. As a result, he must use his hands, feeling where her balance falls in every step. The more each couple practices partnering by Braille, the better they become. No wonder ballerinas often fall in love with their partners.

Figure 14-2:
The promenade while he holds her waist (a) and while she holds his shoulder (b).

While she holds his shoulder

After you've mastered the preceding promenade, it's time for the man to walk a little farther away from the ballerina and complete larger circles on the floor.

To get ready for this promenade, begin by standing apart, just for a moment.

1. **The man faces D-1, with his feet in first position, and lifts his left arm in front of his shoulder, palm facing upwards. Meanwhile, the woman stands slightly behind and to the left side of the man, about two steps away from his left shoulder.**

2. **Before the man gets too tired of standing with his arm out, the woman steps with her left leg toward his arm. She then steps onto her right foot (on *demi pointe*) and lifts her left leg in *arabesque*, while putting her right hand on his left shoulder, and holding his left hand with her left (Figure 14-2b).**

The woman should not push down on the man's left hand. When the man holds his left hand so far away from the body, there is very little strength in it. The woman should be gentle — using her right arm and her own inner strength for support.

Now for the promenade part.

3. **The man steps forward with his left leg and walks around the ballerina.**

   He makes a circle to the left; his distance from her standing leg should always remain the same.

4. **At the end of the full circle, the woman lowers her *arabesque* leg and does a *demi-plié* in first position, brushing into a fourth position *demi-plié*. She finishes by transferring her weight to her left leg, straightening her left knee, and leaving her right leg turned out and bent behind her.**

   In the final position, her knees are together; her right foot is pointed and resting on the floor.

You see this final position very often in ballet choreography, when dancers stand and wait between complicated steps. Every professional dancer in the English-speaking world knows this position as a "B-plus." We're not sure why — we would have given it at least an A-minus.

While she pirouettes

After you become familiar with the promenade in *retiré* from the preceding sections, you can put a spin on it — literally.

In ballet performance, nearly every *pas de deux* contains at least one supported turn. The variations on this move are legion: Sometimes the man holds the woman's waist while she spins; sometimes the woman just holds onto one of the man's fingers — and then there are *whip turns*. Don't even get us *started* on whip turns. For the purposes of this book, we'll concentrate on the standard supported *pirouette* from fourth position.

1. **The woman stands in a fourth position *demi-plié* with her left foot in front. Her arms are in low fourth position with her right arm forward. Meanwhile, the man stands behind the woman. His weight is on his left leg, which is in *demi-plié,* and his right leg is extended out to the side, leaving room for the woman's leg behind her.**

   His arms are outstretched, and his hands rest oh so tenderly on her waist (Figure 14-3a).

   Why does the man stand with his arms outstretched, rather than closer in to the woman's body? The answer to that question would become painfully clear if you tried the alternative. As the woman turns, her *retiré* knee can easily knock into (and damage) a sensitive part of the male anatomy. At one time or another, every male dancer has been "tagged" by a ballerina's knee during partnered pirouettes.

Figure 14-3:
The
partnered
pirouette.

a.   b.

2. **Now then. The woman performs a pirouette (see Chapter 10), but with one exception: She has to adjust her arms (usually in middle fifth position) for the presence of her illustrious partner. She brings her arms slightly in toward her body so that they cross, with her forearms touching, each hand reaching almost to the opposite elbow, yet keeping the same rounded quality as in middle fifth position.**

When a woman is being partnered, she should never drop her elbows in against her body. There's a reason for this: Her torso doesn't belong to her. It's her partner's domain — and she shouldn't put anything (like arms) in his way.

Try a single pirouette — the woman remembering to spot. When the woman begins to turn, the man brings his right leg into first position. As she turns, the man keeps his left hand steady and makes any balance adjustments with his right hand. He should keep each thumb firmly alongside its corresponding index finger, to ensure that it doesn't get caught in clothing, or anything else, as she turns.

3. **As the woman comes around to the front, the man puts on the brakes, using his hands to stop her. At the finish, the woman opens her arms into second position (refer to Figure 14-3b); then she closes in fifth position with her right foot in back, with a *demi-plié*.**

Well done.

What Did You Have for Dinner Last Night? Lifting Safely

Some of the most beautiful and exciting moments in ballet involve *lifts*. The man hoists or throws his ballerina into the air with the greatest of ease — or so it seems. Lifts often inspire gasps from audiences, who usually clamor for more. As a result, many lifts occur at least twice within a dance.

A huge amount of trust is required on the part of both dancers to ensure the success of any lift. Good timing is also a must — it can mean the difference between beauty in motion and total disaster. Dancers need to practice each lift until it is comfortable and secure. After all, ballet is live theater, and anything can happen once the curtain rises.

In the first act *pas de deux* of the ballet *La fille mal gardée,* there is a spectacular moment where the leading man, Colas, lifts the ballerina, Lise, way over his head. Lise wears a romantic length tutu, which comes down to just below her knees. One night at a major North American ballet company, Lise's tutu became plastered to the sweat on Colas's face, and he could see no longer. With Lise still lifted over his head, Colas walked directly into the orchestra pit. Both dancers were only bruised — but no dancer fails to remember this cautionary tale whenever this ballet is performed.

A simple lift (soubresaut)

The simplest lift is called the *soubresaut* ("soo-bruh-SOH") lift. If you happen to be the person being lifted (in this case, the woman), your part in this lift is the same as the *soubresaut* that we tell you about in Chapter 12.

If you are doing the lifting (the man, in this case), then you must first master the correct lifting posture, in order to protect your back against injury. Here's the golden rule: Never bend forward when lifting. Instead, bend your knees, keep the back upright, and press your abs strongly in, as if trying to press your belly button against your spine.

1. **After assuming the correct lift posture, the man takes hold of the woman's waist (Figure 14-4a).**

   Notice the position of the man's hands: He presses his palms inward, creating the main source of support for his partner.

   For the man: Be especially careful not to dig your thumbs or fingertips into the ballerina's ribs. Save that form of torture for emergencies — say, if you ever find yourself stuck under a horse.

The woman stands in fifth position with her right foot in front, and she clasps her partner's wrists as he takes her waist. Meanwhile, the man stands in a semi turned-out second position *demi-plié*, back straight.

2. **When he is ready to lift, he lets her know. She then does a smooth** *demi-plié* **(Figure 14-4b), rebounding easily into a short lift.**

   As he begins to lift her, she presses down against his wrists, and keeps her shoulders down. The man lifts her partway — not yet extending his elbows completely (Figure 14-4c).

   She presses her legs and feet together as she rises into the air, and prepares her landing gear by releasing her toes just before touching the floor — going into another *demi-plié*.

   In a lift such as this, a man's work is never done. After the woman is up, he must also support her weight all the way down to the floor. In essence, he lifts her both up *and* down.

When both partners have mastered the timing of this joint activity, then they can attempt a full arm extension in the following lift.

Figure 14-4:
A simple
soubre-
saut lift.

Lifting pointers for men and women

To accomplish a successful lift, *both* partners need to be on their toes, figuratively speaking. Men should remember these pointers:

✔ Be patient when trying to find the woman's balance. Look for the elusive "sweet spot," where she is perfectly balanced. Persevere — it is there.

✔ Never drop your ballerina — especially not on purpose. Besides the fact that you can cause long-term injury, it just isn't nice.

✔ Never exclaim how heavy your partner is while lifting her. And try not to grunt.

Here are some steps to success for women:

✔ Trust your partner completely. He will never drop you (as long as he's read this sidebar). And if he does, it's his responsibility to stop your fall with his own body.

✔ Maintain your own positions, but let your partner find the perfect balance; that's his job. Give him the time to fix something if it goes wrong.

Foot-changing lifts (changement)

The next lift involves the *changement de pieds* from Chapter 12. The preparation for this lift is identical to the *soubresaut* lift (see the preceding section). But the lift itself goes higher: The man fully straightens his elbows.

With this added height, the woman has time to change her legs in the air. She changes them immediately; then she holds fifth position in the air until her partner has the good sense to lower her down. She lands in fifth position (now with the other leg in front, of course), and immediately goes into a *demi-plié.*

After both partners are comfortable with the simple *changement,* the woman can try changing her legs in the air *twice.* (This is the same *entrechat quatre* that you can read about in Chapter 13.) That way, when she lands in fifth position, the same foot is in front as when she started. She can even try changing her legs three times (*entrechat six*) or four times (*entrechat huit*). The only limit is the amount of time that the man can hold her up.

For an added challenge, the woman can let go of her partner's wrists, and perform a full *port de bras* while in the air. She starts with her arms in low fifth position during the *demi-plié,* lifts them through middle fifth position as she goes up, brings them to high fifth at the summit of the lift, opens them to second during the descent, and finishes in low fifth on the landing. Look Ma, no hands!

Darting across the floor (sissonne fermée)

Many of the steps that we show you in other chapters throughout this book can be done in the context of a lift, as well. If you're being lifted while you do them, you feel as if you are defying gravity. As a result, you have much more time to accomplish these motions. The feeling is like moving in slow motion on the surface of the moon, but without so many breathing problems.

The *sissonne fermée* is a perfect example. If you do one by yourself (see Chapter 12), you have about one second to go through the entire sequence of motions. But when somebody is lifting you, you can take your time. Here's how it's done:

1. **The woman stands facing D-2, in fifth position with her right foot in front, arms in low fifth position. The man stands facing D-2, in first position, and puts his hands on the woman's waist. They both do a *demi-plié* together (Figure 14-5a).**

2. **The man begins to lift the woman. As she is lifted halfway, she keeps her legs together and brings her arms up into middle fifth position. Meanwhile, the man steps forward with his right leg (Figure 14-5b).**

3. **As the man continues to lift upwards, the woman opens her legs and arms into a first-position *arabesque*. Meanwhile, the man steps across in the same direction with his left leg, just as he reaches the full height of the lift (Figure 14-5c).**

4. **The man carefully lowers the woman back to the floor, and simultaneously steps out with his right leg. The woman lands gently on her right leg in a first position *arabesque demi-plié* (Figure 14-5d). Then the man closes his left leg into first position. Finally, the woman closes her left leg in back of the right in fifth position, and lowers her arms into low fifth position.**

The man must make sure not to bend forward when lifting the woman — to preserve the health of his back. The woman must also make sure that her body is not parallel to his, so that she doesn't accidentally kick him with her back leg.

This stunning lift is hard to beat for beauty. When done right, it really does appear as if the woman is flying through the air.

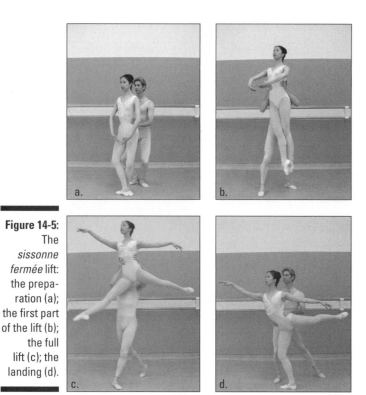

Figure 14-5:
The *sissonne fermée* lift: the preparation (a); the first part of the lift (b); the full lift (c); the landing (d).

Don't Try This at Home! Lifts to Look for in Performance

This chapter introduces you to the various moves that two people can do together onstage. But we've deliberately left out a thing or two, until now.

Here are some lifts *not* to do — not without the supervision of a trained professional and a good insurance policy, anyway. Even the pros ask for help from "spotters" when they first try these new and frightening lifts. Look for these lifts the next time you watch a ballet, and forgo the trip to the hospital.

The *fish dive* gets its name from the position of the ballerina at the end. It's a very popular ending for a *pas de deux*. The ballerina comes running toward her partner (just like a gymnast about to leap off a springboard), takes a flying leap in the air, and lands face down in the arms of her trusted partner (Figure 14-6a).

Figure 14-6: Lifts to avoid (except at the theater) include the fish dive (Evelyn Cisneros and Anthony Randazzo) (a) and the overhead *pressage* (Evelyn Cisneros and Alexander Topicy) (b).

© Marty Sohl (2)

The *shoulder sit* sounds simple enough — the ballerina ends up sitting on her partner's shoulder. But you have to ask yourself — *how did she get up there?* Usually, the ballerina runs and jumps, turns in the air, and aims her gluteus maximus in the general direction of her long-suffering partner's waiting shoulder. Alternately, the man can lift her, then quickly get his hands out of the way as she lands on his shoulder. This lift takes hours and hours of practice, before the ballerina can consistently land safely without slipping off the back of his shoulder and onto the floor. Whoops.

Finally, we offer a view of the *overhead pressage* (Figure 14-6b). For the man, this move probably requires more upper body strength than any other. Not only must he hold his partner in the air for several moments, but he must often carry her around the stage before placing her lovingly back on the floor. "How many ballerinas can you bench?" is a question often overheard in the ballet locker room.

Chapter 15

Exploring Choreography

*W*hy do some ballets send you into fits of ecstasy, while others leave you snoring in your seat? What separates the great ballets from the not-so-great?

Well, assuming that the dancers onstage are competent, the most important difference is in the *choreography*. Choreography is the art of designing a dance — putting old steps together, or inventing new ones, in order to create a visual experience, express an emotion, or tell a story.

The word *choreography* comes from the Greeks roots *choreo* (dance) and *graph* (write). "Those who can't dance, dance-write," ballerinas are fond of saying. (Okay, not really. Most of the great choreographers are or were wonderful dancers themselves.)

In ballet, choreographers have the power to direct your eye any way they choose. Done right, choreography can be a constant source of interest, awe, and delight. In this chapter you can discover how choreography works — and how to try your hand at it yourself.

Classical Ballet Constants

As varied as the great ballets can be, they all have a few things in common. These constants can be a great help to you when you're trying to decipher their choreography — or create some of your own.

First, the ballet technique and vocabulary that you encounter throughout this book shows up in *every* classical ballet. As you may remember, dancers do all their moves with their hip joints turned out. Whenever a foot is lifted off the ground, that foot is always pointed. Every move begins and ends in one of the major positions of the legs and arms. And there's not a single classical ballet out there that isn't simply brimming with *battements tendus, arabesques, attitudes, dégagés, soutenus, pirouettes, double tours, cabrioles, fouettés,* and everything else in Chapters 6 through 14. This is simply the language of classical ballet — just as English is the language of Shakespeare.

Second, classical ballets usually have at least a hint of a story line. (For example, a pivotal moment from *Giselle* is depicted in Figure 15-1; here the title character protects her beloved from the curse of dancing till death, as any good woman would.) But choreographers hardly ever let the story get in the way of the fun. Act II of *La Bayadère*, for example, takes place entirely in one guy's dream — just so 32 females, identically clad in white, can glide gracefully down a zigzag ramp, dancing slow-motion *arabesques* and *tendus effacés* in complete unison as they go. (More on that later in this chapter.) The point of the story line is to create a world in which the choreographer's vision can flower.

Figure 15-1:
Lucia
Lacarra
and Yuri
Possokhov
in *Giselle*.

© Lloyd Englert

Third, it's fair to say that nearly every traditional classical ballet treats its men as brilliant, bounding, acrobatic Olympic athletes, and its women as lighter-than-air visions of feminine perfection. Chauvinistic, yes — but classical choreography nearly always reflects this prejudice, and any ballet that doesn't is seen as a wry commentary on tradition.

Fourth, there is *always* a principal couple — one most awesome ballerina, and her equally inspiring Cavalier. Story-wise, the goal of these two is to live happily ever after, or die trying, Dance-wise, the point is to highlight those gorgeous partnering moves you can find out about in Chapter 14.

Finally, nearly all classical ballets contain certain traditionally structured sequences to make those moves possible. (See Chapter 17 to find out about the *grand pas de deux* and its components, the *adagio,* the male and female variations, and the coda.) When one of these numbers begins, you can sit up and say, "Aha! Here it is. This is where I'm supposed to be impressed."

Applaud Aurora from *Sleeping Beauty* as she balances forever *en pointe* in *attitude;* bravo to that Bluebird from the same ballet as he jumps and beats his legs until he's ready to regurgitate for his young — and what about that nasty Black Swan from *Swan Lake,* and her 32 vengeful *fouettés?* These are masterful moments of the classics.

Applying the Steps to the Great Choreography

Believe it or not, all ballet dancers, from Petipa to you, started each day with the same basic steps, in the same order, at the barre and in center floor. Now, like Baryshnikov, you are ready to try putting them together in some of the greatest choreography ever created.

Oh, sure, we'll stick with some of the less involved combinations. But these are real steps, from the real ballets. So read on — and be assured that your commitment has not been in vain.

Swan Lake: Black Swan pas de deux and coda

When it comes to classical ballet, the *coda* is showoff time. Here the dancers create fireworks for your pleasure: Men beat their legs with each jump; women do all those *fouettés;* everyone jumps as high as possible, ending with spectacular turns and poses.

One of the exciting elements of any coda is the element of *repetition*. For example, the coda of the *Black Swan pas de deux* from *Swan Lake* begins with the *grand jeté* (see Chapter 13), danced repetitively in a circle and at full height, like a gazelle bounding around the stage. So dust off your Swan Lake recording and put on the Coda from Act III.

Start in the D-6 corner, standing on your left leg, with your right leg extended in front of you in a *battement tendu* to the front, arms in second position. (If you were really dancing this ballet, you'd start offstage in the wings.) Ready? Take two large, aggressive steps on your right and left legs, building up momentum.

Now bring your right leg into the air in a *grand battement* as you bring your arms in through middle fifth position (Figure 15-2a). Pushing off with your left leg, allow the *grand battement* to lift you into the air. Split your legs as far apart as they will go without tearing anything, and lift your arms into high fourth position with the left arm up (Figure 15-2b). If you were actually dancing this ballet in performance, the audience's first impression of you would be in midair, bounding onto the stage like this.

Figure 15-2:
The Black
Swan
grand jeté

a.

b.

Land on your right leg. Now, alternating legs, repeat the same steps: two giant steps leading into a *grand jeté* with the left leg. And so on.

When you reach the corner, continue to alternate and travel around in a circle to the left. Keep going until you run out of gas, oxygen, or room; but you are not likely to run out of music.

You have just completed your first coda from your first classical ballet. Bravo!

Giselle: The Wili Chug

In the second act of the ballet *Giselle,* the spooky Wilis (the ghosts of broken-hearted virgins pictured in Figure 15-1) are cursed to haunt the men who dare venture into their forest. Perhaps as part of their curse, the Wilis are required to perform a daunting physical task: with one leg behind them in arabesque, they chug, in perfect rhythm and exquisite unison, from one side of the stage to the other.

As you might expect, this move in such lengthy repetition, with one leg lifted back, gives your *gluteus maximus* something to scream about. And speaking of curses, you may well hear some if you sit close enough to the stage during a performance of *Giselle.*

Start as far to the D-7 wall as possible. Stand on your left leg, with the right leg in B-plus position (see the description of the *promenade* in Chapter 14 for a review of this pose), and your arms in low fifth position. Slide out with your right leg through fourth position *demi-plié,* facing D-3. Lift your left leg behind you and your arms into a first position *arabesque* in the Romantic style, as shown in Figure 15-3a.

Now for the "chug": Move forward about 6 inches all at once. Don't try to put any bounce in your step — imagine that you are balancing a glass of water on your head. Now continue hopping, until you arrive at the opposite wall. You are now free to bring your left leg down into the B-plus position. Cross your arms to relax them (Figure 15-3b).

Figure 15-3:
Doing the
Wili Chug
from *Giselle.*

Now you get to do something that even the Wilis don't — repeat the move to the other side — if for no other reason than to even out those glutes. There's nothing more dangerous than a lopsided Wili.

La Bayadère: Entrance of the Shades

The Entrance of the Shades from the dream sequence in *La Bayadère* is one of the most challenging of all for the women of the *corps de ballet*. Even though their entrance technically consists of only two moves, the sequence is beautifully hypnotic — not least because these two steps are repeated for up to five minutes at a stretch, depending on how slowly the conductor takes the music.

Picture this: a high ramp, extending from one side of the stage to the other, then back again, and finally reaching the floor on the third pass. Onto the top of this ramp, one at a time, enter the Shades — dreamlike white ghostly figures not unlike Wilis (see the preceding section). As each enters, the entire group performs an extreme *arabesque,* lifting the leg so high that the body is forced to bend forward at the hip — followed by one step back to a *battement tendu* to the front. They repeat this combination over and over, each time moving forward ever so slightly.

If this section is danced well, the audience bursts into applause out of sheer appreciation for the beauty and control that these women display. Then the Shades go on to do a complicated *adagio* section, lifting their legs in unison. Yikes.

It is your turn to shine in the Shade. Start at the D-7 wall, standing on your left leg, with your right leg behind you in the B-plus position, arms in low fifth position. Take two steps toward D-3: right, left. Then, with the third step, slide your right leg into *demi-plié.* Lean slightly forward and lift your left leg high behind you in *arabesque.* Bring the arms to an exaggerated first position (Figure 15-4a).

After you reach your deepest *arabesque,* bring your left leg down into fourth position behind the right in a *demi-plié,* and bring the arms into middle fifth position. Next, transfer your weight back onto your left leg, do a *battement tendu* with the right in *effacé devant* (see Chapter 9), and bring your arms into the position shown in Figure 15-4b. You are now ready to repeat the two steps into another *arabesque.* And so on, and so on, and so on.

Figure 15-4:
The Entrance of the Shades from *La Bayadère.*

Dancing with a Modern Flair

After you experience some of the classical ballet positions in this book, you can play with 'em a bit. In other words, let your technique *evolve,* just as the art form has evolved over the years.

But that doesn't mean that you should distort the steps completely. Instead, experiment with slight alterations. By making one simple change, you can sometimes make a step look completely different. For example, once you're in a pose, you may choose to move the balance slightly off to one side — or stick out your hips to alter the look.

Figure 15-5a shows a very classical *développé à la seconde* from *Swan Lake.* Note the tutu, the arms in perfect high fourth position, even the composure of the face — everything about this pose just shouts "classical".

Now look what can happen when an old step goes "modern." Figure 15-5b, from William Forsythe's *The Vertiginous Thrill of Exactitude,* shows the same *développé à la seconde* — but this time, the weight of the body is far off the ball of the left foot, the body is leaning off to the left, to achieve a higher leg position, and the arm position is exaggerated as well. This pose is simply a modern form of an old classic.

Now it's time to go contemporary — combining elements from the classical and the modern. Figure 15-5c, from Val Caniparoli's *Lambarena,*. is the same basic position: the legs are still turned out, feet are pointed, body is upright, and the dancer is *en pointe.* But the position of the arms and head are very unconventional. The ethnic costume also gives the impression that the choreographer is exploring a unique style.

Figure 15-5:
The *développé à la seconde* in three different versions: classical (Evelyn Cisneros), modern (Parrish Maynard), and contemporary (Evelyn Cisneros).

© Lloyd Englert/© Marty Sohl/© Lloyd Englert

Basic Guidelines of Choreography

When you decide to choreograph your own dances, using variations on the moves in this book, you have complete freedom of expression. And that's as it should be.

But artists of all kinds have found that they flourish best when they voluntarily submit to certain limitations. The series of ballet gestures, for example, is a "limitation" that somehow sets the imaginations of the great ballet choreographers free.

The ideas in the following sections, culled from centuries of great choreography, give you a framework for your freedom, a vehicle for your own artistic vision. All forms of expression are valid — but these ideas can help you get started successfully.

Finding your inspiration — music or theme

What makes a choreographer want to create a particular dance in the first place? Most choreographers say that they are usually inspired by one of two things: the music or the theme.

When you hear a certain piece of music, are you swept away in an ecstatic whirlwind? Do colors and shapes and movements immediately suggest themselves to you? Are you lost in time and space? If so, we know a good doctor who can help. But failing that, the piece sounds like a good candidate for choreography.

If there's one basic rule of choreography, it's this: The gestures should somehow reflect the music. What sets the successful choreographers apart is that their gestures embody the music beautifully, as if each musical phrase had been written just for them.

An example most people can visualize is the dance of the Sugar Plum Fairy from *The Nutcracker*. As the celesta begins to play its tinkly tones, the ballerina dances nimble, delicate little steps, seeming to flit across the stage. Although different choreographers may have set different steps to this music over the years, nearly all of them have tried to create something appropriately delicate.

You might like to know that in the professional world, every single minute of dance onstage is the result of approximately two hours of choreography and rehearsal. But hey, don't let that stop you.

Another form of inspiration is the need to tell a story. Storytelling is one of our oldest pastimes, and dance has always come in handy for that purpose. Does a certain story call out to you, just *needing* to be expressed somehow? Then why not make that the basis for a dance?

When telling a story in dance, first decide whether you want to create a simple narrative from beginning to end, or something more complex.

Say, for example, that your theme is the story of Hansel and Gretel. Just think of all the ways you could tell that story. You could opt for the linear approach, showing Hansel and Gretel wandering through the forest, dropping breadcrumbs, getting lost, happening upon a candy house, and getting fattened up. Or you could start at the end of the story, with the kids leaping breathlessly onstage to tell you what they just experienced.

Or, your dance could simply focus on character at one point in a story. How does the wicked witch feel when the kids bake her alive? Maybe she could do an interpretive dance to let us know. This expression of one instant in time, telescoped out to show the emotional weight it contains, is the basis for 99 percent of all poems, operatic arias, and popular songs — and it works for dance as well.

Knowing how you want the piece to look

Great choreographers almost always talk about their "vision" of their work. Choreographers are proud of their visions and will tell you about them until you ask them to stop.

Quite literally, choreographers create an image of the dance in their minds before attacking the nitty-gritty of the choreography. Whether or not they envision the actual steps at first, they can imagine the overall "look" of the piece. From there, they can begin to choose the steps that best fit that vision.

The vision can include costumes, set, and lighting designs — although in the professional world, special designers are hired to flesh out the details of this portion of the vision.

Working from this internal vision, choreographers then write down their ideas using *dance notation* — or simply dance it themselves on videotape.

Developing a vocabulary for the dance

As you can see by referring to Figure 15-5, the same basic step can be danced in many different ways. So when you choreograph a piece, you have a nearly infinite number of steps to choose from. The *vocabulary* of the dance refers to the particular gestures and movements that you *choose* to use — the ones that seem to reflect your own character and make up your personal style.

The order in which you put the steps is important, too. The steps should seem to flow from one to the next. For example, an *arabesque* looks good when followed by a *failli*. But it looks bad followed by a backflip. You just feel these things.

After you begin to experiment with various sequences, you're likely to find some that feel just right for you. When that happens, you can repeat those sequences again and again — thereby creating a vocabulary that you can call your own. George Balanchine, for example, was famous for following a *sauté* in *arabesque* with a *jeté*. That was his trademark — just as Bob Fosse made a name for himself with bowler hats and turned-in legs (also known as pigeon toes — think *Cabaret*).

Using your full space

Here's another useful rule for choreographing your own work: Use the full amount of space that's available. By the end of the dance, every area of the stage should have been stepped on at least once.

You should even consider using non traditional areas — where you'd never think of dancing. Staircases, hallways, railings, and other levels of flooring come to mind. (Or puddles — as Gene Kelly discovered in *Singin' in the Rain*.) The unexpected is often where the most inspiration lies.

When covering your space, we suggest varying the shape of your dance. If you begin with a move on a diagonal; then try adding a circular pattern later. Or vice versa. Stretch your imagination — and keep your audience on their toes.

Ending as you began

One way to make a dance feel artistically whole is to "come full circle." And one way to accomplish this is by starting and ending the dance with the very same pose.

An even more advanced version of this technique is to end in a slightly "evolved" version of the starting position. For example, if the dance is a duet, consider switching the parts at the end, so that the woman ends up as the man began, and vice versa.

This technique gives the dance a feeling of completion, and it can sometimes be quite poignant and moving. Who knows — you may have your audience in tears. In a good way.

Getting Inspired by Others

Every field has its heroes. There's not a golfer alive today who hasn't been influenced by Tiger Woods; not a filmmaker who hasn't been influenced by Steven Spielberg; not a governor who hasn't been influenced by Jesse Ventura.

So it is with ballet. All great choreographers go through a phase where they choreograph a lot like their idols or mentors. And that's fine. There's no better way to learn than by example. Eventually, the great choreographers find their own voice, and then *they* serve as examples.

It would be impossible to name all the great choreographers of the past century. But here are a few whose work you may want to emulate at first. We suggest you seek out performances of their work, either live or on videotape. They'll keep you inspired for at least a few years.

George Balanchine

If you think of George Balanchine (1904–1983) as a brick dropped in a pond, his ripples touched most everyone who followed him, including his disciple, Jerome Robbins (of *West Side Story* fame).

George Balanchine was born in the Soviet Union and moved to Europe, then to the United States in 1933, where he founded what is now the New York City Ballet. Mr. B., as some of his dancers affectionately called him, could be considered the Beethoven of the dance world.

He set the evolution of ballet on a completely new path. In his ballet classes, he experimented with classical technique, always searching for new possibilities. He asked his dancers to use their hips differently than the classical structure ever used them. He became fascinated with the speed of dance, pointe work, and very thin female dancers. (He married about half a dozen of 'em — but that's another story.)

Balanchine was sublimely musical. Many of his ballets *are* music in motion. When you watch them, you feel as if you are looking into the mechanics of music itself. After the better part of a century, his works still feel fresh, and those who were fortunate enough to dance his ballets feel blessed by his talent.

Balanchine, by the way, was intensely aware of what made ballet great. He wrote a book praising the work of the great choreographers, including himself: *101 Stories of the Great Ballets.* He would have called it *Ballet For Dummies* if he had thought about it.

Jiri Kylian

Jiri Kylian (born in 1947), founding Artistic Director of the Nederlands Dans Theatre (Holland), is one of the most innovative choreographers today. Trained in classical ballet, Kylian has found his choreographic voice in an absolute marriage of modern dance with traditional technique. Exploring the possibilities of strength, force, and momentum, he has created lifts and partnering never before seen. Considering the number of years ballet has been around, that is truly an enormous accomplishment.

From a dancer's perspective, Kylian's choreography is very demanding. He integrates the use of the entire body into a technique — multiplying the opportunities for injury and other mishaps. For the audience, his ballets can be demanding as well: He gives you a lot to watch at once. But for dancers and audience alike, Kylian's work is supremely rewarding — especially when it goes well.

William Forsythe

The American choreographer William Forsythe (born in 1949) trained in both ballet and modern technique — and it shows. He first made a name for himself with off-balance steps and active use of his dancers' hips. He was one of the first choreographers to incorporate speaking, singing, and yelling — and oh yeah, dancing — into his vocabulary.

If experimental theater met ballet, it might look something like the work of Billy Forsythe. He's not for everyone, perhaps, but he's definitely for us.

Mark Morris

Born in the United States in 1956, Mark Morris was trained in music, ballet, ethnic dance, and modern dance. He made his international reputation in Europe; he is now Artistic Director of Mark Morris Dance Group in New York.

Morris adds natural or organic movements to his ballet combinations, lending a look of freedom to his dances. He uses men and women in nontraditional ways, and each dance is sublimely crafted.

Mark Morris was strongly influenced by Balanchine, and his dances are as musically descriptive as those of his predecessor. He seems to use certain dancers to represent certain musical instruments. The result is *visual music* — full of beauty, and full of fun (Figure 15-6).

© Lloyd Englert

As you explore the world of ballet, we invite you to discover your own favorite influences. Who knows — maybe our next book will be about you.

Chapter 16

What the Heck Are They Saying? The Art of Ballet Mime

*W*hen you get right down to it, ballet is a very bizarre art form. Here you have these dancers, who are human beings just like you and me, with mouths and lips and everything — and yet they *never speak*.

Sure, many different disciplines impose restrictions of one kind or another. Haiku poems use only three lines. Pointillist paintings use nothing but dots. Tai chi uses only smooth gestures. And in soccer, you can't use your hands.

But here's the difference between soccer and ballet. In soccer, you have to get the ball into the goal. In ballet, you have to communicate, somehow, that Giselle has a congenital heart condition, and although she loves to dance, if she exerts herself excessively, she will die and spend eternity as a ghost, in a forest haunted by the spirits of unmarried virgins.

Try doing *that* with two feet and a ball.

Telling a Story with Gestures

Enter *ballet mime* — the strangest thing to hit the ballet stage since *pointe* shoes. Ballet mime is a set of conventional gestures that can be used for all occasions. (All ballet occasions, that is.) And that's nothing new — humans have codified their gestures since the beginning of recorded time.

The making of mime

In ancient times, many religious ceremonies included specific mime movements among their rituals. From these ceremonies, actors began to incorporate stock mime gestures into their performances. It was in Ancient Greece, during a performance of a play by Aeschylus, that the legendary dancer Telestes performed the first recorded mime in 467 B.C. Greek troupes brought the art form to Ancient Rome, where it separated from the spoken word completely, and *pantomime* was born. In the fifth century the poet Nonns wrote of a dancer "with nods his only words, a hand his mouth, and fingers for a voice."

From there, you see, it's just a short step to Marcel Marceau.

Somewhere on the comprehensibility spectrum between American Sign Language and semaphore, ballet mime has baffled balletgoers worldwide. More than a few dazed spectators have been known to ask, "What the heck are they saying?"

Although it looks exceedingly weird to the uninitiated, ballet mime is surprisingly easy to pick up on. Once mastered, this ingenious device allows balletgoers to comprehend even the most convoluted plot twists during the course of an evening-length ballet. Hence, stories of Shakespearean complexity — like *Romeo and Juliet* or *Othello* — can be translated into gestures and understood wordlessly onstage.

We know that most ballet technique is very complex. But finally, here's an aspect of the art form that doesn't take years of practice to perfect. After reading this chapter, you will not only understand what the heck the ballet dancers are "saying," but you'll also be able to say it yourself.

Not to mention the incredible advantage you'll have at your next game of Charades.

Understanding the Basic Principles of Ballet Mime

Just like everything else in ballet, mime has rules. No matter where you see a ballet performance, most likely the dancers are abiding by these rules.

First and foremost is the concept of speed — or lack of speed. Ballet mime must be performed very slowly and clearly. Most people in the audience (except for the balletomanes who have every step memorized) don't know what to expect. You must allow the audience the time to see and decipher your movements. For that reason, most ballet mime is choreographed very specifically to the music. Each gesture happens deliberately, on a particular beat.

Coupled with speed is the concept of size. Most ballet mime movements are big and broad so that the spectators can make out the gestures. Don't forget — a lot of your audience is a hundred feet away.

The number of mime gestures that can occur in a row is almost unlimited. But the more convoluted the plot, the more important it is to keep the action moving. So while you mime your story, you can be dancing a sequence of steps as well. Even in the simplest of mime gestures, dancers often stick out a pointed foot, or go up into a lovely *arabesque*.

One of the most moving moments in ballet mime comes from *Swan Lake,* when Prince Siegfried swears eternal fidelity to Odette, the lovely yet cursed Swan Queen. As he proclaims his love (using a gesture that you can find in this chapter), he steps up on his tippy-toes in fifth position — as if he's finding the highest possible point from which to assert his undying affection. Talk about romantic!

Mastering the Most Common Gestures

Armed with the gestures in this chapter, you should be able to understand the story of nearly *any* classical ballet. And more than that, you will soon be able to use ballet mime to tell your own story. So put that guitar away.

The personal pronouns

These gestures allow you to turn any character onstage into the subject of a silent sentence:

- **I (me, my):** Simply gesture to yourself with a relaxed hand. It's not polite to point — except with your foot.
- **You (your):** Gesture to the other person with a relaxed hand.
- **Y'all:** Make a broad gesture, encompassing the entire group. Especially good for ballets set in the South.

✔ **We (us, our):** Gesture to yourself, then to the other person or people, as if to say "Me, you."

✔ **He/she/it/they:** Look at the person you are addressing. Then gesture to the appropriate third person (singular or plural) you want to describe.

"Yes" and "No"

Just as you might expect, nod your head up and down for "yes," and shake it from side to side for "no." But in ballet, these gestures are much slower and more fluid than in real life, and therefore they take on a dramatic significance.

By the way, for an even *stronger* "no," cross your lower arms in front of you, palms down, and open them outward, as if clearing off a table.

Hungry

Place one hand over your stomach, and rub it in a circular motion — clockwise or counterclockwise.

To mime the question "Are you hungry?" simply do the gestures for these words in sequence: "You hungry?" The answer: "Yes."

Sleeping

Lift your arms to one side at shoulder height, hands to elbows. Then lower your head to rest on your arms, face forward, tilted 90 degrees, with lowered eyes (Figure 16-1).

This gesture is not meant to simulate sleep, but rather to talk about sleep — as in the following two examples:

✔ **"I'm sleepy":** Put the gestures for these three words together: "Me slept no."

✔ **"I don't want to sleep":** In this case, the first two gestures are the same as "I'm sleepy." But for the final gesture, use one arm to push away and off to the side, with an air of dismissal. The combined effect is "Me sleep? Fuhgeddaboudit."

Figure 16-1:
The gesture
for sleeping.

"Come here"

Extend your hand, palm up, to the person you want to beckon. Now bend your elbow, bringing your palm back toward your chest in a semicircular motion. If you *really* want them to come, continue the circle, bringing your hand down and out, and repeat this gesture at least once more.

If you're dealing with a group, elevate the entire gesture so that it's visible to everyone. At its height, your arm reaches an open high fifth position.

Depending on your facial expression, its uses are many and varied — from "Gather round and hear what I have to say," to "Come here, sexy!"

Beautiful

In ballet, the most chivalrous and chauvinistic of arts, the gesture for *beautiful* refers only to women. However, it can be *performed* by both men and women.

Start by holding your right hand over to the left side of your face — or vice versa. Then, with a swooping action, make a circle around your face, going down and around in at least one circle, with your head held still and your face forward (Figure 16-2a). As if to say, "Now *that's* one good-looking head."

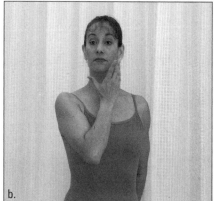

Figure 16-2:
The gestures that mean beautiful (a), handsome (b), and strong (c).

Handsome

In the interest of equal time for guys, the original ballet mimers invented a gesture for *handsome* as well. Both men and women can do the move, but it can only refer to a man. (With the possible exception of leotards, there is no such thing as unisex in ballet.)

Face forward and bring one hand in front of your face at forehead level, palm inward, fingers extended but relaxed — as if your hand were a mirror. Now draw your hand down slowly to the bottom of your chin, and pause for a moment (see Figure 16-2b). You handsome devil!

Strong

If you've ever been a weight lifter, you have an advantage here.

Stand facing a corner of the room or stage, with your arms at your sides. Now lift both arms together, bringing them halfway between your front and sides. When your elbows reach shoulder height, begin to bend them. As you keep raising your lower arms, make your hands into fists, with firm biceps — Schwarzenegger-style (refer to Figure 16-2c). Anyone can do this gesture — but only when talking about men.

Rich

Hold out one hand, palm cupped upwards, as if holding a pile of coins. With the other hand, slowly pretend to extract several coins, and wriggle your fingers as if dropping them back into your hand. Repeat this action three times. That's what Franz does in the ballet *Coppélia*, while describing the rich Bürgermeister.

Love

Because nearly every story ballet is about love, this is one of the most common mime gestures for both men and women. Today's men usually use a very simple gesture — crossing their hands over their heart (Figure 16-3a).

But for both men and women, there's a more complex version too. Start with your hands at your sides. Now, keeping your elbows down, bring up your hands and hold them under your heart, palms up, one cupped under the other. At the same time, lift your torso ever so slightly, as if inhaling.

Despite its striking similarity to a bra commercial, this is one of the more common gestures in ballet.

Swearing eternal fidelity

Oh, there is nothing more valiant than a ballet hero — whether man, woman, or elf — swearing eternal allegiance to one person, cause, or thing.

Step forward, with both feet facing front. Keep your left hand at your side. Lift one arm, elbow slightly bent, till it is overhead in front of you, with your index and middle fingers held together, like a Boy Scout with a missing finger.

If you want, you can make this gesture even more powerful by placing your other hand over your heart (as in Figure 16-3b). Now you're swearing fidelity *and* love — quite a combination.

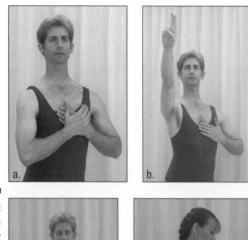

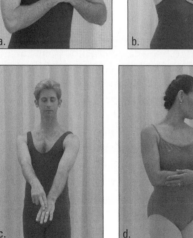

Figure 16-3: The gestures for love (a), swearing eternal fidelity (with love) (b), marriage (c), and baby (d).

TIP

As you make this gesture, look straight out to the audience, with an expression of Deepest Affection, Solemn Allegiance, Temporarily Hurt Pride at Being Underestimated, or Dedication to a Lofty Goal — preferably all at once.

Marriage

Both men and women can do this one. First, hold your left hand out in front of you at about hip height, palm down, with your fingers slightly spread. Now, extend the index and middle fingers of your *right* hand, and lift your right hand higher than the left. Finally, place those two right fingers on your left ring finger, as if to point to a wedding ring (Figure 16-3c).

BALLET BACKSTAGE

Ever wonder why ballet dancers often point with *two* fingers rather than one? It's because of the distance from the audience. From the second balcony, two fingers are twice as easy to see.

By the way, this gesture works even if there *is* no wedding ring — it's the *concept* of marriage we're dealing with here.

Baby

Hold both arms in front of you, hands to elbows, as if cradling a baby in your arms. Looking down, gently rock the imaginary child from side to side (refer to Figure 16-3d).

This gesture is not meant to depict an actual baby, but just to "talk" about a baby. In a classical ballet, if you want to depict an *actual* baby, you use a bunch of swaddling clothes in the shape of a baby.

Happiness

This gesture is most often associated with the character of the Sylph in the ballet *La Sylphide*. But its meaning is so universally understood, you can use it in any situation.

Bring your hands together in front of you at about chest height, and angle them slightly to the left, with the fingertips of your right hand resting in your left palm. From that position, clap three times quickly — then switch sides and repeat (Figure 16-4a).

The Sylph in *La Sylphide* actually dances a complicated step while doing this gesture. That's one happy fairy.

Sadness

Facing forward, place one relaxed hand over your face, fingertips just below one eye, and draw the hand downward, tracing the tracks of your tears. Meanwhile, slowly tilt your head and eyes downward (see Figure 16-4b).

Alternately, bring both hands in front of your eyes, looking at your palms. Now slowly lower your hands until they are beneath the chin. At the same time, lower your eyelids and lower your head slightly.

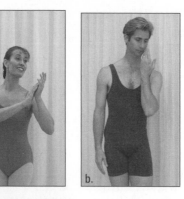

Figure 16-4: The gestures for happiness (a), sadness (b), and anger (c).

Anger

The challenge here is to unleash your wrath while maintaining grace and elegance at the same time. One way is to stand facing away from the other person, arms crossed, with an indignant expression. You might even add a foot stomp — as the character Lise does in Act II of Sir Fredrick Ashton's ballet *La fille mal gardée.*

But if you're really, *really* angry, you need to act a bit more threatening. Stand in a belligerent posture, with one foot forward. Lift both arms in front of you, elbows bent, fists clenched and slightly vibrating (refer to Figure 16-4c). Put 'em up!

"Stop!"

In other words, "Halt!"

Hold up one arm at shoulder height, elbow straight, palm facing the other person, while looking directly into his eyes (Figure 16-5a).

Figure 16-5:
The gestures for "Stop!" (a), "Go!" (b), and sword-fighting (c).

"Go!"

Or more to the point: "Go now if you value your life."

Look at the other person. Now bring up your arm that is closest to the direction in which you want him to go. Point in that direction, using *two fingers* so that he'll leave twice as fast. You can even add a *battement tendu* if you're really serious (as in Figure 16-5b).

If you want him to go back the way he came, then as you point, look *away* from him with disdain. That way, you make it clear to the audience that your gesture is not toward *him,* but toward the exit.

Swordfighting

Take fourth position, with your legs in *demi plié*, parallel to the front of the stage. Now bring your arms into a typical "*en garde*" position: Bring one arm behind you, rounded with the palm up. Pretend you have a sword in the other hand, and fight with your invisible partner. Move forward and back as you improvise swordfighting gestures (refer to Figure 16-5c).

If this sounds familiar to you, you've probably seen *The Nutcracker*. This gesture, simplified, is a classic move from Act II.

"Are you sick?"

It takes two people to convey this question. Person A (the questioner) stands to the left of Person B (the Sick-Looking Person). Person A steps toward Person B, while keeping her body facing forward. Person A then places her right palm over Person B's forehead, as if checking for a fever (Figure 16-6a). Finally, Person A drops her hand and looks questioningly at Person B.

This gesture occurs in *La fille mal gardée,* in which Person A (the Widow Simone) checks Person B (her daughter Lise) for fever. As it turns out, Lise is just feeling guilty over kissing her boyfriend. Long story.

Figure 16-6: The gestures for "Are you sick?" (a), "No, I'm fine — nothing's wrong (cough, cough)" (b), and death (c).

"No, I'm fine — nothing's wrong"

This gesture is the answer to the question, "Are you sick?" Person B steps away from Person A. This accomplishes two purposes. First, it creates emotional distance, as if to say, "How could you possibly think such a thing, Person A?" Second, it creates *physical* distance, enabling the next move. Person B then crosses her wrists in front of her body, palms down, and then opens her arms to the side — "enough of that!" — while shaking her head "no" (refer to Figure 16-6b).

By the way, in most story ballets, Person B's answer to "Are you sick" is almost *always* "Nothing's wrong."

Person B then dies.

Death

Fall on the ground in a heap. No, we're kidding. This gesture isn't used for actual dying, but simply to *talk about* death.

Bring both arms up above shoulder height, stretched forward. Now draw them together in a downward diagonal motion, so that your wrists cross in front of your body at about waist level. Keep your elbows straight, with your hands clasped into fists, and hold for a moment (Figure 16-6c). This is the ballet equivalent of a skull and crossbones.

Dance

It's one thing to dance a ballet. It's quite another to *talk about* dancing — and that's the purpose of this gesture.

Bring your arms overhead, going through second position to high fifth position. Then, cross your arms so that one wrist is over the other, with space in between. Circle your arms in the air at least twice (Figure 16-7).

Although the *plots* of story ballets aren't usually about dancing, you'd be surprised how often the subject comes up. Choreographers use it at every opportunity — especially in the scene where some queen or another says to her guests, "Why don't you dance for us?"

Figure 16-7:
The gesture
for dance.

"Please?" and "Thank you!"

To say, "Please," clasp your hands together in front of your chest (or put your palms together, prayer-style), and move them away from your body, toward the person you are pleading with, until your elbows are almost straight (Figure 16-8a).

If that doesn't work, more desperate measures are needed. Throw yourself at the other person's feet and wrap your arms around his legs (as in Figure 16-8b).

To say, "Thank you!" start with your hands at about chest height, palms down (as if in the middle fifth position, in front of the body). Now turn your hands over, palms up, and lower them, while simultaneously lowering your chin with profound gratitude, allowing your eyes to drop in deep humility.

Depending on the character and the situation, this action can also be performed with one single hand (refer to Figure 16-8c). The King, for example, couldn't be bothered to use both hands. But the young heroine, recently spared from marrying her evil stepfather, would definitely use two.

For gestures of *extreme* gratitude, or in less formal situations where there are no kings around, a simple hug or kiss works, too.

"Could you direct me to the Ladies' Room?"

Okay — there's no mime for that. But you may need to invent your own at a ballet performance. (See Chapter 17 for more information on attending ballets.)

Figure 16-8: The gestures for "Please?" (a), "Pretty please?" (b), and "Thank you!" (c).

Famous Examples of Ballet Mime

Ballet mime is used most effectively in story ballets. These ballets almost always have a pivotal moment when the action depends on the telling (or retelling) of some important detail. Sometimes it's the backstory — background detail that we couldn't possibly know otherwise. ("Ever since his hunting accident, he can only sit down when it rains.") Or perhaps it's the introduction of a new character. ("Watch out for this guy. Swans seem to follow him around.")

In these story ballets, of course, much of the ballet mime simply consists of imitative gestures. For example, there is no official mime gesture for *mouse* — after all, how often would you need it? — but a dancer can make his meaning very clear by putting his curled fingers up under his chin like whiskers and scurrying around like a mouse. We're talking *no shame* here.

Here are three of the most famous examples of ballet mime in action. They make generous use of imitative gestures — as well as much of the mime vocabulary in this chapter (in **bold type)**. You can find out much more about these three ballets in Chapter 19.

Swan Lake: Odette describes her plight to Siegfried

When the Swan Queen waddles into Prince Siegfried in the woods, she tells him of her curse: The evil Rothbart has turned her and all her friends into swans. The mime is set to a specific section of the music, and the dancers usually act out the words of the mime story, which goes as follows:

Siegfried: Who are **you?** (*He gestures to her and makes a questioning motion.*)

Odette: **I** am the Queen of the Swans (Figure 16-9).

(*At this point, the prince bows deeply in respect. She continues:*)

Odette: An **angry** man has made **me** into a Swan. But if one **handsome** prince **swears eternal fidelity to me, I** will be a swan **no more!**

Figure 16-9:
Swan
Lake —
Odette
(Evelyn
Cisneros)
shows
what she's
made of
(feathers).

© Lloyd Englert

The Nutcracker: The Prince recounts the battle with the mice

In Act II of *The Nutcracker,* Clara arrives in the Land of Sweets escorted by the Prince. The Sugar Plum Fairy, who reigns over this kingdom, asks the Prince to explain why they have come. The Prince tells her of his climactic battle with the Mouse King. This mime is choreographed to specific phrases of Tchaikovsky's masterful score. It usually goes like this:

> Prince: **Come** and **gather around** one and all. While **Clara was sleeping**, I was watching over **her**. (*He pantomimes being vigilant.*) Suddenly **I** saw *mice!* **They** were huge, and their leader was an enormous Mouse King. (*He makes a "big" gesture to indicate their size.*) What was **I** going to do? **I pulled out my sword and began to fight him. He** was winning! (*He pantomimes being pushed backward in the swordfight.*) But then **Clara** took off her shoe and hit the Mouse King on the head! (*He gestures to Clara, then pantomimes that action.*) That distracted the Mouse King long enough for **me** to stab him with **my** sword. **I** rescued Clara from danger! (*And he bows deeply, to great applause.*)

Giselle: Mom delivers a lecture in advanced cardiology

The first act of the ballet contains a scene in which Giselle's mother catches her dancing around the village, and scolds her for it. At first we think Mama is just old-fashioned, but we soon learn the real reason: Giselle has a weak heart. As the villagers gather around, we find out that mother knows best:

> Mother: **Your** heart isn't good. **Everyone, gather round** to hear what **I** have to say. Over there in the forest (*she points*) is a cemetery (*she makes a cross*). Every night, up out of the ground (*she gestures upwards*) come spirits called *Wilis.* (*She portrays the famous Wilis by placing one hand over her face and drawing it down, to imitate the veils that Wilis wear — see Figure 16-10*). Giselle (*indicating her daughter*), if **you dance, you will die**, and become a *Wili.* (*This time she portrays the Wilis by imitating their arm movements.*) **You** will be cursed to fly around every night. **I** can't bear to look at **you** and think of **you** as a *Wili!*

> *At this point, she begins to cry. Giselle runs up to her, kisses her, and says,*

> Giselle: Mama, my heart is fine. **I'm OK! Nothing's wrong!**

Famous last mimes.

Figure 16-10:
Giselle's mom (Anita Paciotti) explains that Giselle must not dance, or she'll die.

© Andrea Flores

Chapter 17

Watching Ballet in Action

*I*f you read some of the technical chapters in this book — and you're still awake and haven't wandered off to the hardware store — you know how much trouble professional dancers go to in order to perfect their art. Now you get to watch the pros in all their glory, plying their trade so brilliantly onstage.

But attending a ballet performance by a professional ballet company can feel like attending a convention of geneticists, scuba divers, or Hungarians: You're entering a huge room filled with people using a language few people understand, dressed weirdly, and following rules you haven't yet mastered. And that's just the *audience*.

Never fear: We, your intrepid authors, are here to help. This chapter can save you from embarrassment and confusion. By the time you finish this chapter, you'll be as savvy as the biggest balletomane at the Bolshoi.

Getting Ready

The age-old question among balletgoers is, "How much should I prepare beforehand?" Well, a little preparation goes a long way.

You certainly don't need to be closely acquainted with the ballet or ballets on the program in order to enjoy a performance. But people do tend to like what they know. So after you've spent anywhere from $5 to $150 on a ballet ticket, why not invest another $14.95 to buy a CD of the ballet music you're about to hear?

Sit back and listen to the music. Read the little booklet that comes with the CD, written by a ballet expert in tiny print. These notes usually give a complete synopsis of the story of the ballet — telling who's related to whom, who falls in love with whom, who kills whom, who is left in abject grief and misery at the end; that sort of thing.

If you don't listen to a recording before you go, you should at least glance at the notes in the program after you get to the theater. You can find out interesting things about the composer who wrote the music and the choreographer(s) who created the dance — what was happening in the world during their time, and what ideas they were trying to convey.

Some ballet companies also offer informal preconcert talks. These talks are usually very informative, and sometimes entertaining. The talks usually begin up to an hour before the performance, and they are usually free. Call ahead and find out.

Arriving Early

Make sure to get to the theater early. People-watching is one of the comical joys of ballet-going. Plus, many ballet companies won't admit latecomers until the first intermission — and that can easily mean a wait of 45 minutes or more.

If you happen to arrive *really* early, take a walk around the inside of the theater. Very often, the building is a beautiful old opera house with lots of interesting nooks and crannies — like San Francisco's War Memorial Opera House, home of the San Francisco Ballet. Stroll down to the orchestra pit and peer inside; the musicians' warm-up exercises are fun to watch. You can even wander upstairs to the loge, where the luminaries sit in their private boxes, with champagne, caviar, and chocolate truffles. Truly an entertainment in itself.

If you arrive with a thick coat or jacket, check it in the lobby for comfort. After you're seated, check and double-check that you've turned off anything that beeps, buzzes, rings, or plays *La cucarach*a. Your neighbors (not to mention the dancers) will be glad you did.

Can I Wear a Codpiece to Romeo and Juliet?

People often stress out about what to wear to a ballet. Don't get uptight — wear whatever you want. There are no dress requirements in force at the ballet. Except onstage, that is.

At ballet performances, the younger audience members often dress very casually. In fact, the cheap seats or standing room area may be occupied by young dancers and students at the local ballet school, sporting nothing fancier than a leotard and sweatpants. Many of the older people in attendance may dress up a bit — a jacket for men, a dress or nice pantsuit for women. Some may even wear a tuxedo or pearls — especially at a benefit performance or gala. Of course, they have a right to dress up, and many enjoy the chance to look special. We, your iconoclastic authors, on the other hand, believe that formal dress can be a distraction, making it that much harder to relax and really get into the performance.

True, the ballet *can* have a certain degree of ceremony and dignity. But these things are peripheral to the true purpose of the event: experiencing a masterful human expression. You don't need a suit and tie for that. You need eyes and ears.

A pointer: If anyone, at any time, disapproves of your dress, do the following: Turn to the person, smile, and ask, "What did you think about those absolutely stunning *grandes pirouettes à la seconde* in Act One?" This always works, no matter what the dancers have just danced.

A Pre-Ballet Food-Lover's Manual

Herewith, the cardinal rule in dining before the ballet: Try to avoid creating a situation in which you're constantly dashing to the rest room.

As a form of after-dinner entertainment, enrichment, and fun, an evening of ballet is hard to beat. But there's a major difference between a ballet performance and, say, a television show. At the ballet, you're entertained by live human beings who must maintain concentration and composure (not to mention that killer *arabesque*) for extended periods of time. The act of standing up, sidling past 2,337 knees, and bolting for the exit can actually disturb the dancers — and, of course, the audience.

And here's another warning: The line for the ladies' room at today's ballet performances often stretches around the block. Bad planning is the cause — the average opera house holds well over 2,000 people, and the average ladies' room holds 10. (The men, on the other hand, are usually in and out of theirs in an instant.) True fact: Several ballet companies have been forced to lengthen their intermissions for exactly this reason. We offer two suggestions for women:

✔ Don't overindulge, liquid-wise, before the ballet.

✔ Try cross-dressing.

All this boils down to a solution that experienced ballet goers figured out a long time ago: Eat *after* the ballet.

Knowing Where to Sit — and Getting the Best Ticket Deals

Every ballet company in this country — and we mean *every* single one — has financial worries. Maintaining a big professional ballet company costs millions upon millions of dollars a year. With an annual run of *Nutcrackers* as their only sure-fire hit, all ballet companies need financial and moral support. So we would feel extremely guilty showing you how to save money at an American ballet performance.

So instead, we're going to give you tips on how to save money at a ballet performance in the country of *Vulgaria.* The Vulgarian National Ballet, as you are probably aware, is state-funded. And to be honest, we don't really care whether the government of Vulgaria makes enormous profits this season.

The Vulgarian National Ballet on a Budget

by Elena Cisnerova and Semyon Speckinski

Fact number one: The best seats in a theater are not necessarily the most expensive. The back of the balcony often offers the best of all possible worlds: a great overview and great sound.

The farther back you sit, the easier it is to see the whole stage, the entire set design, and the complete array of fancy costumes — not to mention broad strokes of choreographic genius. Take *The Nutcracker,* for example. In some versions, there's a wonderful moment in the Waltz of the Flowers where all the female dancers join together and create an enormous flower by spreading all their arms at once, Esther Williams style. Stunning effects like this are best seen from on high.

Furthermore, if you're right at the back of the balcony, you often can hear the sound reflected at you from the ceiling. It sounds as if you're actually right next to the orchestra; sometimes you can even hear the whispers of the players and the muffled curses of the dancers. Seats right in front of the stage, where the glitterati often sit, have the worst visual perspective and the worst acoustics. You get too much of one thing and no blend of sound. Let the visual and aural flavors mix by sitting farther back.

On the other hand, it's loads of fun to watch the dancers sweat and strain, and you can see them best from up close. So what to do? Well, binoculars are always a good investment. (You can rent them at most opera houses if you don't have your own.) You might also try buying a ticket way up in the balcony, and — at some point before the intermission — scanning the expensive section for empty seats. After intermission, you're free to take an unclaimed seat. That way, you can have the best of all possible worlds: a wonderful overview and excellent acoustics before intermission, a great close-up view after intermission, and a cheap ticket.

But what if you take an unclaimed seat after intermission, and then the seat's rightful owner shows up? Produce your own ticket, look surprised, and exclaim in Vulgarian, *"Hôppala! ez hëlás plàtu Orkêste A-5? Jô dumalo shto bîlaj Tritja Bälkôn ZZ-96! Jô tolka reqüalá."* ("Oh, is this seat Orchestra A-5? I thought it was Third Balcony ZZ-96! I'm so sorry.")

Actually, just a friendly smile will suffice. Remember: You always have your own seat to go back to.

Fact number two: Just before the ballet begins, ticket prices sometimes drop precipitously. Look into so-called *rush tickets* (especially if you're a student), which can be discounted by as much as 90 percent. These tickets are usually available half an hour before the performance. You might also find high-class scalpers standing in front of the theater or opera house. These folks can't use their tickets, but they don't want them to go to waste. Sometimes they ask for the original price; sometimes they're willing to sell them more cheaply; and sometimes they just give 'em away. Look respectable and honest, and try to avoid being spotted by the Secret Police.

Fact number three: If you're low on cash but don't want to forgo the entire ballet, try arriving during the intermission (around 8:45 p.m., Eastern European Time, for most ballet performances.) At intermission, for whatever reason, some people always go home. Usually, they're happy to give you their seats. Stand in the lobby (or outside, on the front steps), and ask politely. As students, we used to do this occasionally. Now we do it all the time.

Corollary to fact number three (and don't forget, you didn't hear this from us): Tickets are almost never checked after intermission. That's all we're going to say about *that*.

Fact number four: Many ballet companies offer an open dress rehearsal. Mostly, the dancers run straight through the program that they're preparing; this is the final rehearsal, after all. But often the artistic director, choreographer, or conductor stops to fix something onstage or in the orchestra. This can be fascinating, especially if you can see and hear what's being corrected. Often, these open dress rehearsals aren't announced to the general public — call ahead to find out.

Who to Bring, Who to Leave at Home with the Hamsters

Another age-old question concerns children. What is the appropriate minimum age for watching a ballet?

We don't believe that there's any minimum age. Kids can and should be exposed to live ballet as early as possible. But if they're likely to start crying during the performance, you may want to stand or sit near the exit, rather than in the middle of the audience.

Of course, every ballet program is different: Some programs feature several short ballets, and others consist of a single long one. To determine whether a particular ballet is appropriate for a particular person, consider the subject matter, the length of the dance (or the length of each act), and that person's attention span. With a little effort, you can find the perfect ballet program for just about anyone.

Ballets to Attend — or Avoid — on a Date

A ballet is a wonderful event for lovers (and lovers-to-be). Ballets often include a love story, and ballet has been synonymous with romance for centuries. Just think: Beautiful music! Graceful pirouettes! Tights!

Well, okay — music and pirouettes.

To impress your beloved with your consummate taste and romantic instinct, you can hardly do better than an evening of ballet. If you want this well-planned evening of romance to lead to *further* romance, however, you should take certain things into account:

- **What kind of ballet company are you going to see?** If it's a large professional company, you almost can't go wrong. (See "What is the ballet *about*," later in this list.) If it's a modern dance group, the experience may be cutting edge, mind expanding, and possibly fun. If it's a group of people in white, wearing wings, check around to see if anyone's playing a harp nearby. If so, you're probably dead.

- **What style or period of ballet are you going to see?** This question is more important than you may think. Ballets come in all different styles and characters. *Classical* ballets are extremely stylized, with complex conventions that can appear stilted to the beginner. (Great for that first date with the President's daughter.) *Romantic* ballets often explore concepts of love, nature, and ghosts; the dancing is concerned with feeling, emotion, and nursing one's inner child. And in *contemporary* ballets, almost anything goes.

✔ **What is the ballet *about*?** Many ballets are based on stories. These stories are always described in the program book. Because some of these stories tend to cause embarrassment in romantic situations, you may want to avoid certain ballets on a date. For example:

- *The Rite of Spring* **(music by Igor Stravinsky, original choreography by Vaslav Nijinsky, 1913):** A truly incredible ballet, set to the most influential piece of music in the twentieth century. But it's violent, dissonant, and oh-so-graphic. A virgin girl is sacrificed to the god of Spring, forced to dance until she dies. Rated R.

- *The Invitation* **(dissonant music by Matyas Seiber, original choreography by Kenneth MacMillan, 1960):** A story that explores the topic of Victorians Behaving Badly, this ballet takes place in an elegant outdoor garden. It begins with polite and rigid formalities, progresses to a satirical cockfight, and devolves into a violent rape scene. Gruesome and graphic.

- *Othello* **(music by Elliot Goldenthal, original choreography by Lar Lubovitch, 1997):** This brilliant retelling of the story of the Moor of Venice, immortalized by Shakespeare (and described in more detail in Chapter 20), is full of violent sounds and images — ending with the jealous Othello strangling his wrongly accused wife. Save this one for marriage.

On the other hand, depending on your relationship, some of these ballets may be just what you need.

Enjoying the ballet program

The program booklet is critical to enjoying the ballet you're about to experience. This booklet sometimes costs a few bucks — but it's usually worth the price.

You can expect to see the following elements in any self-respecting program book:

✔ A list of the ballet or ballets that you're about to see

✔ A short explanation of each ballet, its composer, and its choreographer, including some relevant history

✔ Pictures (and possibly short biographies) of the dancers

✔ An advertisement for a jeweler

Understanding What You Are Watching

If you watch a ballet without knowing about the *form,* it looks like one step after another, after another. But every ballet actually consists of many identifiable sections. Once you understand just a few simple concepts, the whole structure of the ballet becomes clear before your eyes and ears.

Many ballets begin with an *overture.* As in a musical play or opera, the overture is simply a musical introduction, played by the orchestra with the curtain down. Its purpose is to set the mood of the opening scene, or of the ballet as a whole. (And it sometimes serves another purpose too — to allow latecomers to sit down.)

When the curtain goes up, the music often changes. If this is a *narrative ballet* (also called a *story ballet*), the first scene usually gives you some background information. It often takes place in a big public square, or banquet hall, with opulent scenery and tons of "extras" milling around. During this scene, you may see a lot of ballet mime. (For *much* more on mime, see Chapter 16.)

At some point in the action, everyone goes off to the sides of the stage (or exits the stage entirely), except for a small number of characters, who stay in the center. That's your cue that these dancers are about to launch into a formal dance number.

Pas de deux — step of two

Throughout this book, we make occasional casual use of the term *pas de deux,* but we save the thorough explanation for this moment. *Pas de deux* means, literally "step of two." Early on, choreographers realized that by having two people participate in a beautiful step *together,* they could create some of the most stunning effects in ballet. (For more on the possibilities of partnering, see Chapter 14.)

What's more, after the stunning debut of the *pas de deux,* choreographers rushed to outdo themselves, creating the *pas de trois* (for three dancers), the *pas de quatre* (for four), the *pas de cinq* (for five), and so on. Every one of these dances consists of several separate sections of music in which the dancers show their stuff — individually and together.

The grand pas de deux

The grandest *pas de deux* of all usually comes in the final act of a classical ballet. It's called, appropriately, the *grand pas de deux,* and it displays the exquisite skill of the principal couple. The two in question are usually a man and a woman, and they're usually in love.

This beautiful dance almost always consists of four distinct parts, or *movements,* each set to a totally different kind of music.

Adagio

The first section of a *grand pas de deux* is the *adagio* — and it's just chock full of the slow, deliberate, graceful movements that you can read about throughout this book, especially in Chapters 9 and 14.

The focus of the *adagio* is always the woman, and the man is there largely to support her — literally. He holds her while she does long and luxurious *développés* and *arabesques.* He holds her while she does *pirouettes* — either lightly at her waist, or with one finger, which she grasps. Sometimes she just stays in a lovely pose, *en pointe,* while he promenades around her. During climactic moments, the man lifts the woman, very slowly and with control, and at the very end they join together in a dramatic pose.

Appropriately, the music in this section is usually slow, intense, and passionate, and it displays the whole orchestra in all its glory.

When the *adagio* is over, the man and woman unlock from their final coupling and take a bow. Then the woman runs offstage and collapses, panting, in the corner. Somebody brings her a cup or bottle of water, and she gets ready to dance again. But you don't get to see any of that.

Male variation

Meanwhile, onstage, the man gets ready to perform his big solo, known as the *male variation.* After watching the ballerina's exit with great longing and affection, one arm gesturing tenderly in her direction, he *slowly* walks across the front of the stage, then turns and walks to a back corner. If you look carefully while his back is to you, you may see his entire torso heaving. He's trying to catch as much breath as possible.

When he reaches the corner, a new kind of music starts — often loud, much faster than before, and with very heavy beats. This music makes great use of the deepest instruments of the orchestra to create a feeling of machismo and power.

This is, in fact, the man's great chance to show his mojo. He does multiple jumps, double turns, or *cabrioles.* (See Chapter 13 for more on *cabrioles.*) He may do a long *pirouette* or two, with one foot partly extended back in *attitude.* At the end of his variation, he usually does a spectacular turn, ending in a dramatic pose, usually down on one knee with arms outstretched. "Ta-DAAAAH!" If he has calculated right, he's facing the audience.

Female variation

After his moment of glory, the male dancer runs offstage to great applause — and the woman, not quite fully rested, comes back on. The music starts again; this time it's usually very soft, in a measured tempo, and with hushed beats like little cat feet. This music often makes use of the high, soft, tinkly instruments of the orchestra, to create the most traditionally "feminine" feeling possible. We're talkin' *Sugar Plum Fairy* here.

This is the chance for the ballerina to show off her awesome *pointe* work. Notice how delicately she rolls up onto her toes, stays up there, and then rolls back down again. Notice how long she can balance on one foot in various positions; for example, she's able to hold that killer *arabesque* pose, *en pointe,* for longer than it took you to read this sentence.

Adding a manège or diagonal

Toward the very end of any male or female variation, the dancer may do a *manège* ("mah-NEJ"). Simply put, this means that the dancer travels around the stage in a circle, while performing a set of steps again and again. He or she may vary the degree of difficulty, lengthening or shortening the steps to make the dance more interesting, or to match the accents in the music.

Alternately, the dancer may end the variation with a *diagonal*. This is exactly what you'd think it is: The dancer goes to a back corner of the stage and comes forward in a diagonal line to the opposite front corner, while dancing a complicated step or series of steps over and over — and bringing the house down.

Coda

The last movement in any *grand pas de deux* is called a *coda,* or "tail." This movement often includes the most technically difficult steps of the entire ballet. You can imagine how tough this is, toward the end of the ballet when the dancers are already exhausted.

The music to the *coda* is almost always fast, energetic, and cheerful, using all the instruments of the orchestra. The man and woman take turns running on and off the stage, showing their stuff one after the other.

The man often performs *pirouettes* in second position (with one leg sticking straight out), *double tours,* or big leaps while beating his feet back and forth six, eight, or even ten times (*entrechat six, huit,* or *dix*). The woman may do *fouettés,* multiple turns such as triple *pirouettes,* and big split jumps.

Toward the end of the coda, the man and woman join together for multiple turns and a lift or two. At the end, they do a big pose like a fish dive or a shoulder sit (see Chapter 14). This is probably the single most spectacular section, dance-wise, of the ballet.

You can always tell when a big classical ballet is about to end: The music swells, and all the characters come onstage at the same time.

Ballets without a story

Of course, not every classical ballet tells a story. But even without a story, the structure remains similar. You can find a *grand pas de deux,* for example, in an abstract ballet — even when the dancers in question aren't expressing their eternal love.

The classical ballet is the foundation for the structure of contemporary ballet as well. Although many choreographers choose to take liberties with this structure — and you should be ready for anything — the resulting ballet is usually well aware of its classical roots.

Life in the Wings

Whenever we go to work at the ballet, we enjoy watching a performance from the wings. The drama going on backstage (see Figure 17-1) is just as compelling as the drama onstage. On any given evening, the production staff and the dancers are engaged in a hilarious human comedy.

After dancing so exquisitely onstage, the ballerina may dash off in crisis — nearly smacking into a setpiece that four stagehands are moving. Her costume's falling off! Her partner dropped her during the lift! As a seamstress rushes in to fix her costume, the ballerina blows her nose, wipes the sweat off her face with Kleenex, swigs a mouthful of water and spits it out — into the proper receptacle, of course.

Meanwhile, the male dancer rushes offstage, swearing about the conductor's tempo. His ankle hurts; he quickly massages it. He adjusts his dance belt, which has been digging into all the wrong places. The wig designer comes forward to fix his wig, which nearly came off during his last *double tour.*

Then the stage manager cues the lights, the music swells, and both these admirable troopers run, smiling, back onto the stage.

Figure 17-1:
Backstage
at the ballet.

Unstrung Heroes — The Ballet Orchestra

Some of the most important members of the ballet company are underground — in the orchestra. The music in a ballet is of paramount importance. After all, a ballet danced in silence wouldn't be interesting for very long.

An orchestra is a world unto itself, made up of practically every kind of instrument you can name. It's also a fascinating microcosm of the human race, containing every personality type imaginable. Orchestra life has its great excitements, its challenges, and its amazing frustrations. (You can read all about them in *Classical Music for Dummies*.)

The orchestra musicians are the stars of a classical music concert, but at a ballet performance, they're relegated to a small (and usually cramped) orchestra pit. Audiences and ballet companies often undervalue the contribution of these fine virtuosos, who sit hidden from view. And yet, ballet dancers absolutely depend on the musicians — and their conductor — to create the mood, and set the tempo for the dance.

For *much* more on the music, and the people who love it, see Chapter 5.

Basking in the Afterglow

When the ballet is over, you may feel the urge to meet the dancers. We encourage you to give in to this temptation. Go outside and stand at the stage door of the theater or opera house. Most likely, every single one of the dancers will come out that way.

It's a well-kept secret: Most ballet dancers are just as friendly as you and me. (Well, just as friendly as *me*, anyway.) They *love* to meet their fans, and they are usually very gratified when someone expresses sincere appreciation for what they do.

After watching the dancers strut their stuff so magnificently onstage, you may be surprised by how normal these people seem in real life — and how much shorter they appear when they're not standing on their toes. When you get right down to it, ballet dancers are human too.

Part V
The Part of Tens

The 5th Wave   By Rich Tennant

"Oh, the ballet was fine. But coming out, Dolores and I did a pas de deux down the theater steps and almost broke our necks."

In this part . . .

If you've dutifully traversed the pages of this book from the beginning, congratulations — you've waded through some truly complicated stuff. And if by chance you've also read it, you are in wonderful shape to face the world of ballet without fear.

Now it's time to relax. This part is truly for those low attention span moments, times when you need a break from the rigors of *Dummies* text. Herewith, Scott 'n' Evelyn's Top Ten Lists.

Chapter 18

The Ten Most Commonly Used Ballet Steps

In This Chapter

▶ Steps you see again and again

▶ Twists and turns

▶ Count 'em — 32!

You'd be forgiven for thinking that ballet is made up of thousands and thousands of different steps. Over the centuries, choreographers have invented countless variations of the basic moves.

But certain ballet steps *do* come up over and over, in nearly every ballet combination, and in nearly every classical ballet. Once you can recognize these steps — and maybe even do them — you're halfway there.

Small Knee Bend (Demi-Plié) in Fifth Position

The small knee bend, which you can read about in Chapter 6, might just be the most common step in all of ballet. This versatile little step is the preparation for almost every jump, and landings too. You also see it before pirouettes. And many other steps start and finish here — the *glissade,* for example. Even the slow lifting of the legs in *adagio* goes through the fifth position *demi-plié*.

We'd be hard pressed to name a single ballet that doesn't use this step.

Leg Stretch (Battement Tendu and Dégagé)

As we show you in Chapter 6, the *battement tendu* is a step that anyone with two legs can do. It consists of extending one leg, with a straight knee, and pointing the foot. In the basic *tendu*, the foot never leaves the floor, and in the *dégagé* variety, the foot goes up to about 45 degrees off the floor.

These motions often come up in preparations for other moves, like jumps and turns. Both men and women dance them often.

Développé

The *développé* is usually danced at the highest of heights by the ballerina, either alone or supported by her partner. She bends one knee, lifts it as high as she can, and then straightens the leg, pointing her foot proudly to the sky, to the ooooohs of the audience. (See Chapter 8 for an awesome view.) The more slowly and deliberately she does this move, the more ooooohs she gets, so count on seeing a slo-o-o-o-ow *développé* during any *grand pas de deux*.

Leg Lifted Back (Arabesque) in First Position

The *arabesque* is the most stereotypical ballet move — and the pose that most ballet dancers strike when there's a photographer nearby.

An *arabesque* looks absolutely stress free, which is, of course, never the case with dancers. In *arabesque*, the dancer lifts one leg behind the hip, with a straight knee. Depending on the flexibility of the dancer, this leg can rival the shoulders or head for height. Meanwhile, the rest of the body is upright, as if there were nothing sticking out. See Chapter 8 for more.

Our favorite *arabesque* takes place in a *pas de deux*, where the ballerina takes several luscious seconds to raise that leg. The more you understand how difficult this move is to do smoothly, the more impressive it is.

Leg Lifted Back and Bent (Attitude)

Chapter 8 shows you the *attitude,* which looks just like an *arabesque,* except that the knee of the raised leg is bent.

To a dancer, this bent knee makes all the difference. The back *attitude* is the perfect alternative for the *arabesque,* easing the weight of the lifted leg and allowing the leg to lift higher. This move comes in handy whenever the dancer has a sore back or feels a muscle spasm coming on — the *attitude* gives the dancer a break without sacrificing the line.

You can also see dancers do *pirouettes* while in the *attitude* position — and ballet just doesn't get any more beautiful than that.

Outward Turn (Pirouette en Dehors) from Fourth Position

Ballet technique offers many turns, or *pirouettes,* to choose from. (See Chapter 10 for an in-depth look at *pirouettes*). But the most common begins in fourth position. From here, the dancer can gather the force needed for multiple turns.

You find the outward turn from fourth position in nearly every classical ballet. Check out the male variation of the *pas de deux* for an almost guaranteed set of exciting turns.

In performance, when the dancer goes exactly to center stage, you can bet that *pirouettes* are coming. When they're done, watch the dancer's face. If he or she seems pleased, they probably went well. If the dancer runs offstage immediately — or if he ends the turn sitting on his rear end — they didn't.

Forward Jump with Split (Grand Jeté)

If you try all the jumps in Chapter 13, you'll never forget the *grand jeté.* In this boisterous jump, you run, kick one leg up into the air in front of you, and then hurl your body up into the sky, doing a split in midair. The best dancers can do all that with freedom, abandon, and perfect technique. Others may need surgery.

In the ballet *Swan Lake,* in the coda of the Black Swan *pas de deux*, Siegfried leaps out from the wings and does a whole circle of these jumps. (You can find out how in Chapter 15.)

The Gliding Step (Glissade)

The gliding step usually shows up between larger steps. As you can discover in Chapter 11, the *glissade* gives the dancer a tiny break from difficult technique. Look for this step just before *jetés* of any size; it even comes up in preparation for some turns and lifts.

The Famous Fouetté — Count 'Em, 32!

Fouettés gives balletomanes something to count. These whipping turns show off a ballerina's strength, balance, and endurance to the nth degree.

As you may remember from Chapter 10, this turn starts at center stage, with a *pirouette.* Then the ballerina keeps turning, and turning, and turning. With each revolution, she does a *demi-plié* on her standing leg and whips the other leg around to face the audience. Every good ballerina should be able to do this 32 times — theoretically, she could go on forever, like a perpetual motion machine.

If you'd like to see this feat of the feet, watch the Black Swan in *Swan Lake.* You can also find 32 *fouettés* in the ballet *Don Quixote,* and occasionally in *Le corsaire.*

Double Turn in the Air (Double Tour en l'Air)

This step is almost exclusively for men — and it's a prerequisite for a contract with nearly every ballet company in the world.

The man starts in fifth position, bends his knees, and thrusts himself up into the air, making *two* complete revolutions before landing in perfect fifth position again: *Ta-DAAAAAH!*

Chapter 19

Ten Best-Loved Classical Ballets

*I*f your local ballet company is producing a full-length classical ballet, chances are it's one of the ten in the chapter. And for good reason — these ballets are true masterpieces, ever popular and nearly-always fresh.

Herewith, in chronological order, a look at ten classical ballets that have stood the test of time.

La Sylphide

Music by: Jean Schneitzhoeffer. **Original choreography:** Philippe Taglioni. **First performed:** Paris, 1832. **Another celebrated version:** Music by Hermann von Lovenskjold; choreography by August Bournonville; first performed in Copenhagen, 1836.

La Sylphide ("The Sylph," or spirit) was groundbreaking in many ways. It is credited with being the first Romantic ballet — full of ethereal settings and supernatural creatures. The satin shoes and flowing white costume of the sylph changed the ballet world forever. And this is the ballet where, in 1832, Marie Taglioni (daughter of choreographer Philippe Taglioni) danced *en pointe* for the first time — and brought about the age of the *prima ballerina*.

The plot: On the morning of his wedding day, James, a Scottish farmer, falls in love with an elusive vision of a magical sylph (Figure 19-1). As he ponders the vision, an old witch appears and predicts that he will betray his fiancée — but he scoffs and sends the witch away offended. The wedding begins. James is just about to put the ring on his fiancée's finger when the sylph appears out of nowhere and snatches it. James runs after her, abandoning his own wedding.

James chases the sylph into the woods, where he runs into the witch. She offers him a magical scarf that will bind the sylph's wings so that he can catch her. The scarf works as promised, but it also kills the sylph. (*That wasn't on the warning label.*) James is left alone and disconsolate, and his fiancée marries his best friend.

Figure 19-1:
La Sylphide:
The Sylph
(Muriel
Maffre)
appears to
James as
he sleeps.

© Lloyd Englert

Giselle

Music by: Adolphe Adam. **Choreography:** Jean Coralli and Jules Perrot. **First performed:** Paris, 1841. **Additional choreography:** Marius Petipa.

One of the great Romantic ballets, *Giselle* concerns itself with forest spirits, death, and forces of nature. It also has the quintessential "white act" — the second act of the ballet, in which everyone is wearing white.

The plot: In the Rhineland, Count Albrecht impersonates a farmer to woo the beautiful peasant girl, Giselle. She agrees to marry him, despite the advances of another peasant, Hilarion, who suspects that Albrecht is an impostor. Giselle wants to dance — but her mother warns her that she has a weak heart.

A hunting horn announces a Prince and his entourage. The Prince's daughter gives Giselle a gold necklace when she learns they are both engaged. Hilarion interrupts and exposes Albrecht as a nobleman, and the prince's daughter reveals that Albrecht is in fact *her* fiancé. The frail Giselle goes mad and dies of a broken heart.

Act II takes place in the forest near Giselle's grave. The ghostly Wilis, virgins who have died of unrequited love, are summoned by their Queen to initiate Giselle into Wili-hood. Hilarion stops by, and the Wilis force him to dance to death. Now Albrecht arrives. The Wilis trap him and command him to dance as well. But new-Wili Giselle dances with him until the clock strikes four, when the Wilis lose their power (Figure 19-2). Saved, Albrecht cries at Giselle's grave.

Figure 19-2:
Giselle:
Giselle with
Albrecht
(Joanna
Berman and
Pierre-
François
Vilanoba) as
the morning
bell tolls.

© Lloyd Englert

Don Quixote

Music by: Ludwig Minkus. **Original choreography:** Marius Petipa. **First performed:** Moscow, 1869.

The plot: Based on the epic masterpiece by Miguel de Cervantes, this ballet depicts some of its highlights. An aging nobleman, Don Quixote, becomes obsessed with stories of ancient chivalry. A little bit bonkers, he imagines that he himself is a brave knight, and sets out to rescue the lady of his dreams, Dulcinea. Having transformed a beggar, Sancho Panza, into his trusty squire, he leads a charge against the "enemy" that he sees everywhere. He fights against imaginary rivals, puppets in a theater, and even windmills.

Although Don Quixote is the title character, his role is usually portrayed by senior dancers past their prime. It is the fiery young lovers, Kitri and Basilio, who get the best dance in the ballet — the Wedding *pas de deux*.

Coppélia

Music by: Leo Delibes. **Original choreography:** Arthur Michel Saint-Léon. **First performed:** Paris, 1870.

This charming ballet is often performed by smaller ballet companies because it doesn't call for an entire phalanx of world-class dancers. In fact, the role of the mad scientist is sometimes played by the artistic director.

The plot: The ballet tells the story of a man, a woman, a mad scientist, and his doll named Coppélia. Man loves woman, but is infatuated by mad scientist's extremely lifelike doll. Woman impersonates doll to fool man and mad scientist. Chaos ensues, but all is forgiven. Man and woman make up and get married, to great merriment.

La Bayadère

Music by: Ludwig Minkus. **Original choreography:** Marius Petipa. **First performed:** St. Petersburg, Russia, 1877.

This ballet is most famous for its "white act," The Kingdom of the Shades, often performed by itself. As the act begins, 32 ghostly women in white make their way down a zigzag ramp, doing an *arabesque* with each forward step, and performing a complex series of motions in unison (Figure 19-3). Ballet doesn't get any more exquisite than this.

The plot: The beautiful *bayadère* (temple dancer) Nikiya is in love with the young warrior Solor. But Solor is engaged to the Rajah's daughter. At the betrothal, Nikiya is commanded to dance. Afterward she receives a basket of flowers, containing a deadly snake, courtesy of the Rajah's daughter. She dies.

Solor dreams of being reunited with Nikiya in the Kingdom of the Shades. Awakening, he realizes a minor detail — that he's still engaged. At the wedding, Solor sees a vision of Nikiya. He says his vows to her, instead of to his real fiancée. (Whoops!) The infuriated gods destroy the palace. Nikiya and Solor are reunited in spirit, in the Kingdom of the Shades.

Figure 19-3:
La Bayadère:
The San Francisco Ballet's *corps de ballet* in Act II — otherwise known as the White Act.

© Marty Sohl

Swan Lake

Music by: Peter Tchaikovsky. **Original choreography:** Julius Reisinger. **First performed:** Moscow, 1877. **Revised choreography:** Marius Petipa/Lev Ivanov, St. Petersburg, 1895.

This was Peter Tchaikovsky's first ballet score, but the first production in Moscow didn't catch on. Several versions of the choreography exist, but we are indebted most to Marius Petipa and his St. Petersburg production of 1895. The San Francisco Ballet performed the first American production.

The plot: While hunting, Prince Siegfried spots a magnificent swan. As he takes aim, the swan turns into a beautiful woman, Odette. She explains that she is a princess who has come under the spell of an evil sorcerer. By day she must be a swan, swimming in a lake of tears, and only at night can she assume human form. The spell can be broken only if a virgin prince swears eternal fidelity to her. (Luckily, Siegfried just *happens* to answer to that description.) But, she says, if he refuses her, she must remain a swan forever.

Siegfried falls head over heels for her — but through the treachery of the evil sorcerer, Siegfried unintentionally proposes to another woman at a party the next night, thinking she is Odette. (Long story.) Doomed, Swan Lady determines to kill herself; Siegfried, who's *really* sorry, throws himself into the lake with her, and the pair are transformed into lovers in the afterlife (Figure 19-4).

Figure 19-4:
Swan Lake: Odette and Siegfried (Evelyn Cisneros and Anthony Randazzo) in a final embrace, with the *corps de ballet* in front of them.

© Lloyd Englert

Sleeping Beauty

Music by: Peter Tchaikovsky. **Original choreography:** Marius Petipa. **First performed:** St. Petersburg, Russia, 1890.

Despite great music and masterful choreography, Tchaikovsky's second ballet was initially no more popular than his first. The production was criticized for being "too lavish," and Tchaikovsky's incredibly gorgeous music was dismissed by the Czar as "very nice." The ballet quickly gained popularity, though, and within 3 years it had been performed 50 times.

The plot: Baby Princess Aurora is being christened. The evil Carabosse, whose invitation has been overlooked, bursts in and curses Aurora: On her sixteenth birthday she will prick her finger and die. But the good Lilac Fairy weakens the curse, proclaiming that instead, Aurora will fall into a deep sleep, from which she will be awakened after 100 years by the kiss of a handsome prince.

Cut to Aurora's sixteenth birthday party. A mysterious guest (actually the evil Carabosse) presents her with a gift. Why, it's a lovely spindle! Aurora pricks her finger. The Lilac Fairy sends the whole court into a long sleep.

After several years — say, about a *hundred* — Prince Desiré is out hunting when he sees a vision of Aurora, supplied by none other than the Lilac Fairy. She leads him to the castle, where he must do battle with Carabosse. Finally he enters, he kisses Aurora, everybody wakes up, and they have a wedding, complete with some (probably extremely stale) cake.

The Nutcracker

Music by: Peter Tchaikovsky. **Story:** Loosely based on a story of E.T.A. Hoffmann. **Original choreography:** Marius Petipa/Lev Ivanov. **First performed:** St. Petersburg, Russia, 1892.

Tchaikovsky's final ballet, *The Nutcracker* has become the most popular ballet of all time. This ballet provides the financial fortunes of most of the world's ballet companies, which stage it every year at Christmastime. In the United States, *The Nutcracker* was premiered by the San Francisco Ballet.

The plot: It's Christmas Eve, and Clara and her family are throwing a big party. Enter the mysterious Drosselmeyer, who presents Clara with a beautiful Nutcracker as a gift.

After all the guests have gone home, the Christmas tree grows to enormous size, and the toys underneath it come to life. They are threatened by a group of mice, led by the Mouse King. Clara's beloved Nutcracker leads the toy soldiers in battle against the mice (Figure 19-5). Clara distracts the Mouse King and the Nutcracker defeats him. The Nutcracker is then transformed into a prince.

In Act II, Clara and her Nutcracker Prince travel to the Land of Sweets, ruled by the Sugar Plum Fairy. The prince tells the Fairy his amazing story — and she invites all the tasty treats of the kingdom to dance for their guests. The characteristic dances — including those of Spanish Chocolate, Arabian Coffee, Chinese Tea, the Russian Trepak, the Reed Flutes and the Sugar Plum Fairy herself — are the highlight of this beautiful ballet. Finally Clara and Prince go back home . . . or Clara wakes up, take your pick.

Figure 19-5:
The Nutcracker: Battle of the soldiers and the mice, at the San Francisco Ballet.

© Marty Sohl

Romeo and Juliet

Music by: Sergei Prokofiev. **Original choreography:** Leonid Lavrovsky.
First performed: Kirov Theater, Leningrad (St. Petersburg), 1940.

Many people contend that Prokofiev's *Romeo and Juliet* is quite simply the
greatest ballet score ever written. Prokofiev composed the music in 1935-36;
since then, this music has inspired an incredible number of great choreographers to try their hand at Shakespeare's story.

The plot: The Capulets and Montagues are feuding. Romeo Montague meets
Juliet Capulet when he crashes a party at her house in disguise. Romeo falls
for Juliet big-time; on the balcony, they secretly proclaim their eternal love.

The forbidden lovers are secretly wed by Friar Laurence, who hopes to end
the family feud. But that is not to be: In the marketplace, Juliet's cousin
Tybalt fights with Romeo's friend Mercutio, and kills him. Romeo avenges
Mercutio's death, killing Tybalt, and is sent into exile.

Juliet begs Friar Laurence for help. He tells her to take a vial of sleeping
potion that will make her appear dead. Her family will bury her in the family
tomb. Meanwhile Romeo, tipped off by Friar Laurence, will return and take
her away, and they'll live happily ever after. That's the plan, anyway.

That evening, Juliet takes the potion. The next morning her family finds her
"dead"; distraught, they bury her. Romeo hears of Juliet's "death" and returns
home grief stricken. But he never received Friar Laurence's message. Believing
Juliet to be dead, Romeo drinks a vial of poison. Juliet wakes and, seeing the
dead Romeo, stabs herself.

Cinderella

Music by: Sergei Prokofiev. **Original choreography:** Rotislav Zakharov. **First
performed:** Bolshoi Theater, Moscow, 1945.

After the great success of *Romeo and Juliet*, Sergei Prokofiev was asked to
create another ballet score. The result was *Cinderella*. Many different choreographers tried their hand at this the ballet — and one of your faithful authors
has danced the title role in *five* different versions.

The plot: The ballet is a variation on the familiar fairy tale. Sweet girl, wicked
stepsisters, Fairy Godmother (in this case a magical old beggar woman who
repays Cinderella for her kindness), handsome prince, glass slipper — you
get the idea.

Chapter 20

Ten Great "Contemporary" Ballets

*I*n this chapter we use the word "contemporary" loosely — after all, some of these ballets are nearly a century old. But these ballets use so-called "classical" ballet technique in a totally new way, breaking free of many old conventions and giving the art form a fresh new personality.

Here are ten of our favorite "contemporary" ballets, in chronological order. See them if you can!

The Rite of Spring

Music by: Igor Stravinsky. **Original choreography:** Vaslav Nijinsky. **First performed:** Paris, 1913.

This groundbreaking work is the granddaddy of contemporary ballet. Subtitled "Scenes from Pagan Russia," this ballet depicts an ancient ceremony in which a virgin is forced to dance to death, to propitiate the god of Spring. Not exactly a day at the beach (unless you live in certain parts of South Florida). Igor Stravinsky's music is brutal, and Nijinsky's provocative choreography is steeped in primitivism. The ballet shocked the audience: At the first performance, the shouts of the audience drowned out the music. The result was a riot, literally — and the first recorded fistfight in the history of ballet.

Although *The Rite of Spring* is seldom performed in the original choreography, this ballet cast a very long shadow. The boundaries of ballet had been shattered, and nothing was the same afterward.

Serenade

Music by: Peter Tchaikovsky. **Original choreography:** George Balanchine. **First performed:** White Plains, New York, 1934.

George Balanchine was one of the most influential choreographers of the twentieth century. Born in Russia, he studied music as well as dance. He worked for the *Ballets russes* in Paris (the same folks who had put on *The Rite of Spring* years earlier). He later moved to New York and became the legendary founding Artistic Director of the New York City Ballet.

Serenade was Balanchine's first ballet in America. He choreographed it in a workshop for the School of American Ballet, using whatever dancers happened to be in class at the time. As a result, the ballet has an improvisatory quality that keeps it exceedingly fresh.

Balanchine created the dance to the *Serenade for Strings* of his beloved countryman Peter Tchaikovsky, whose connection with some of the greatest ballets is well known. (See Chapter 19.) Brilliantly musical, Balanchine matched all the musical gestures in Tchaikovsky's luscious score with perfect physical gestures. There is no plot, but the ballet reflects the shifting moods of the music.

Balanchine was not interested in breaking the mold of classical ballet technique, as Nijinsky did in *The Rite of Spring*. Instead, he expanded ballet technique, keeping it relevant for the twentieth century. The ballet world owes him a huge debt.

Pillar of Fire

Music by: Arnold Schoenberg. **Original choreography:** Anthony Tudor. **First performed:** Metropolitan Opera House, New York City, 1942.

Anthony Tudor was one of the great English choreographers. His most well-known dances are deeply dramatic and passionate. In America, he created several ballets for the American Ballet Theatre, and had a huge effect on that company.

This ballet is set to the piece *Verklärte Nacht* ("Transfigured Night") by Arnold Schoenberg. This piece, for string orchestra, is wildly expressive and passionate — the perfect music for Tudor's character.

The plot: A young woman, Hagar, is secretly in love with her friend. But the friend seems more interested in her younger sister. Lonely and afraid that life is passing her by, Hagar goes off with another man for a quick fling. When she returns (possibly pregnant), she is shunned by her community. But her friend firmly takes hold of her and expresses his undying love for her. Her love has transfigured him.

Rodeo

Music by: Aaron Copland. **Original choreography:** Agnes DeMille. **First performed:** Metropolitan Opera House, New York City, 1942.

In 1942, the same year as *Pillar of Fire,* the great dancer and choreographer Agnes DeMille (niece of epic film director Cecil B. DeMille) was asked by the Ballet Russe de Monte Carlo to create a ballet for that company. The result was *Rodeo,* subtitled "The Courting at Burnt Ranch" — a story of a tomboy-ish cowgirl (Figure 20-1) and her attempts at love. (Long story, but it combined ballet traditions with the spirit of the Old West — all set to terrific music by Aaron Copland, including the famous "Hoe-down.")

The ballet was a sensational success. Agnes DeMille herself danced the leading role at the Metropolitan Opera House in 1943, and the audience gave her 22 curtain calls and standing ovations. This triumph brought her to the attention of Richard Rodgers and Oscar Hammerstein, who tapped her to create the dances for their musical, *Oklahoma!*

Figure 20-1: *Rodeo:* The cowgirl (Joanna Berman) in midair.

© Lloyd Englert

Fancy Free

Music by: Leonard Bernstein. **Original choreography:** Jerome Robbins.
First performed: Metropolitan Opera House, New York City, 1944.

While George Balanchine was Artistic Director of the New York City Ballet, Jerome Robbins was one of his most talented dancers and choreographers; he later became Artistic Director himself. Robbins continued Balanchine's expansion of classical ballet technique.

Fancy Free was Jerome Robbins's first ballet — and it was an enormous hit. Its zestful and youthful mood seemed to embody the spirit of the American big city. The ballet, with wonderful music by Leonard Bernstein, was later turned into a Broadway musical and movie, *On The Town*. Robbins went on to choreograph many Broadway shows, including the legendary *West Side Story*.

The plot: On a hot summer night in New York City, three sailors on shore leave pick up two beautiful women. They quickly realize that this math doesn't work; so they stage a competition. In a bar, each sailor dances a characteristic variation, trying to outdo the others and impress the women. But the women can't decide among them. The three sailors fight, and the women slip away. The sailors make up — but when a third woman comes their way, we see that they haven't changed a bit.

La Fille Mal Gardée

Music by: Ferdinand Hérold, adapted by John Lanchberry. **Original choreography:** Frederick Ashton. **First performed:** London, 1960.

Sir Frederick Ashton was one of the most inventive of all choreographers. Like Balanchine, he took classical technique and expanded the possibilities.

This ballet is a hilarious comedy: sparkling and delightful from beginning to end. Every dance is inventive, funny, and touching. It's as if the whole ballet were made up of greatest hits, with no filler. Unexpected props — like ribbons and a butter churn — become important elements of the dance. There's a real live pony in one scene, complete with a very large pooper scooper. There's a dance for "four chickens and a rooster," in full-body suits, complete with headpieces. There's a dance for harvesters with sickles. There's a spinning dance, a Maypole dance, a tambourine dance, a dance where the men whack sticks together in time to the music — and the longest, most embarrassing choreographed kiss (16 counts of slo-o-o-o-w *adagio* music) in the history of ballet.

The plot: Peasant girl Lise loves Colas. But her mother, the widow Simone (played by a man), disapproves and wants her to marry a rich simpleton. Lise sneaks off with Colas even as her mother signs the contract to marry her off to the simpleton. The usual complications ensue, all is forgiven, and Lise and Colas live happily ever after.

Song of the Earth

Music by: Gustav Mahler. **Original choreography:** Kenneth MacMillan. **First performed:** Stuttgart, 1965.

Kenneth MacMillan was a student of Frederick Ashton, and his early ballets are full of Ashton's influence. But in *Song of the Earth,* MacMillian finally broke free and found his own voice. Ironically, this was Ashton's favorite of MacMillan's ballets.

For his music, MacMillan used the profound and unforgettable song cycle of Gustav Mahler, *Song of the Earth (Das Lied von der Erde).* MacMillan's great success was in embodying the depth of the music in movement.

This ballet is mostly abstract — it has only the hint of a plot. A Man and Woman, symbolizing all mankind, become aware of the Messenger of Death. In the final song, death threatens this human relationship, but the lovers are reunited spiritually at the end.

Forgotten Land

Music by: Benjamin Britten. **Original choreography:** Jiri Kylian. **First performed:** Scheveningen, Holland, 1981.

The brilliant choreographer Jiri Kylian created a vocabulary of movements that no one had ever seen before. His ballets show an astounding talent for using controlled force. His steps are physically more demanding — and potentially more dangerous — than most classical ballet steps: head rolls, *pirouettes* and *bourrés* danced on the knees. His work is known to be hard on the knees, shoulders, back, and neck. But the result is gorgeous.

Forgotten Land, inspired by an expressionist painting by Edvard Munch (painter of "The Scream"), is set to the heartbreaking Sinfonia da Requiem by Benjamin Britten. There is no real plot; the ballet consists of a series of dances against the backdrop of a lonely seashore. Six couples live by the sea, which is constantly reclaiming their land. The ballet begins and ends as dancers stretch and arch their backs against the draw of the ocean, reaching longingly, despairingly, for a lost homeland.

In the Middle, Somewhat Elevated

Music by: Thom Willems. **Original choreography:** William Forsythe. **First performed:** Paris, 1987.

Like others before him, the American choreographer William Forsythe felt limited by the classical technique and craved more freedom and abandon in his work. As this ballet's quirky title suggests, Forsythe's work displays his own unique style. "Billy" (as his dancers call him) has explored the outer limits of dance — using angular, almost-off-balance steps and partnered positions, all at high speed. His style includes an element of improvisation, and he uses aspects of theater — including speaking, singing, and even yelling.

In this particular ballet, the item in the middle (somewhat elevated) is a pair of golden cherries. What exactly they have to do with this dance is anybody's guess. But if you get a chance to see this ballet, don't spend too much time looking at those cherries, or you'll miss what might otherwise be named the "X Games of Ballet."

The Hard Nut

Music by: Peter Tchaikovsky. **Original choreography:** Mark Morris. **First performed:** Brussels, Belgium, 1991.

In *The Hard Nut*, the brilliant American choreographer Mark Morris has taken the familiar story of *The Nutcracker* (see Chapter 19) and transported it to the Swinging Seventies (set to Tchaikovsky's original music, of course). The result is a totally original ballet that both satirizes and pays tribute to the original. Mark Morris has found a way to translate our most cherished ballet traditions for the modern world.

The party scene comes complete with television, fighting kids, Barbie dolls, hot pants, and sloshed guests. Some of the females are played by guys, especially in the Waltz of the Flowers.

Although this ballet is a riot, some of the choreography is surprisingly beautiful and moving. One of the most delightful scenes is the waltz of the snowflakes, in which successive waves of dancers enter the stage with handfuls of white confetti and fling them into the air — in perfect rhythm.

Othello

Music by: Elliot Goldenthal. **Original choreography:** Lar Lubovitch. **First performed:** New York City, 1997.

Lar Lubovitch invented his own ballet vocabulary, mixing some elements of classical technique with incredibly demanding athletic moves. Lifts are dramatic; characters climb on top of each other; dancers roll their heads in unison.

Lubovitch's vocabulary of gestures is so emotionally specific that the dancers can express a wide variety of emotions *through* these gestures, rather than "acting" their parts through particular facial expressions. This ballet never fails to make a very powerful impression.

The plot: The story of Othello existed long before Shakespeare wrote his play, and Lubovitch's ballet is based on the original story. Othello, the Moor of Venice, is deeply in love with his wife Desdemona. His ensign, Iago, is jealous of the favor that Othello is bestowing upon his friend Cassio. So Iago cooks up a scheme, making it look like Cassio and Desdemona are having an affair. Enraged, Othello punishes Cassio, and strangles his innocent, loving wife. Realizing his error, he kills himself — to absolutely gorgeous music. Ah, tragedy.

Chapter 21

The Ten Best Ballet Terms for Cocktail Parties

● ●

*1*f you were a strip of wallpaper in the gentlemen's restroom during intermission at the ballet, you might overhear this typical (and extremely realistic) ballet conversation. How much can you understand?

Answer: None; you're a strip of wallpaper.

Frank: Yo, Tony! What's shakin'?

Tony: Not much, buddy boy. Repaired another 72-cubic-foot Freez-O-Matic today. Ain't they the worst?

Frank: Fuggedaboudit. Faulty Freon tubes left and right. Gimme that side-by-side Kenmore any day, I always say.

Tony: Didja get a loada that *prima ballerina* tonight? Whoa, what a dancer.

Frank: You got that right. I've never seen such *line.* She musta practiced with a tape measure.

Tony: Yeah, how about that *pas de deux* — did you catch that amazing *pointe work?* Quick, but delicate, like a Rapid R-53 staple gun.

Frank: And those 32 *fouettés* in the *coda* — it was like she was drillin' a hole in the floor at 900 rpm with an 18-volt Black & Decker cordless.

Tony: Yeah, but what's with her partner? No *turnout* at all during his *variation.* Sheesh!

Frank: Yeah, what does he think he is, a Ramelson 11/64-inch Straight-Handle Skew Chisel? *(Moves to the washbasin.)*

Tony: And he totally messed up his *manège.* Turned it into a *diagonal* halfway through. He really coulda used a plumb bob level. Whadda louse.

Frank: Got something caught in his *dance belt*, I guess.

Tony: *(laughs)* Okay, Frank, you take care now. See you at Beethoven's Ninth next week.

Frank: You can count on it.

This conversation uses all eleven of the Ten Best Ballet Terms for Cocktail Parties:

- ✔ **Coda:** Literally, "tail" — the final part of a *pas de deux,* where both dancers do the most complicated steps.
- ✔ **Dance belt:** The equivalent of a jockstrap for male dancers, providing support in all the right places.
- ✔ **Diagonal:** One way to end a *variation:* The dancer goes to a back corner of the stage and comes forward in a diagonal line to the opposite front corner, while dancing a complicated step or series of steps over and over.
- ✔ **Fouetté:** A turn on one leg, in which a ballerina "whips" the other foot outward on each revolution. This turn is sometimes done 32 times in a row.
- ✔ **Line:** The overall imaginary line (or shape) created by all the parts of a ballet dancer's body during a pose or a step.
- ✔ **Manège:** Another way to end a *variation:* The dancer travels around the stage in a circle, while performing a set of steps again and again to wild applause.
- ✔ **Pas de deux:** Literally, "step of two" — a dance for two dancers, usually male and female, and usually consisting of several contrasting sections: the *adagio,* or slow section, the male variation, the female variation, and the *coda* (or tail).
- ✔ **Pointe work:** The steps that a ballerina does while balancing on the tips of her toes, while wearing toe shoes (also known as *pointe* shoes).
- ✔ **Prima ballerina:** The "first dancer," or most important female dancer in a ballet, or in a ballet company.
- ✔ **Turnout:** The dancer's ability to rotate the hip joints outward, ideally to 90 degrees — the foundation of classical ballet technique.
- ✔ **Variation:** The portion of a *pas de deux* where one dancer gets to show his/her stuff.

Now that you understand these terms, see if you can understand the following conversation, overheard in whispered tones behind the curtain just before the performance:

Odette: Gosh, I hope my *diagonal* in the *pas de deux* goes well tonight. Last night it turned into a triangle.

Siegfried: But I thought it was lovely.

Odette: *Lovely?!* It was totally off. That reminds me — I need to use much more *turnout* tonight in my *variation*. Last night my knees were touching each other the whole time!

Siegfried: Really? I *adored* your variation.

Odette: You're just being nice. Oh! I completely forgot to practice my *fouettés* from the *coda*. I was actually aiming for 64 last night, but I only managed to do three.

Siegfried: But they were three gorgeous ones. And I especially loved your *pointe work* in the *manège*.

Odette: *Loved it?* I fell at least four times.

Siegfried: That wasn't your fault. You were distracted by my *dance belt*. It really distorted my *line*.

(At this point the Artistic Director walks across the stage.)

Artistic Director: And how's my *prima ballerina* tonight? Ready?

Odette: Ready!

Chapter 22

Ten Fascinating Facts about Professional Ballet Dancers

*B*allet dancers give their life energy in order to transform the theater into another world — to involve the audience so completely that they forget about their daily grind. This is the ultimate reward for any live performer.

But in order to create this illusion, ballet dancers have a daily grind of their own. For every single hour of new choreography that you see onstage, dancers put in about 60 hours of rehearsal time. Here's a look at the true lives of ballet dancers.

The Discipline Needed to Be a Dancer

Most professional ballet dancers decide on their career when they're in their early teens — and most begin training before the age of 10. At that early age, they choose to set aside team sports, school parties, and hanging out at the mall for *battements*, *dégagés,* and hanging out at barres.

Young ballet students practice for an average of ten years before they are ready to join the ranks of professional dancers. That's ten years of daily stretches, classes, and rehearsal — and then the work *really* begins.

After they get into a large professional ballet company, dancers spend about 30 hours per week in the rehearsal studio — plus up to 15 hours warming up. Outside the studio, dancers spend time getting physical therapy, massage therapy, and chiropractic care, sewing five to ten pairs of *pointe* shoes per week, cross-training at the gym, putting their hair into the requisite bun (for women), adhering to a special diet, and refraining from any activity that could jeopardize an optimal performance — usually for a small salary.

Some young dancers eat, drink, and think of nothing else but ballet — inspiring the term *bunheads.*

A Dancer's Schedule: A Day in the Life

A dancer's day usually starts with a hot bath or shower to loosen up the muscles, followed by light stretching at home. At the studio, it's back onto the floor for *serious* stretching, followed by the structured warm-up known as *ballet class.*

Ballet class is offered nearly every day at every professional ballet company. Some dancers choose to skip class and warm up on their own, but the class offers an opportunity to do it together, under the watchful eye of a ballet master. Ballet class begins with the same barre and center floor exercises that we show you in Chapters 6 through 13, and continues with imaginative combinations of steps — danced to the accompaniment of a long-suffering (but cheerful) rehearsal pianist.

After class, dancers have about 15 minutes to change into dry dancewear, have a snack, complain about ballet class, and fill up on water. Now the serious rehearsing can begin. Dancers often rehearse for three hours at a stretch, with five-minute breaks each hour. Afterward they get an hour for lunch — and then it's back to the studio for three more hours of rehearsal. In a typical rehearsal day, a dancer may rehearse as many as six different ballets.

On performance days, the dancers generally have only two hours of rehearsal. Then they try to fit in a massage, dinner, and a nap before going to the theater. In most companies, dancers must sign in half an hour prior to curtain time.

After the performance, most dancers are ravenous; and this is when they eat the most. Then it's home to unwind — and off to sleep, while visions of sugarplums dance in their heads.

What Dancers Actually Eat

In a word, carbs.

Carbohydrates, and lots of 'em, are the staple of any dancer's diet. Bagels and coffee for breakfast, bananas, apples, and orange juice after class, sandwiches and salads and tofu and rice (and the occasional potato chip) for lunch.

Of course, the amount of food consumed at breakfast and lunch is usually small, because rehearsals are coming right up. If you're about to get held upside down in the air by your partner, a light lunch is a good idea.

Dinner tends to be on the hefty side. But even here, carbs are paramount. A large salad, followed by a helping of pasta, is a typical dinner. And some low-fat protein, like chicken, beans, or tofu, helps charge up for the next day.

Of course, dancers don't eat healthy *all* the time. We've been involved in plenty of dancer pizza parties. And most dancers have a drink or two now and then at the end of the day — after eight hours of grueling exercise, why not?

And chocolate's good, too. One piece at a time.

The Hierarchy of a Ballet Company

Not all dancers are created equal. And ballet companies make sure that you know this. Most companies divide their dancers into at least three different levels.

At the highest level are the Principal Dancers. These dancers get most of the meaty roles — Siegfried and Odette in *Swan Lake,* Giselle in *Giselle,* and so on. (At the Paris Opera Ballet, those roles go to an even higher level of dancer — the *étoiles,* or "stars.")

Just below the Principal Dancers are the Soloists. These dancers usually get to dance featured roles, but often take part in group scenes as well.

Below the soloists are the members of the *corps de ballet.* The corps is the largest group of any ballet company, and the heart and soul of any ballet. When you see that line of 32 women in white doing *arabesques* in unison, or the crowd scenes and Wilis in *Giselle,* that's the corps at work.

Below the corps are apprentices, who are usually hired on a yearly basis. They may or may not ever become permanent members of the company. They dance along with the corps most of the time.

And below the apprentices are the students of a ballet school, which is usually attached to any major ballet company. These are the mice and soldiers and party children in *Nutcracker,* and they occasionally get to participate in crowd scenes of other ballets.

There is no guarantee that a member of the corps will ever be promoted to soloist, or that a soloist will ever be promoted to Principal Dancer. As a result, dancers sometimes leave one company for a higher position in a smaller company. (Big fish — small pond.)

The Mysterious Pointe Shoe

Ask a great ballerina if you can try out her *pointe* shoes, and she'll probably back away slowly, shoes behind her back, offering calm, soothing pleasantries, until she's far enough away to bolt into a dead run.

Shoes are a very personal topic for ballet dancers. Eventually, every ballerina has to learn how to balance on the tips of her toes. To help her achieve this feat, she has several pairs of *pointe* shoes (see Figure 22-1).

Pointe shoes are handmade from such things as canvas, newspaper, and acrylic cement. (Just how we, as a species, determined that these materials go well together is beyond our imagination. But suffice it to say that "canvas, newspaper and acrylic cement" are right up there with "peanut butter and chocolate" in the inspired combinations department.) Those materials are shaped into the appropriate form, and then topped with a layer of satin, with a leather sole.

Like ballet slippers, *pointe* shoes have drawstrings to tighten the top part of the shoe. (Don't ever let a *pointe* shoe dealer talk you into buying drawstrings as optional equipment. They're standard.)

The part of the shoe that surrounds the dancer's toes is called the *box.* The box comes in various lengths, widths, and degrees of hardness in various places (such as along the sides). The only thing all ballerinas agree on is that the box should have a flat tip to stand on. Contrary to popular belief, this tip is not made of steel. But the dancer's toes are.

Today there are many different makers of *pointe* shoes, and some have incorporated new materials available today into the construction of a "new and improved *pointe* shoe". But most dancers today are purists, and their *pointe* shoes aren't significantly different than they were a century ago. We highly recommend *pointe* shoes constructed by Freed of London.

When a ballerina gets a new pair of shoes, she has to break them in. She bends and softens the leather soles. She pounds on the boxes for awhile, or slams them in a door a few times, to make them more flexible. She whacks the points of the shoes against a cement floor to soften them a bit and prevent them from making too much noise onstage. No wonder she's so attached to the things.

After all the work that goes into making *pointe* shoes and preparing them for your foot, you'd expect them to last a long time. But nothing could be further from the truth. In the heat of performance, a pair of *pointe* shoes can last for as little as 30 minutes before the box becomes too soft to dance in. A typical ballerina needs three pairs to get through a single performance of *Swan Lake* — and up to 150 pairs a year. That's about 8,000 shoes for a typical ballet company. Luckily for the dancers, the company pays the bills.

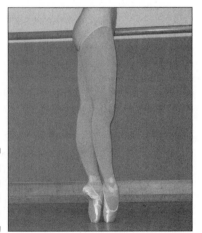

Figure 22-1:
The mysterious *pointe* shoe.

Why Macho Guys Dance

In America, many male dancers start taking ballet because their sisters do — and then discover the challenge and physical workout to be fun. Some are even captured by the thrill of performance. And lots of 'em enjoy hanging around with a bevy of perfect beauties. But no doubt, young male dancers in the United States often have to endure ribbing about their chosen activity.

But in some other countries, like Russia and Cuba, the motivation is different. In those cultures, a male ballet dancer is the equivalent of a sports hero. And why not? The virtuosic pyrotechnics of these professionals are not to be believed. Being the principal dancer of a ballet company is just as cool as being a basketball or football star.

Women, Pregnancy, and Performance

Every woman who has had a child knows how wacko the female body gets during pregnancy. How does a dancer deal with the added stress of pregnancy on her body, when her body *is* her instrument?

For a ballerina, whether or not to get pregnant in the first place is a huge decision. Most ballerinas at the highest level decide to wait until they finish their career before having a baby. Still others decide to retire early while their biological clock is active.

But many ballerinas get pregnant, have kids, and *still* practice ballet brilliantly. We know many professional ballerinas who have safely *performed* ballet into their fourth and even fifth month of pregnancy.

Why Some Ballet Dancers Need Hip Replacements

All classical ballet technique is founded on turnout from the hips. Just think — you walk, run, turn, leap, and land heavily on the floor, all with turned-out hips. After several years, this position can really take its toll on your body.

Some dancers are so determined to be more turned out than anyone else that they end up ruining their hip joints completely. Some need hip replacements as early as in their 40s — and because hip replacements only last about 20 years, that means at least one upgrade on each side. Ouch!

Party versus Performance

Dancers are notorious for loving a good party. (And *man,* are they amazing at discos.) As a result, some dancers walk a fine line — usually early in their careers, as members of the *corps de ballet.*

But most dancers — at least the smart ones — eventually realize that partying interferes with performance quality. As a result, they have to pass up wonderful temptations every day.

Like all art, ballet demands a sacrifice. A huge one. But a dancer who's willing to make that sacrifice is often rewarded with a beautiful career. And when the career's over, they can party all they want.

Early Retirement

Even if a dancer lives right, eats right, makes all the right decisions, gets enough sleep, maintains a healthy lifestyle, and manages to avoid major injuries, he or she can still expect to retire early. A good professional dancing career usually lasts 10 to 15 years. And a typical retirement age is between 30 and 35. What then?

Some dancers go back to school to begin a totally unrelated career. But others choose to pass on the flame. These dancers become artistic directors, ballet masters, choreographers, and dance teachers. Their new passion is keeping the art alive for the next generation.

Why It's All Worth It

So why do dancers do what they do? Why is a dance career worth this daily grind, insane discipline, risk of injury, little pay, no guarantee of promotion, and early retirement?

It's worth it for those rare moments when everything comes together in performance, when the dancers create something bigger than themselves, and when the audience responds enthusiastically as one (Figure 22-2).

And deep down, ballet dancers love every bit of their work. Scratch the surface of the most jaded professional, and you'll find that bunhead who just lives for her art.

Figure 22-2:
Evelyn
Cisneros
and Tony
Randazzo
in James
Kudelka's
The End.

© Marty Sohl

Glossary of Ballet Terms

*A*s you have undoubtedly noticed, just about every move in ballet has a French name. That's because ballet was invented — and perfected — largely in France.

In this glossary and throughout the book, we give you an *approximate* pronunciation for each French word. But here's your handy guide to pronouncing the language a little more accurately.

In French, the last syllable always gets the accent. Most consonants are pronounced just as in English. As for the vowel sounds, one of the most common is the most difficult to pronounce: It's that *awwwwwnnngggh* sound that you can get by talking like a donkey through your nose. In the following table, an asterisk (*) refers to that very sound, or a close approximation of it.

French Pronunciation Guide

These letters	Sound like	As in
a, -as, -at	ah	*pas* ("PAH")
an, ans, ant	*	*dans* ("D*")
au	oh	*pauvre* ("POH-vr")
e	eh *or* euh	*belle* ("BELL") or de ("duh")
é, ai	ay	*étoile* ("ay-TWAHL")
en, ens, ends, ent	*	*battement* ("batM*")
i	ee	*retiré* ("ruh-tee-RAY")
au, aut, o, os	oh	*saut* ("SOH")
oi	wah	*étoile* ("ay-TWAHL")
ou	oo	*coupé* ("koo-PAY")

In general, you don't pronounce a final consonant in French (*corps de ballet:* "COR duh bah-LAY"). You don't pronounce a final E either, unless it has an accent mark.

à la seconde ("ah la se-COND") (Chapter 8): In second position: That is, out to the side. Also, one of the nine positions of the body in *battement tendu*: facing flat front, leg to the side.

à terre ("ah TAIR") (Chapter 6): On the ground.

abdominals (Chapter 3): Stomach muscles, also known as "abs."

adagio ("ah-DAH-joe") (Chapter 6): Literally, "at ease." A slow tempo. Also refers to the traditional series of slow ballet moves in general, or one a slow dance in particular.

adductors (Chapter 3): The muscles of the inner thighs.

arabesque ("ah-rah-BESK") (Chapter 9): The position with one leg lifted behind you.

attitude ("ah-tee-TUDE") (Chapter 8): A position in which one leg is extended off the ground, but bent. This can be forward, to the side, or to the back.

balancé ("bah-lahn-SAY") (Chapter 11): The classic waltz step — plus turnout, of course.

ballet mime (Chapter 16): A set of pantomime gestures that have specific meanings in ballet, to help advance a story.

balletomane (Chapter 16): A ballet connoisseur.

barre (Chapter 2): The long horizontal cylinder, usually attached to the wall, that ballet dancers use for warming up every day of their career.

battement tendu ("bat-MAHN tahn-DUE") (Chapter 6): A move in which one leg slides out along the floor to the front, back or side, all the way to the tip of the pointed foot, with a straight knee.

beat (Chapter 5): In music, the length of time it takes to tap your feet once. Also (Chapter 13), to flap your legs like wings.

Bolshoi Ballet (Chapter 17): Literally, the "big ballet." The legendary Russian and dance company, based in Moscow.

bourré ("boo-RAY") (Chapter 11): The traveling step: consists of about a million teeny, tiny baby steps danced in sequence, usually *en pointe,* to create a deceptively seamless traveling line.

box (Chapter 22): The part of the pointe shoe that surrounds the dancer's toes.

bunhead (Chapter 22): A young dancer who eats, drinks, and sleeps nothing but ballet.

cabriole ("kah-bree-OLE") (Chapter 13): A step in which the legs make a traveling beat at 45 degrees to the front or to the back.

Cecchetti method (Chapter 4): One of the traditional schools of ballet technique, from which most of the technique in this book is derived.

center floor (Chapter 9): The wide open space where exercises are danced without the aid of the barre.

chaîné ("sheh-NAY") (Chapter 10): See *tours chaînés déboulés.*

changement de pieds ("shahnj-MAHN duh pee-AY") (Chapter 12): Literally, "changing the feet." A jump from fifth to fifth position in which the feet switch places in midair.

chassé ("shah-SAY") (Chapter 11): The galloping step.

choreography (Chapter 15): The art of designing and/or creating the steps of a dance.

class (Chapter 22): A structured daily warm-up for ballet dancers, consisting of barre and center floor exercises, designed to improve and strengthen the classical technique.

coda (Chapter 17): Literally, "tail." The final part of a *pas de deux,* where both dancers do the most complicated steps to show off.

combination (Chapter 6): A sequence of movements used to practice a particular step or group of steps; usually set to music.

corps de ballet ("COR duh bah-LAY") (Chapter 9): Literally, the "body of ballet." The "chorus" of a ballet company; the largest group of dancers, who usually don't dance solo roles. The corps is the heart and soul of any ballet company.

cou-de-pied ("koo duh pee-AY") (Chapter 7): A position in which one foot is placed in front or in back of the other ankle.

coupé ("koo-PAY") (Chapter 11): A way to fake it gracefully, allowing you to look really good as you regroup and carry on.

croisé derrière ("kwah-ZAY duh-ree-AIR") (Chapter 9): One of the nine basic positions of the body in *battement tendu*: legs crossed, and *tendu* to the back.

croisé devant ("kwah-ZAY duh-VAHN") (Chapter 9): One of the nine basic positions of the body in *battement tendu*: legs crossed and *tendu* to the front.

dance belt (Chapter 2): The equivalent of a jockstrap for male dancers, providing support in all the right places.

dance notation (Chapter 15): The method by which choreographers write down a series of steps for future reference.

Dansneakers (Chapter 2): Basically tennis shoes designed for dance, with a split sole and a flat tip: giving extra support and making it easier to point the foot, turn, and jump.

dégagé ("day-gah-JAY") (Chapter 6): A *battement tendu* in which the foot comes off the floor to an angle of almost 45 degrees.

demi-plié ("duh-MEE plee-AY") (Chapter 6): Literally, "half a *plié*"; bend your knees as far as you can *while still keeping both heels planted on the ground*.

demi pointe ("duh-MEE PWANT") (Chapter 10): Standing on the balls of the feet.

demi rond de jambe ("duh-MEE RON duh JAHMB") (Chapter 6): Literally, a "half round of the leg." A quarter circle drawn with the foot.

développé ("DAVE-low-PAY") (Chapter 8): A gradual unfolding of the leg, extending it slowly into the air.

diagonal (Chapter 17): One way to end a *variation*: The dancer goes to a back corner of the stage and comes forward in a diagonal line to the opposite front corner, while dancing a complicated step or series of steps over and over.

double tour en l'air ("DOO-bl TOOR ahn LAIR") (Chapter 13): Literally, a "double turn in the air."

écarté derrière ("ay-car-TAY duh-ree-AIR") (Chapter 9): One of the nine basic positions of the body in *battement tendu*: legs not crossed, *tendu* to the side toward the back corner.

écarté devant ("ay-car-TAY duh-VAHN") (Chapter 9): One of the nine basic positions of the body in *battement tendu*: facing a corner; legs not crossed, *tendu* to the side.

échappé ("ay-shah-PAY") (Chapter 8): Literally, "escaped." A move in which your feet "escape" from the cramped confines of fifth position out into the wide open spaces of second.

effacé derrière ("ef-fah-SAY duh-ree-AIR") (Chapter 9): One of the nine basic positions of the body in *battement tendu*: facing a corner, the leg is in *tendu* back, pointing to the opposite corner.

effacé devant ("ef-fah-SAY duh-VAHN") (Chapter 9): One of the nine basic positions of the body in *battement tendu*: facing a corner, legs not crossed, with the *tendu* leg to the same corner.

emboîté ("ahm-bwah-TAY") (Chapter 12): A jump from one leg and land on the other, while keeping the raised leg in *attitude*.

en arrière ("ahn ar-YAIR") (Chapter 6): To the back.

en croix ("ahn KWAH") (Chapter 7): literally, "in a cross." Performing a move in a pattern that imitates the shape of a cross, as drawn by, say, Hobbits.

en dedans (ahn duh-DAHN") (Chapter 6): To the inside.

en dehors ("ahn duh-OR") (Chapter 6): To the outside.

en l'air ("ahn LAIR") (Chapter 12): In the air.

en pointe ("ahn PWANT") (Chapter 9): Literally, "on point." Balancing on the tips of a few toes, in specially designed pointe shoes.

entrechat ("ahn-truh-SHAH") (Chapter 13): A jump straight up, in which the legs beat, the feet going in front of or behind each other. The word *entrechat* is usually followed by a French number: *entrechat trois* ("ahn-truh-SHAH TWAH") (3), *entrechat quatre* (4), *entrechat cinq* (5), *entrechat six* (6), *entrechat sept* (7), *entrechat huit* (8) — to indicate how many times the legs go back and forth.

étoile ("ay-TWAHL") (Chapter 22): Literally, "star." The highest level of dancer at the Paris Opera Ballet.

failli ("fah-YEE") (Chapter 13): Literally, "failed," meaning "giving way." The leg goes through first position into fourth position.

fermé(e) ("fair-MAY") (Chapter 12): Closed.

fish dive (Chapter 14): A spectacular ending move for partners, in which the woman lands face down in the arms of her trusted partner.

fondu ("fon-DUE") (Chapter 7): A one-legged knee bend.

fouetté **turn** ("foo-et-TAY") (Chapter 10): Literally, "whipped." A move where the ballerina executes multiple turns on one leg; she raises and lowers herself on that leg while simultaneously whipping the other leg around and around.

frappe ("frah-PAY") (Chapter 7): Literally, "struck." Striking the floor with the foot.

glissade ("glee-SAHD") (Chapter 11): The gliding step, crab-like.

glutes (Chapter 3): Short for *gluteus maximus:* the rear end muscles.

grand allegro ("GRAHND a-LEG-row") (Chapter 13): The traditional set of big jumps across the floor.

grand battement ("GRAHN bat-MAHN") (Chapter 8): A high kick, Rockette style.

grand échappé ("GRAHN ay-shah-PAY") (Chapter 12): Literally, the "great escape." A pair of jumps that involve changing the position of the feet.

grand jeté ("GRAHN juh-TAY") (Chapter 13): A forward jump with a split.

grand pas de deux ("GRAHN pah duh DEUH") (Chapter 6): The big moment for the principal couple in a ballet to dance together. This dance usually consists of several contrasting sections: the *adagio*, or slow section, the male variation, the female variation, and the *coda* (or tail).

grand plié ("GRAHN plee-AY") (Chapter 6): A big knee bend, in which the heels are allowed to come off the floor.

grand saut de chat ("GRAHN SOH duh SHAH") (Chapter 13): A jump in which the front leg begins bent and ends straight, in a split position in the air.

hamstrings (Chapter 3): The long muscles running up and down the back of the leg.

legwarmers (Chapter 2): Tubes of material worn at varying lengths around the legs to warm up the muscles.

leotard (Chapter 2): A sort of stretchy one-piece unisex bathing suit, meant for dancing.

line (Chapter 21): The overall imaginary line (or shape) created by all the parts of a ballet dancer's body during a pose or a step.

manège ("mah-NEJ") (Chapter 17): One way to end a *variation*: the dancer travels around the stage in a circle, while performing a set of steps again and again to wild applause.

orchestra pit (Chapter 17): The place in front of and beneath the stage of an opera house, where the musicians of the orchestra sit and play.

ouvert(e) ("oo-VAYR", "oo-VAYRT") (Chapter 12): Open.

overhead *pressage* ("pres-SAHJ") (Chapter 14): A move for partners; he lifts her over his head, as if doing a shoulder press.

overture (Chapter 17): A musical introduction to a ballet, played by the orchestra with the curtain down.

pas ("PAH") (Chapter 6): Step.

pas assemblé ("PAH ah-sahm-BLAY") (Chapter 12): Literally "assembled step." Brushing and joining the feet in the air.

pas de basque (PAH duh BAHSK") (Chapter 12): Traveling to the side and forward.

pas de bourrée ("PAH duh boo-RAY") (Chapter 11): The traditional ethnic Grapevine, danced ballet-style.

pas de chat ("PAH duh SHAH") (Chapter 12): The cat step.

pas de cheval ("PAH duh shuh-VAHL") (Chapter 7): The horse step.

pas de couru ("pah duh koo-RUE") (Chapter 11): The running step.

pas de deux (Chapter 6): Literally, "step for two." A dance for two dancers.

pas de trois ("pah duh TWAH") (Chapter 17): Literally, "step for three." A dance, or set of dances, for three people together.

pas jeté ("pah juh-TAY") (Chapter 12): Brushing the foot, drawing a "4" in the air, and landing on one leg.

petit allegro ("puh-TEET a-LEG-row") (Chapter 12): Small jumps.

petits battements ("puh TEE bat-MAHN") (Chapter 7): Little beats of the leg.

petit échappé ("puh-TEET ay-shah-PAY") (Chapter 12): Changing the feet during a jump, from fifth position to second position and back again.

piqué ("pee-KAY") (Chapter 10): Literally, "stung." A move where the ballerina carefully plants one straight leg with a pointed foot on the ground and transfers her weight to that foot.

pirouette ("pee-roo-ET") (Chapter 10): A turn.

pointe shoe (Chapter 22): A specially made shoe that allows the ballerina to balance on the tips of her toes.

pointe work (Chapter 17): The steps that a ballerina does while balancing on the points of her toes, while wearing toe shoes (also known as pointe shoes).

port de bras ("POR duh BRAH") (Chapter 6): Literally, "carriage of the arms." A broad arm movement from one position to another, often accompanied by a movement of the upper body.

prima ballerina (Chapter 17): The first, or most important, female dancer in a company.

prima ballerina assoluta (Chapter 17): This title is reserved for only the greatest of the great, the most legendary, the most sublime, within a particular ballet company. The ballet companies that give out such titles are few, and a title like this is bestowed less than once in a lifetime.

promenade ("pro-muh-NAHD") (Chapter 14): A move for partners, in which the man holds the woman and walks around her, turning her as he goes.

quadriceps (Chapter 3): The thigh muscles, which are the largest muscles in the body.

quatrième derrière ("kah-tree-EM duh-ree-AIR") (Chapter 9): One of the nine basic positions of the body in *battement tendu*: facing front, one leg in *tendu* back.

quatrième devant ("kah-tree-EM duh-VAHN") (Chapter 9): One of the nine basic positions of the body in *battement tendu*: facing front, with the *tendu* leg in front.

relevé ("ruh-luh-VAY") (Chapter 6): Literally, "raised up again": A rise to the ball of the feet. Known in workout circles as a "calf raise." Can be done with straight knees or with a *demi-plié*.

retiré ("ruh-tee-RAY") (Chapter 6): A move where one pointed foot is lifted and placed by the other knee (strongly resembling a number "4").

reverance ("ruh-vuh-RAHNS") (Chapter 13): A reverent "stretch and bow" done at the end of a ballet class, to show respect for the teacher and the rehearsal pianist.

rond de jambe ("RON duh JAHMB") (Chapter 6): Literally, "round of the leg." A half circle drawn with the foot.

rosin (Chapter 2): A substance used by dancers to prevent shoes, feet, and hands from slipping.

royale ("roy-AHL") (Chapter 13): A jump straight up into the air from fifth to fifth position, beating and changing the legs once.

sauté ("soh-TAY") (Chapter 12): A small jump on two legs, landing on both legs.

shoulder sit (Chapter 14): A move for partners. The ballerina usually jumps and aims her gluteus maximus in the general direction of her long-suffering partner's waiting shoulder.

sissonne ("see-SONE") (Chapter 12): A jump from two legs onto one leg.

sissonne fermé ("see-SONE fair-MAY") (Chapter 12): A *sissonne,* immediately closing the raised leg in to fifth position.

sissonne ouverte ("see-SONE oo-VAYRT") (Chapter 12): A *sissonne,* leaving the raised leg up for a moment before closing it.

soubresaut ("soo-bruh-SOH") (Chapter 12): A simple jump in fifth position; or a simple lift, straight up and down.

sous-sus ("soo-SUE") (Chapter 8): A position in which both feet slide together to meet, one directly behind the other. In this position, seen from the front, you appear to have one foot with two heels.

soutenu en tournant ("soo-tuh-NUE ahn toor-NAHN") (Chapter 10): A turn on two legs.

spot (Chapter 10): To look at a particular point in the distance while turning, to avoid getting dizzy. Also refers to the point itself.

sur le cou-de-pied ("seur luh KOO duh peeAY") (Chapter 7): Literally, "on the neck of the foot." Specifically, one foot is wrapped about the other leg where the calf muscle lowers towards the heel.

sylph (Chapter 19): A wispy, ghostlike woman dressed in white; shows up in a lot of Romantic ballets, especially in Act II, which is often known as the "White Act."

tempo (Chapter 5): The speed at which the beats (or counts) of the music come flying at you.

temps levé ("tahn luh-VAY") (Chapter 12): Jumping repeatedly on the same foot.

tendu See *battement tendu.*

tights Tight-fitting stretchy pants with feet, worn with pride by ballet dancers in broad daylight: or onstage.

tours chaînés déboulés ("TOOR sheh-NAY day-boo-LAY") (Chapter 10): A "chain" of repeated turns on two legs.

turnout (Chapter 4): The dancer's ability to rotate the hip joints outward, ideally to 90 degrees: the foundation of classical ballet technique.

unitard (Chapter 2): A leotard with legs.

Vaganova method (Chapter 9): A Russian school of ballet technique, from which the directions of the room in this book (D-1 through D-8) are derived.

variation (Chapter 17): The portion of a ballet where one dancer gets to show his/her stuff.

Index

• •

• *F* •

Notes

Notes

Notes

Notes

Notes

Notes

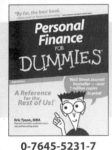  

FOR DUMMIES®

A world of resources to help you grow

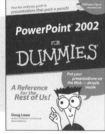

FOR DUMMIES®

The advice and explanations you need to succeed

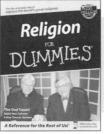